T0268043

MASAI STORY

My Fight for Love and the Future of Indigenous People

*She gave up everything she knew
to learn everything she didn't.*

STEPHANIE FUCHS

with Alexandra Brosowski
English Translation by Dominique Rotermund

TITLETOWN
PUBLISHING

TitleTown Publishing, LLC

P.O. Box 12093 Green Bay, WI 54307-12093

920.737.8051 | titletownpublishing.com

Publisher's Cataloging-in-Publication:

Names: Fuchs, Stephanie, author. | Brosowski, Alexandra, author. | Rotermund, Dominique, translator.

Title: Masai story : my fight for love and the future of Indigenous people / Stephanie Fuchs and Alexandra Brosowski ; English translation by Dominique Rotermund.

Other titles: Esepata: Mein Platz is bei den Massai. English

Description: [Third edition]. | Green Bay, WI : TitleTown Publishing, [2024] | Translation of Esepata: Mein Platz ist bei den Massai (München : Knaur, 2023).

Identifiers:

ISBN: 978-1-955047-65-4 (trade paperback)

978-1-955047-67-8 (eBook)

Subjects: LCSH: Fuchs, Stephanie | Germans--Tanzania--Biography. | Maasai (African people)--Social life and customs. | Interracial marriage--Tanzania. | Village communities -- Tanzania--Social life and customs. | Maasai (African people)--Tanzania--Economic conditions. | Tanzania--Environmental conditions. | Climatic changes--Tanzania. | Climate change mitigation--Tanzania. | LCGFT: Autobiographies.

BISAC: BIOGRAPHY & AUTOBIOGRAPHY / Women. | BIOGRAPHY & AUTOBIOGRAPHY / Cultural & Regional. | BIOGRAPHY & AUTOBIOGRAPHY / Indigenous.

Classification: LCC: DT443.3.M37 F8313 2024 | DDC: 306.896/5--dc23

TABLE OF CONTENTS

THE STORY BEHIND THE COVER PICTURE

The picture that was taken of me that day shows a very important moment of my life with the Masai.

When Sokoine's cousin Saito got married, our whole family set out to attend the ceremony in Olkoilili, a neighboring Maasai village. We had rented several cars in Lengatei and Songe, so all of Saito's and Sokoine's relatives would be able to attend the wedding, and of course we had all dressed up accordingly to the circumstances. I too wore my Maasai robes for once, along with my olkati, a large necklace adorned with hundreds of tiny silver plates. The other women were already waiting in Saito's boma. They had rubbed their skin with olkaria, a mixture of red earth and oil and their faces were beaming. When we climbed into the car, Saito's first wife said to me: "Stephanie, let me apply a little olkaria to your face." I agreed and she ran her forefinger along her neck, bright red with olkaria. Dabbing a little of the mixture on my cheeks, she drew two small patches on my skin with her fingertips in a gesture I found deeply moving.

For half an hour, we jostled over hill and dale, past the village of Lengatei, as we headed towards the forest and Olkoilili. Upon our arrival, we were greeted by the warriors, who had arrived earlier, their naked chests glowing bright red with olkaria. The sun was already low in the sky on that late afternoon, bathing these people I had come to love so much in a golden light which made them appear even more beautiful.

When the men saw me dressed in traditional Maasai clothes, they let out spontaneous cries of joy. One of them, Ninai, whom I was long since fond of because of his kind and quiet nature, came up to me and shook my hand in greeting, saying: "Ah, Mama Yannik, you came! You look good in Maasai clothes! But what is that on your cheeks?" A little embarrassed, I explained to him that the other women had applied a little olkaria to my face.

"Ah, but they did not do it right. Let me."

Seizing the hem of his robe, he moistened it with saliva and rubbed my cheeks to remove the olkaria marks.

Then, pulling a ring off his finger, he dipped it in the red color on his shoulders and pressed it to my cheeks. The two even red circles he drew on both sides of my face are the Ildiloi, the tribal marks burnt on most Maasai's cheeks in their childhood.

CHAPTER 1

Enkong'y naipang'a eng'en

The traveler's eyesees further.

"Rooaar, shh, shh, shh, shh."

I give a huge start. What is that noise coming from the kitchen house? It is super loud. I almost expect my colleagues to come running. It is early in the morning and I have slipped out of our *banda*, our sleeping house, to go to the outside toilet, about fifty meters away.

"Rooaar, shh, shh, shh, shh." There it is again. What is that? I can't see a thing, it is pitch dark. Wild horses could not drag me to that toilet now. One thing is certain: something is lurking in the darkness, waiting to haul a sizeable portion of meat into the bushes. My legs are shaking. I need to hurry back and fast. I start moving backward toward the *banda* as quickly as my fear will allow. The hissing quietens down a little. But the pressure in my bladder has become even worse. Crap. I cannot just pee inside the hut. There's no way around it. Pressed flat against the outside wall of our *banda*, I tiptoe around the hut and quickly do my business before hastily slipping back into our big sleeping room. Everything is quiet in here. My roommates' snoring is the only sound I hear, a fact that leads me to conclude that no one has noticed a thing. I can't hear anything anymore. Perhaps "it" has gone? My heart won't stop pounding in my chest, though, and it is some time before I can go back to sleep.

"Have you been partying for too long, Stephanie?"

Someone pulls the blanket away.

"Hey!" I protest, drowsily straightening up. "Not quite partying, no. Rather an encounter of the third kind."

My colleagues exchange baffled looks as I tell them about my nightly adventure. The mystery is solved, though, when I stride towards the hut's entrance door and bump right into our guides.

"We had some visit, look," Aroni, our guide, says, pointing to huge paw prints in the sand all around the building.

"Leopard," he explains.

My heart sinks into my boots. A leopard!

I realize only now how incredibly lucky I have been. The leopard's paw prints are barely three meters away from my own footprints. I tell Aroni that I have heard the animal.

"There are two reasons why he did not attack you," he proceeds to explain. "Either he was already full or he thought you were too big a prey for him."

"Ain't I the lucky one," I reply with a thin smile.

"His roars were definitely a warning to you."

"Well, I'm lucky I got that right, then."

Over a year before, reading the ad on my way out of the university canteen, I knew nothing of all this, of course. "Volunteers wanted for an environmental project in Zimbabwe!" the note said. Practical training and research semesters are part of the requirements for my biology and environment protection studies. We are not supposed to gain knowledge in lecture halls alone but also in the field. The same goes for our dissertation, as the final paper for my studies is called at the British University of Bath. I eagerly go over the advertisements for the different organizations.

The "Learn From Lion Cubs" ad catches my eye. It sounds so gratifying, and it is actually the most popular program at the time, as I will learn later. The more I read the more skeptical I become, though. Lion cubs, abandoned in the wilderness, are gathered to be bottle-fed and raised in special facilities, thus becoming accustomed to humans. Tourists get to pet and spend some time with these "wild beasts" for a mere 100 dollars. How deviant is that? Li-

onesses have to leave their cubs to hunt for food, often staying away for days
– a very dangerous time for their offspring. Some cubs get lost and become an
all too easy prey for other predators, but then this is the way of nature. Taking
the cubs to some other place is nothing short of kidnapping. Upon her return,
the lioness will search for her cubs for weeks, failing to eat herself and in the
end, falling prey to predators. In my opinion, the project serves one single
goal: to scrounge money for tourists under the guise of animal protection.

I absolutely refuse to support something like that. And I will certainly not pay to promote such utterly unnatural behavior. In the course of my studies, I have come to recognize how questionable some measures allegedly taken in the name of animal and environment protection really are.

This is why I decide to choose another project. In Hwange National Park, in Zimbabwe, I can learn a lot about animal life, elephants, for instance. I will be taught to read their tracks, record their population, discover the paths they take and find out what kind of problems they have to face with poachers, hunters, or simply their coexistence with the local human population. I need to gain experience in national park management and learn how to prevent poaching.

In my dissertation, I write about the conflict between man and beast in Africa. Not everything is black and white, as I have learned in my studies. Who actually needs to be protected from whom? Saving elephants from extinction is crucial, yet when hordes of elephants devour the crops, human survival is at risk. How do these conflicts between man and beast arise, and what must we undertake to ensure the peaceful coexistence of both groups? I hope my taking part in that protect will help me acquire new insight for my work. My choice, however, is not entirely devoid of risk. The Federal Foreign Office advises against traveling to Zimbabwe at the moment, as the current presidential elections are marred by acts of violence and repression following allegations of electoral fraud against long-standing president Robert Mugabe. The country is deemed unsafe, the economy is in tatters, the population shaken and at risk of poverty. Zimbabwe, with its many natural resources and varied landscape, has nevertheless long been considered as the Jewel of Africa.

I won't let myself be deterred by these warnings. The contact person of the African Impact organization is also quite encouraging: "Unrest mostly occurs in the capital city, Harare. That's 700 kilometers away from our camp. There's no need to be afraid. We won't notice a thing down there."

I book a flight and also get a typhus and meningitis shot. My backpack is ready and packed in my student room.

After a brief stop in Johannesburg, South Africa, I board a smaller plane heading for Victoria Falls. The airport is located at the upper part of Zimbabwe. The famous waterfalls share their name with the small town as well as with the airport. After an almost a two hour flight, this part of the journey is finally over too. My excitement rises.

The exit door of the plane opens to a brilliant blue sky. A warm breeze caresses my face as I take in that first impression. Then I step aside to allow the other passengers to disembark. I have finally reached my destination – after a 9,000 kilometer journey. Standing on the small gangway-platform, I gaze upon the premises. A few palm trees line the edge of the airport. No more British drizzle! I traded it at last for the sun, high up in the cloudless sky. The weather is warm, but not too hot. Just perfect.

A small, densely crowded airport awaits me. A great number of visitors are attracted to that magic spot near the Zambian border, where the Zambezi River plunges down into the valley 110 meters below. As I wait at the baggage claim, I think about the Victoria Falls, the broadest waterfall on earth, but it is not the UNESCO World Heritage Site. After some time, I glimpse my huge backpack moving lazily towards me. Something is wrong, though. Surely something is missing? The sleeping bag I had fastened to my backpack is gone. Perhaps it will show up on its own? I think, watching the rotating belt with confidence. After a while, there is no luggage left, the belt is empty, and my sleeping bag is gone. Damn it! Clinging onto my last shred of hope, I head towards a service desk and ask about the lost-and-found.

"Have you found a sleeping bag?" I ask the woman sitting behind the desk in English.

"No, nothing is left!" she replies, shaking her head.

"But it cannot simply dissolve into thin air, can it? Perhaps it is still in the hold?" I insist. But all my questions are met with denial. I can fill in a form in the hope that the item will be found after all. For the time being though, I am upset and clueless. What am I supposed to do without the sleeping bag I was specifically requested to bring along? After a while I manage to calm down. This whole thing has proved quite time-consuming. The people of the organization are waiting for me!

For the first time in my life, I am in the minority, as a white woman. The Victoria Falls are normally a huge tourist attraction, but it seems fewer European tourists have made the journey, what with the troubled presidential election. A little ahead of me in the crowd, I spot another fair-skinned, blond woman about my age, walking up towards the exit, whom I briefly noticed earlier on the plane. I had been far too excited then to realize she too, might be a volunteer. In front of the exit door, my gaze falls upon a man holding a sign that reads: "African Impact - Mona and Stephanie." The woman and I both head in his direction. We look at each other and burst out laughing.

"Hi, I am Mona!" the woman says, introducing herself.

How cool is that! We have both enlisted in the same program and feel at once a sense of community. I am not alone, after all. Mona is 21 years old and studies zoology, which I find rather exciting. For now though, we both turn to the guy holding the sign.

"Hi, welcome to Zim. I am Nathan. I will take you to the Lodge."

Nathan is our driver. He, too, works at the camp. About our age, he was born in the capital, Harare, and studied biology. Just like us, he is white. This actually surprises me, as the proportion of people of non-African descent in Zimbabwe lies below two percent.

We get into the SUV, while our luggage lands in the back of the car. It is a twenty-minute drive to Hwange, Nathan explains to us, the biggest national park in Zimbabwe, stretching to the foothills of the Kalahari-Desert, at the border of the neighboring country, Botswana. I read Hwange acquired national park status as early as 1930, counting among the most important nature reserves of the country today. This shall be my workplace for the next two months.

I gaze out of the window and listen to Mona's and Nathan's conversation. Left-hand traffic does not confuse me. I am actually quite used to it, having studied in England. The British streets, however, don't have much in common with the bumpy dirt roads we jolt over. Nor does the breakneck speed of local drivers.

We soon leave the small town of Victoria Falls behind us and head towards the national park when our Range Rover suddenly swerves into a small path. Shortly after, we find ourselves rushing along a private road towards a group of buildings, past a parking lot and a larger house, resting amidst a splendid garden, around a lavishly planted roundabout, and all the way up to one of the smaller houses scattered around the main building. Have we come here to pick up something or someone?

"Come on, girls, this will be your home for the next two months," Nathan declares.

Mona and I look at each other, not quite believing our own eyes. We had both expected to sleep rough, wild animals sniffing our tent at night. What a surprise! But then we are young and flexible and who would find fault with such luxurious accommodation anyway? Certainly not us students! Nathan explains to us that only a few people volunteer to take part in that program. Setting up a camp just for them would not make much sense. Part of the local crew, the manager, other national park guides, rangers, the park's nightwatchers, and two cooks are also accommodated here.

"We have a deal with the owners," Nathan tells us. "Our local helpers and members live in their villages. They walk or ride their bike to get here, or else we pick them up."

Nathan, too, shares a room with a ranger on the compound.

Our eyes widen with amazement during the subsequent tour. Two large main buildings stand right next to the entrance, housing the restaurant and the administration. Ten sand-colored brick houses of various sizes, some of them circular, covered with dried palm leaves reminiscent of thatched roofs, spread across the entire area. We also make out two wooden houses on stilts in the distance.

"They offer an especially nice view of the park. Great for tourists," Nathan declares, smiling.

There is even a pool with an outdoor bar at the back. Mona and I look about us in awe. We finally stop in front of one of the small circular stone houses. Nathan opens the door and beckons us inside. Excited, we follow him into the house and find ourselves inside a beautiful room with floor-to-ceiling windows and a private bathroom. I definitely won't miss my sleeping bag here.

The lodge borders directly on the national park. We enjoy a breathtakingly beautiful view of the vast nature before us, occasionally catching a glimpse of its inhabitants hiding in the thicket of bushes. As we will learn in the following weeks, we will get many animal visits here. The pool also serves as a watering hole, which is at times actually quite entertaining but can also prove rather frightening. In all cases though, it never fails to be exciting!

As it is, I will never get to use the pool we admired on the day of our arrival, more because of the cold than due to the presence of animals. But I don't know that yet. Even though the days are fairly warm, with temperatures ranging from 20 to 27 degrees, as soon as the sun sets in the early evening, it gets bitterly cold, with temperatures dropping sometimes to five degrees.

The next surprise awaits us at dinner. We are served a three-course meal. What an unexpected luxury! We are being accommodated like regular tourists, just like our driver has assured us. Sitting at the table with our team, we are introduced to the others, some of whom are also housed in the lodge, while others live in the neighborhood and come here every day. Besides Nathan, whom we already know, I only manage to remember Jabolani's name. I forget the others' names at once. Sometime during the main course, exhaustion kicks in. No long night for me. We leisurely stroll back to our house after dinner and bid the others goodnight for what is to be our first night in Africa. Little by little I wind down and relax, suddenly realizing at the same time how tense and excited I have been. But I feel good now. Tired, but glad. I am here now. The place is much more beautiful than I would have dared to hope. Mona seems nice, and we will get started tomorrow.

The quiet is deceptive, though. A loud noise pulls me out of sleep. "Hoo-hoo, hoo-hoo…" It is a minute before I manage to get my bearings. Where am I? Strange bed, strange room. I look about, puzzled, in the soft light of dawn. Oh yes, right. I am in Zimbabwe. But what was that noise? It was certainly no dream. There it is again! My watch shows five o'clock in the morning. I have been fast asleep and dreaming until that odd sound tore me from sleep, and not too gently. I listen closely in the morning hush. "Hoo-hoo, hooi-hoo…" There it is again. What kind of gigantic bird might that be? But as I lay in bed, wondering whether I should go and see for myself, sleep overcomes me anew.

"Did you hear them?" Jabolani, the guide we met yesterday, asks during breakfast.

"The loud bird?" I reply. "Yes, I did, it woke me. What was it? I wanted to get out and shoo it away, but I fell back asleep."

He gives me a strange, disbelieving look, then bursts out laughing.

"It's a good thing you stayed inside. Your bird was a hyena, prowling very close to your house."

"But I thought…" I stammer, taken aback.

After the first shock, I realize nature here will not be stopped by stone houses or garden fences. I need to learn how to deal with that, and fast.

"Don't ever run!" Nathan says to us, explaining the basic rules. "Running turns you into a welcome meal for lions, cheetahs, hyenas, or other animals. They are used to their prey fleeing before them, and they will catch everything that moves."

Mona and I stare at him wide-eyed.

"If you stand still, though, they won't know how to react. Because the only thing that flees is prey, they will wonder what stands before them without moving. Scream! That unsettles them even more because they don't know the sound. Hopefully, they will reach the conclusion that you are not edible after all."

Sounds perfectly logical to me. Jabolani's lesson is almost too simple.

After breakfast, we ramble through the compound when a splendid green lizard suddenly flits across the road.

"Hey, he is amazing!" I cry out in surprise, chasing after the animal to observe it.

As I reach out to brush aside the tall grass, a snake slithers across the road, hissing, and snatches the lizard barely one meter away from my hand. I freeze, realizing what has just happened, and jump backward hastily. Mona lets out a scream. So do I.

"What did the snake look like?" Jabolani asks me later.

"Kind of checkered and brownish-white. Quite bulky too, except for its head that was flat and broad."

"Mmh, it seems this was our first encounter with a puff adder," he replies, grinning.

"Are they dangerous?" I ask.

"Venomous and responsible for most snake bites in Africa," he goes on to explain.

I feel funny all of a sudden.

"Most snakes are rather scared of humans, though," Jabolani continues reassuringly. "They feel the vibration of our footsteps and usually flee. Unless they are hungry, that is. But you should avoid reaching into the grass."

We are assigned Jabolani and Nathan for our first day of work.

"We will give you a short tour so you will get to know the park better," Nathan says.

Before we set off, he informs us about how we should behave. Animals are not the only dangerous creatures around; so are the poachers, who proceed ruthlessly to get their hands on elephant tusks. We give him a cautious, respectful smile.

"Never set off on your own. Always make sure to wear sturdy, closed shoes. Check the wind direction so the animals won't catch your smell. Be careful while you're on the move. Something might be hiding just about everywhere. Big or small." Such are the most important rules he provides.

I look at the two heavy rifles the men carry with them, and I swallow hard, suddenly realizing the whole thing might actually turn out to be life-threatening. There is no fooling around either with poachers or lions, elephants or any other hungry beast. I have never seen a weapon up close before, and I have to admit it does feel a little weird. But then, we are not on our own, fortunately, and I feel quite safe in the presence of the two guides.

Jabolani is Nathan's counterpart and a perfect addition as a second guide. Over sixty, he grew up in the area and belongs to the Ndebele community. The Shona make up the largest ethnic group, accounting for 70% of the population, as he informs us later. An experienced tracker, Jabolani will walk through the area with us a lot.

We set off to the national park, which is the largest in the country, for the first time. I know we will only get to see a small part of the almost 15,000 square meter nature reserve, and yet the thought we might see elephants, rhinos, giraffes, lions, leopards, impalas, and cheetahs in the wild makes my heart race. 40,000 elephants were registered at the last estimate, two years ago, in 2006. Our chances are actually high. Little do I know exactly how high. We get into the open off-road vehicle and set out.

Warm wind caresses my face. Very much aware of the extraordinary moment I'm experiencing right now, I embrace the impressions left by the ride. The park is huge, and the vegetation is very varied. The section of the park we presently drive through is covered with a lot of trees, dense thickets and high steppe-grass. Huge camel thorns and mopane trees offer ample shade, their juicy leaves providing food for the larger herbivores. They are also an indication of the presence of underground watercourses that can retain sufficient moisture during the brief wet seasons. A wide landscape suddenly opens before us and our vehicle jolts across dry, sandy ground dotted with deep holes. I spot a group of giraffes in the distance. How utterly surreal. I almost pinch myself. Until now, I have only ever seen the gigantic animals on TV. Spotting them in the wild is a very moving and at the same time, very surreal experience. Never would I have believed that I would actually make it out of my small Hessian village into the big wide world. And yet I did it. It is real, as real as the giraffes standing a mere hundred meters away from us.

Our territory lies within the green part of the national park. Other sections, closer to the Kalahari Desert in the south-west, present a more barren landscape, as Nathan informs us. He also tells us that besides smaller lakes and rivers, over 60 artificial waterholes, equipped with pumps, ensure the preservation of the park's abundant animal population. Checking the waterholes will be one of our most important missions.

During our one-hour drive, we already get to see many incredible animals. Antelopes, zebras, and warthogs crossing our path, tails wagging. At last, Nathan stops the car next to a large clearing.

"High time for a little walk," he declares.

We don't need to be told twice and readily climb out of the car to follow our guides.

Jabolani takes the lead, pointing to tracks on the ground such as twisted branches, flattened grass or droppings, and telling a story for each trace, along with its source and the matching animal. He plucks leaves off branches and rubs them between his hands so we might sniff them. Mona and I hang at his every word. After a while, we try to make out lions' or other animals' paw prints on our own.

"Shh, shh," Jabolani murmurs suddenly, stooping and pointing in a certain direction. "Elephants, three bulls!"

I can hardly breathe.

At first I feel them. The ground vibrates beneath my feet and the trunks of the trees in the small clearing where we duck and cover tremble and shake. There is a rustle of leaves. A tiny beetle hurtles by. Then I hear heavy breathing and a drawn-out snort, as if one would kindle a fire using a gigantic bellows. The vibration increases, and I suddenly see them. Enormous, grey-brown mountains, less than ten meters away from me. Three elephants. Thoughtfully moving their massive feet, they gracefully make their way through the landscape, heading right in our direction.

My heart misses a beat. Do the others feel the same? I stay stock-still, not daring to look at anyone. Even though we have been told how to behave, there is definitely a very significant gap between theory and practice. Jabolani drops into a crouch and with one finger on his lips, gestures at us to do the same. I barely dare to breathe. We are lucky. Right in front of our hiding place, another cluster of trees seems obviously appealing to the animals. The wind is on our side too and blows right into our face, so the elephants cannot smell us. The group pauses. The biggest bull briefly lifts his trunk, sniffs and looks about. The two others wait, swaying slightly on their feet, their trunks feeling the ground, their breath blowing on the dry ground.

Facing these massive giants here, in the wild, is an incredible feeling. I am both scared and completely fascinated. The faint grin on Jabolani's face does not escape me. My fear dissolves, and a warm feeling spreads through me.

"Let's take a picture," Jabolani suggests.

Seriously? Has the man gone insane? I cannot believe my own ears. I am so scared I can barely move!

"Come Stephanie, they can't smell us, and they seem quite peaceful right now," Jabolani says soothingly.

The experienced guide saw right away that the bulls were not in musth. The annual testosterone surge turns the usually quite peaceful creatures into very aggressive and unpredictable animals.

Jabolani insists. Taking the camera from me, he presses the button. No doubt my fear will be plain to see for anyone looking at the picture later. I stand stooped, not daring to straighten up. Long after the impressive encounter, while we are already on our way back, I can still see the massive trio in my mind's eye. I came to Africa exactly to experience that exact feeling. At that moment, in that small forest in Zimbabwe, I am merely filled with warmth and a kind of faint longing. Twelve years later, I know what home feels like. I know what it feels like to finally belong. Back then though, it was the first time I had ever felt that way.

A few days later, we have settled in and found something like a regular daily routine. There are no fixed working hours here, our work depending on whatever needs to be done. Counting the animals and following their tracks, observing them, looking out for poachers' wire traps and taking them apart so they can no longer cause any harm, checking the waterholes, and collecting animals' carcasses – all this is part of our core missions in the weeks to come. The national park appears quite different in the gathering dusk, filled with other sounds and noises, other creatures too. As we drive through the darkness, countless pairs of eyes are reflected in the sweeping light of the car's headlights. Some animals, startled by the bright light, jump right in front of our car. The pistes, however, are in such a bad state that we drive slowly most of the time, and except for a fright now and then, no one gets hurt.

But working during the day might also end up badly, as Mona and I learn a few days later.

"Today, we need to clear the weeds obstructing one of the waterholes on the west side of the park," Jabolani tells us. "The animals get caught in them or have limited water access."

At first sight, the job does not sound particularly spectacular. Yet once on-site, we realize the extent of the mess. Liana-like weeds twine around one another in thick clusters, while thorny bushes, dragged by violent storms, have become entangled with the weeds and form an insurmountable barrier. Larger animals such as gnus, zebras, or buffalos cannot gain access to the water, while smaller ones risk getting stuck in the thicket. The plants have grown so dense and thick in some parts that they have created backwater ponds, turning the water into a foul-smelling, disgusting soup swarming with flies. Wild animals are certainly not squeamish, but one look at the water is enough to convince anyone that the whole thing is positively teeming with bacteria. And so we set to work.

"You need to tear out these long things with stump and stem," Nathan says, showing us how it is done. "Otherwise, they grow back much too quickly."

We all get started courageously. Although we work close to the edge of the water, the job is arduous and sweaty, the damn things showing great

13

resistance. At times, I have to use all my strength to pull the roots out of the ground. Sweating like crazy, I am soon covered with mud and drenched with sweat and water, so much so that I fling my hat aside and take off some of my clothes. Quite pointless, as it turns out. The sun shines bright, just like it does every day, and we are so focused on our work that we do not realize how hard it beats down on us for hours on end. This, of course, is not without consequences. At some point, I start to feel giddy.

"Does anyone have some water left?" I ask around.

"I think that's enough for today," Nathan replies. "We did a good job here, and you look really worn out, girls."

Not only do we look worn out, we also truly are so.

My head pounds badly on the way back, and something flickers before my eyes.

"Can you please stop?" I ask, barely managing not to vomit inside the car and taking two shaky steps aside. We have both got massive sunstroke and are done in for today. A cold shower, a darkened room, a bucket kept close to the bed, and lots of sleep are the only effective antidotes. On the next day, our legs still feel a bit wobbly, but apart from that, we are fine.

"Oh boy, we should have taken better care of you!" Nathan says, contrite.

We are given a free day to fully recover and spend the rest of the day reading in the shade.

We have quickly adjusted to our new circumstances and every day jump into the Range Rover without a second thought. I absorb everything like a sponge. Some things, such as a close encounter with death, I experience for the first time. During one of our rides, we notice several black bumps lying on the ground in the distance. Dead water buffalos. The animals must have been lying there for quite some time, their massive bodies already extremely swollen and bloated, the smell of decay lingering in the air. I will never again forget that smell. I also smell it when we pull carcasses out of poachers' wire snares. Locating these, along with other kinds of traps, is a crucial mission. In the evening, I ponder over the hard work, rubbing my aching hands. It is not the nicest part of my stay, but I am still glad we do not end up finding ourselves in the unpleasant circumstance of actually catching poachers red-handed. I certainly would not like to experience that.

During one particularly long drive, Nathan mentions our commitment.

"It's quite funny, actually. You are paying thousands of dollars to help me do my actual job," he declares, clearly baffled.

I have a different view of things; the money we pay to take part in volunteer programs also finances important public work. As I see it, there is profit on many different levels. I learned so much here and got to experience things I would never have been able to experience in Europe.

We spend our free time in a very relaxed manner. Our days are so packed that we enjoy rather quiet evenings. We don't want to party, even though procuring beer or other beverages would have been no trouble. We don't spend all our time together though, nor do we take all our meals as a team. From time to time, Nathan's girlfriend comes to visit. She is part of the lion program.

"Sometimes I need a break," Nathan explains. "Don't get me wrong. But from time to time, smart-talking tourists, in particular, do get on my nerves."

I can really understand that. We, too, appreciate being on our own sometimes.

We rarely get to see life around the lodge, only venturing into the neighboring villages whenever we need to buy some personal items. The very nasty stomach flu that had me completely on my knees constituting one big exception to that rule. After having spent three days swaying between my bed and the toilet, Jabolani packs me into the Rover and drives me to Dete, a small town of a thousand souls. The options inside the simple hospital are quite limited, though. A person wearing a white coat presses a little on my belly before handing me a couple of aspirin. And with that, we set off back home. Two days later, the whole thing is over, and I am fit again.

As much as I enjoy my time here, I miss the academic aspect of our work. Contrary to what we had been led to expect, the program is not very scientific, despite the claims of the members of the organization.

"Yes, we will take you to the farmers! We will prepare a questionnaire for you so you can conduct some research for your dissertation."

On-site, however, I quickly realize nothing of the sort has been prepared. There is no questionnaire, no research analysis, and no meaningful figures. This is why I am all the more glad when Nathan offers me to take part in a very special trip.

"Would you like to talk to a farmer who experiences a lot of trouble with hungry elephants?" he asks me after a fortnight.

"Definitely!" I reply eagerly at once.

I don't need to give that a lot of thought!

"And I can also show you our sample plant project we use to draw natural boundaries around the farms."

Sounds thrilling.

On the next day, I meet Thabani, a farmer faced with a huge problem. Hungry elephants regularly devour his corn crop. On a neighboring farm, one of the field hands was even killed by the animals. Thabani finds himself fighting for his existence and his survival.

We talked together for about an hour, and the man told me willingly about his hardships. I dutifully take notes so I will at least gather some material for my dissertation. The elephants are not to blame. They know no boundaries and follow their own trails, sweeping over whatever farm has been built on their trail due to wrong land management.

At the beginning of my studies, I considered myself an animal rights activist. The animal world is threatened by humans and I must do everything in my power to counter this. But I began to develop a deeper understanding of the different connections; I realized things could not be solved with such all-or-nothing thinking. Although many species around the world are indeed being driven out of their natural habitat and threatened by hunting, the same fate also befalls a lot of humans. While there are now large national parks in Africa for wild animals, farmers and indigenous communities find increasingly less suitable habitats, which in turn leads to many conflicts. And this brings me to my subject.

What I only ever learned about in theory before, I now get to experience first-hand in Zimbabwe. There is a massive difference between learning about nature conservation from afar and actually experiencing it. Retrospectively, I realize how important such moments turned out to be for me, fundamentally changing my view of things. Nature protection can only ever work in relation to people. One needs to talk and listen to people and come up with solutions so man and beast might coexist in peace.

After our visit to the farm, Nathan takes me to a special plant project. Once again, I have no clue as to what actually awaits me when I spot something that very much resembles countless gigantic pineapples in the distance. Bulky short trunks with huge, sword-like, thick leaves. As we come closer, the plants remind me of aloe vera.

"These are sisal agaves," Nathan explains. "See the sharp thorns on the edge of the leaves? That's the difference with the aloe."

"How do you plan to use them? Why are they grown here?" I ask.

"They make for very efficient barriers, protecting fields and farms. Even the mighty elephants don't trample over them."

This could be a way to support the farmers without killing the elephants. I shall include these essential findings in my dissertation, which I am due to begin after my six-week stay in Zimbabwe. It is my final year at the university. Once I am finished, I will reorient myself.

CHAPTER 2

Metum orrip tuli kiteng.

No cow for the idle one.

I spend most of my days on the campus to complete my courses while simultaneously working on my dissertation and spending countless hours in the university's gigantic library for my research. I work at the San Francisco Fudge Factory three times a week to pay for my rent and living expenses. It is one of the best jobs I have ever managed to secure until now. Not only does it offer the most delicious varieties of fudge, but the owners, Maureen and Mark, are also the best bosses ever.

"Well, it looks like we will lose you soon, I am afraid," Mark says, grinning.

All my work colleagues are definitely very patient listeners and have heard my stories about Zimbabwe by now.

I love my life in Bath. And yet, for all that, I cannot picture myself living here forever. I have already come up with my next plan for Africa and have applied for a job as a research associate in a camp in Tanzania. As it is, I am to go to London a few weeks later for a job interview. Will it go well, I wonder?

Every day, I check my mailbox and my emails with great anticipation. Until, in the end, the long-awaited letter finally arrives. My heart hammering wildly, I tear open the envelope, the logo of the organization stamped on its upper corner.

"We are sorry to inform you..."

A rejection. I am infinitely disappointed. The letter says something about a lack of experience and other, more qualified candidates. To hell with it, I think to myself, shaking off the frustration. I won't be deterred by that letter and continue my research. Still having a little money left from my aunt's inheritance, I book a six months stay with the same organization that has rejected my application - with the difference that I won't receive any wages, quite the contrary actually, as I have to pay a lot of money to become a volunteer. I will work for three months in a bush camp in the Ifakara region, in the south of Tanzania, and spend the following three months on Mafia Island, working on a marine research program. I click on the send button to email my application. It's a good feeling. I just took the next step towards the future.

"Hi, I am Emma! Are you going to Selous, too?"

The woman sitting next to me seems nice. Together with a large group of volunteers, we have come to London at the invitation of the Frontier organization. We are assigned to our different projects and get to know each other. We also learn about the difference between a national park and a nature reserve.

National parks are state-run, while Selous is a privately managed large nature reserve. Hunting is forbidden in national parks, but photo safaris are allowed.

"It is quite easy to tell the difference between a nature reserve, a safari area, or a national park," James, the project leader, explains. "When the animals flee in panic before the arrival of your car, you are in a nature reserve. They associate your vehicle with the possibility of getting shot. Unfortunately, poachers don't abide by the rules in nature reserves or in national parks. That is why you will always be escorted by armed guides, apart from the security patrol."

This time, I will not be traveling to Africa on my own but with Emma. We will meet the other volunteers on site. My anticipation grows during the coming weeks, and I can hardly wait until it is finally time to leave in January. I don't have much time to ponder over things, though, having to work really hard for my studies. I feel really happy after having passed my last exam and having been given great marks for my dissertation by my professor. All the hard work I put in was definitely worth it. I cannot quite believe yet that I am finally done.

Mama

"Mama is dead."

I hear my brother's voice on the phone, but I don't comprehend yet what he is saying.

"She took her own life."

His words pierce through my heart like a sword. Mama, dead…

I should scream. Or faint. Wake up from a dreadful dream. But I am standing stock-still in my students' room in England, holding the receiver in one hand, unable to grasp what is happening to me.

It has happened then, I think, startled even as the words come to me. She did it. She actually did it. I am shocked, but I am not surprised. One of our aunts had told us that my mother had already attempted to take her own life several times. As a teenager, as a young woman, and later as a mother, when my twin sister and I were babies. She remained in hospital for two weeks back then. We were too young and thus utterly unaware of these dramatic events.

I have feared this very call my entire life. And now the day has come. My eyes wander to the calendar hanging on the wall. It is the 9th of July, 2009.

I cry for my poor mother, who lost her love of life at a very early age. She came to Germany from France as an au pair nanny when she was only 19 years old, fell in love here, and got married before drowning in sadness. And now she is dead.

It is a thirty-minute walk to my twin sister's home. She also lives in Bath and works in a hotel. Today is her day off.

"You'd better sit down."

I need a moment to collect myself.

"Mama is dead."

In a daze, I repeat the words I have heard from my brother only one hour before. We fall into each other's arms, sobbing.

I know now that my mother suffered from severe depression her whole life and would have required urgent help. When we were children, we had no word for it; people did not talk that openly about mental disorders back then. Getting help is not easy. All the more so when the person cannot accept any help in the first place. I recall the crippling sadness that weighed upon our flat like a cloud of fog and was etched deeply on our mother's face. The three of us always felt that she was unwell, but we had no means to change her condition. My parents separated when my twin sister and I were two years old and our brother six. The three of us became the most important thing in her life, but when we escaped from home with great relief, she was suddenly stripped of her mission.

Today should be a day of celebration. My fellow students have donned their nicest clothes and received their university diplomas. They now stroll along the streets, get drunk and party all night. I, on the other hand, find myself standing in the graveyard of a small Hessian town, watching as my mother's coffin is slowly lowered into the ground.

One of the greatest days in my life has become one of the saddest.

Would my mother have attended the celebration in England? Would she have felt proud seeing her daughter on stage as she received her diploma? Probably not. It has been a long time since we have celebrated anything together. My mother sank into her own dark world much too soon. She had no strength left for bright moments.

I wish it would all have come differently. I ardently wish my mother had not been ill.

As I take my leave of her, I make a promise to myself – I shall not waste or give away my life. On the contrary, I shall endeavor always to remember and feel its value. I shall get out into the world and discover my own mission.

Tanzania

As the doors of the plane close on a grey, wintery London day, I am about to embark on a new chapter of life in an entirely different world. We travel via Cairo to Dar es Salaam, the largest city in the country. Five million women, men, and children live in the former capital city of Tanzania. On the gangway, the warm air blows into my face as if coming right out of a hairdryer. I get a strong sense of déjà-vu and take a deep breath. Standing next to me, Emma, who experiences this for the first time, bursts out laughing. Then we plunge into the hustle and bustle of the metropolis' airport, grab our travel backpacks from the belt, and follow the flow of people drifting towards the exit.

"And here I was, thinking London was overcrowded, but this is unbelievable!" Emma cries enthusiastically.

I know what she means. Everything is fuller, louder, hotter, and much more colorful. In front of the airport building, we look about us searchingly. I hear someone whistle.

"Hey Stephanie, I am Stella! I will be your driver for the next two days," an unknown woman says by way of introduction.

I am baffled. I had not expected a female taxi driver.

"I often work with Frontier. We will surely see a lot of each other."

Chattering away happily, Stella leads us through Dar es Salaam's chaotic traffic. Honking and swearing, she entertains us in a mix of the country's two official languages, English and Swahili. I have read that 125 languages are spoken here by just as many ethnic groups. Stella takes us to a small hotel where we are to spend one night. Tonight, we will meet the other volunteers, as well as the women and men on the team. In the morning, we will set off by bus to Ifakara, the main town of the Kilombero district, about 400 kilometers away.

Dar es Salaam is awesome. It feels like we have just landed in the middle of Tanzania's beating heart. On our way from the airport, we stare in amazement at the city's skyline and the huge harbor, where container ships dock alongside ferry boats. Huge skyscrapers rise to the sky as we cruise through green, clearly expensive neighborhoods and poverty-stricken areas - quite a contrast. The deeper we progress into the heart of the city, the livelier and busier it gets. Throngs of people wearing colorful clothes weave in and out of the crowd on narrow streets, dangerously close to the honking and jostling lines of cars. The sidewalks are not used as much by pedestrians; rather, they serve as extended shop floors. People circumvent carts brimming with melons and bananas, street vendors and traveling merchants, and market women selling all manner of goods. Many women balance large parcels on their heads or pull small carts behind them.

It is a good thing that I don't have to drive around here; not only do the people stand right in the middle of the street, but they also jump in front of fast-approaching cars most adventurously. Seeing children in the midst of all this frenzy makes me really scared, and I keep holding my breath or crying out in fear as I picture a fateful collision. Very surprisingly, though, nothing of the sort happens.

The car stops in a narrow alley in front of a small hotel. As soon we step out of the air-conditioned vehicle, the heat washes over our faces. Pew. My body will probably need a few days to adjust to the tropical sun after coming from the cold British winter. I feel a little giddy, and we decide against going for a stroll through the streets, choosing to rest in our darkened room until our meeting in the evening.

"Wake up, you late riser!"

All right, this might be a slight exaggeration. After all, morning is just dawning. But then, as we were told yesterday, the buses have to leave very early for very, very long journeys.

Emma nudges me gently. It is a moment before I manage to wake up fully.

"Today is the day it finally starts," she cries happily, even more excited than I am.

We both put to good use our last opportunity to take a shower. Who knows when and how we will get another chance? Our backpacks are packed and ready in no time. Stella is there, waiting for us in front of the hotel. We are supposed to meet the others at the bus stop. If things did seem hectic the day before, during our taxi ride, they reach an entirely different level at the bus terminal. Except we are now part of the frantic hustle. It is still dark, desperately overcrowded, chaotic, and loud. Help! We are lucky to have Stella with us. We could never make it to the right bus without her. Tanzanian signage leaves us clueless. I completely fail to understand which bus is heading where or where we are supposed to get on our bus.

Here, too, countless market women and vendors are waiting for willing customers.

"Mister, Madam, please, buy this, buy that, you need this!" they call as we make our way past them.

White women are spoken to in English, of course. I stagger after the quick-moving Stella, doing my best not to bump into anyone - quite a hopeless enterprise, as it turns out.

"Your bus is over there," Stella says, pointing to one of the many vehicles. "But you still need some food, girls! You will be traveling for an entire day."

No lack of choice here. The faces of many men and women beam with longing expectation. After all, they have to pay for their living with their earnings. Biscuits, power banks, earbuds for mobile phones, bread, and many other goods are thrust into my face. I decline most of them, though, exhausted by the loud shouting and blinding light of the stalls. In the end, we settle on buying some fruit, bottles of water, and bread. When we reach the bus, a huge file of people has formed. Our colleagues are already waiting in line. That's quite a load off my mind. We part with Stella and walk up the passenger stairs of the large coach. Peace and quiet? Of course not! We are riding on an African bus; not only do we share the space with a large number of chattering men, women, and children of all ages, but also with various kinds of animals. Traveling with clucking hens is a first for me and could actually prove quite funny, if it wasn't for the chicken droppings which I'm not too keen on. Emma and I exchange a smile. We take the whole thing easy. After fifteen minutes of no little turmoil, people have found their seats and somehow managed to cram their luggage and belongings above or under their seats, on the roof, or on their lap. The bus is packed to the brim. I am glad we managed to secure seats. Not everyone is as lucky as the central aisle is full of passengers. Our relief, however, is short-lived. We have just left the bustling city behind us when the bus suddenly stops by the side of the road.

"Is this already the first stop?" I ask Emma.

That would actually have been nice.

"Hey, the bus broke down, unfortunately. You all need to get out!"

What? I cannot believe what the driver has just announced. Perhaps I did not quite catch his words with all the din around? It turns out I have, though. The bus broke down, and our journey ends here. Lovely prospect. After all, there are only 380 kilometers to go.

"You'd better get used to it right away," Billy, whom we know from London, says, grinning. "Bus breakdowns are a daily occurrence around here. As are accidents..."

Well, what a relief! A breakdown is definitely the better option of the two.

To think that I had just been enjoying my seat... Now, barely one hour later, I find myself standing in the central aisle of the replacement bus, which is not so much a replacement as simply the next bus. This means two busloads of people and animals now have to squeeze inside one vehicle. Air conditioning? Nope. That's all I needed. During the forty or so minutes we have been waiting by the side of the road, the rising heat has crept into my bones, and after only a few minutes on the bus, sweat is running down my body. Eight hours of standing, that's something. But then, hey, I am young, right? I keep reminding myself to muster up some measure of courage. After two hours, though, my whole body hurts. We try to alternate places so that one of us at least – in our group of six people - gets to enjoy the only seat we managed to secure. It is a small relief. Looking out of the window, I observe the fleeting landscape to distract myself. It seems highly unlikely that I should manage to doze off for a bit, and I might as well concentrate on sightseeing.

The bus is plowing through an endless green sea of rippling rice fields. Rice? It is the first time in my life that I have seen rice fields. The route of the bus crosses right through the Mikumi National Park, our very first safari, making for a nice compensation for the torture we are subjected to. If our circumstances are uncomfortable, the vista is breathtakingly beautiful: antelopes, huge elephants, and even lions, lazing by the side of the road or else playing and crossing our path. It is worth it. It is a good thing the overcrowded bus cannot speed on such bumpy ground.

"This is where you will be sleeping. Pick one of the beds."

Yes. Truly rustic circumstances. I am standing inside a large *banda*, which is what this type of building is called, with a dozen camp beds to the right and left. It is spacious enough, though, and has lots of fresh air. We are staying inside an open, simply built house on stilts and piles, topped with a thatched roof and hoops hanging from the ceiling to fasten the mosquito nets. The house is furnished with a few tables and some open shelves. We drop our backpacks on our beds and join the others for the tour.

I have already come to understand that my second stay in Africa will be quite different from the first. And not only because we are living in a rustic camp in the middle of the bush instead of in some luxurious lodge. This time, we are taking part in a scientific wildlife protection support program that has been running for some time. The program aims to identify the routes chosen by wild animals, especially elephants and buffalo herds, both inside the reserve and in the area bordering the adjoining national park. More and more farmers have settled within this vast expanse of land, and the coexistence between humans and wildlife is increasingly full of conflict. It is a topic I am very familiar with, having written my dissertation on that subject. To make a change, one must know the facts; this is why we are here.

Even the temperatures are different. We arrived during the shorter wet season that lasts from November to February. Every day, the thermometer steadily reaches 30 degrees and above. In about eight weeks, though, the second wet season will begin in the middle of March, bringing very heavy rainfall.

"Make sure you pack closed, broken-in walking shoes," Billy, our team leader who has come with us on site, advised us in London. "You will walk many miles through the grounds. And don't forget a hat with a flap."

"Does anyone have a problem with elephant dung?" he asks us as we gather in front of the *banda*.

We shake our heads.

"On average, elephants eat up to about 250 kilos of leaves, twigs, grass, and fruit daily. Fear not, though; only a quarter of that comes out the other end."

Our daily routine will include spotting, assessing, and examining elephant and buffalo feces in the following months. We learn how to read the tracks left by the animals and follow their paths, locate them via our GPS, and then collect and analyze the data.

A larger camp is located closer to the action, and more locals are working with us. We have more demanding work. This is what I had in mind, I think to myself. I am quite satisfied.

"Please remember to put your shoes somewhere above ground and always check for scorpions or other creatures hiding inside before wearing them!" Billy says, bringing me back to reality in a flash. I am familiar with that warning and intend to heed it.

After Billy's introductory words, Emma and I continue our tour. The guides and the security staff stay at the far end of the camp in huge, cream-colored tents. The clattering of cooking utensils and some singing echoes from the kitchen house where our food is being prepared, a fireplace with a grill rack right next to it.

The most strategic places are slightly hidden from sight. Our toilet consists of a hole in the ground, about fifty meters away from our sleeping accommodation. A small - let's call it a wall - surrounds it, enabling one to enjoy the view of the open sky while being safe from prying eyes.

The same goes for our outdoor shower, which, to be honest, is not quite worthy of the name. To take a shower, one has to walk about a hundred meters toward a small stream, fill a few buckets of water, and splash oneself with it. After a few days, we get more daring: whenever it is possible, and we feel sure no one is watching, we head for the little brook and simply jump into it, naked.

Procuring drinking water proves slightly more time-consuming. Billy shows us huge black water tanks used to collect water during the two annual wet seasons. After the brook has dried up, the water we use for showering is also rationed. We have to make do with half a bucket. During that period, we drove the truck loaded with a jumble of huge canisters and buckets to the local water pump.

The pump consists of a small, silvery hand knob one has to work to coax water from the depths of the earth, and more often than not, in front of the pump is an endless line waiting. Many children and women in the area often walk several miles to provide clean drinking water for their village. It is here that I learn to consider the value of water with completely new eyes and a humble soul. How carelessly did I stand in the shower under running water? How thoughtlessly did I use to leave the tap running? I had read, of course, that many million people around the world have no access to clean water, but there is a huge difference between reading about something and experiencing it up close.

No shoving and jostling here, however. Everyone waits patiently in line. When our turn comes, we form a chain and fill bucket after bucket. It is a game of patience; as it turns out, the water trickling out of the pump is nothing more than a small rivulet. When no volunteers are available, the driver comes here alone and gives some small change to the kids standing by the pump to pay for their helping him.

I like these encounters by the water pump very much. No one is scared of the *mzungu* – the white woman – or too shy to talk to her. Quite the contrary.

"Can I touch your hair?" the children keep asking, unused to soft, flowing hair.

They want to touch it, sometimes even braid it. Everyone is friendly and open, and there is a lot of laughter. This is one of the reasons I chose to come to Tanzania: I want to meet people and get to know and understand them. I am not shy either; quite the opposite, actually.

"Why don't we take our meals together? Why is there a separation between black and white people?" I ask on the second day after our arrival in the camp.

Our group of volunteers does not share its meals with the wildlife reserve's guides and security staff.

"To be honest, we've never really given it a thought," Billy replies. "That's just the way it is."

"I have not come all the way to Tanzania to have meals only with the English group," I say, seizing my plate with determination before heading towards the kitchen house where all the black members of the team have just taken place.

"*Habari*!" I call across the room.

Habari - meaning Hello - is one of the few Swahili words I have learned so far. The guides do not speak much English either, which means we communicate in an international way – using our hands and feet.

"*Karibu*!" they answer heartily.

This is how I get to learn the word "welcome." The local team obviously appreciates my efforts and the interest I express, and soon the ice is broken. Learning about fauna and flora is all very good and important, but it is only half as interesting if one does not get to know the people who actually live in the country. Before long we all sit together at one table. I learn quite a lot, not only about locals, but also the language, a fact that will later prove very useful.

I wake up in the middle of the night with a dreadful headache and ghastly abdominal cramps. I feel awful and barely make it to our distant toilet. Diarrhea, lovely. I don't mind the lack of comfort at all, honestly, but when you've got diarrhea? After a few frantic trips to the toilet, I find myself shivering and hovering above the hole, fervently longing for the ceramic bowl of our lodge in Zimbabwe. I would trade just about everything for a comfortable sitting toilet. Within hours, I turn into a perfect picture of misery. My colleagues advised me to rest and fed me water and tea. I cannot get anything down. All I manage to do is sleep. I feel battered. Three days later, my condition has not improved.

"We need to see a doctor."

I allow Aroni, our guide, to take me to Ifakara without resistance. The bumpy ride is torture for my ravaged body.

A blood test in a small medical center finally brings some clarity: malaria. It has hit me hard. I am given a prescription. In the pharmacy close by, I stare with disbelief at the small package handed to me by the pharmacist. It contains exactly one tablet. This is supposed to make me better? Well, they must know what helps, I think to myself, obediently swallowing the tablet.

The following day is sheer hell. I feel even worse than on the day before. The room is spinning around me; my head feels like it weighs a ton, and I am so dizzy I can barely stand on my feet. I feel hot and feverish and unbelievably exhausted. The state I am in is hard to describe. I feel a little as if I were on drugs, or at least this is how I imagine it would feel like - stunned, numb, aloof. Sleep is the only thing that helps. After a few days, I feel a little better, and I can once again drive into the wild and work with the men and women on my team. I consider malaria as checked off - a huge mistake, as I shall soon come to learn.

A few weeks later, the whole thing starts again: headache, limb pain, exhaustion, dizziness. I return to the hospital and take another test. Then, I sit in a tiny room and wait for the result.

"It's a bit of a miracle that you can still stand on your two feet."

At first, I do not understand what the doctor means.

"You've got so much malaria in your blood that you should collapse on the spot!"

I cannot believe what he is saying, and I proceeded to tell him what happened to me before.

"No wonder, then. You were given the tablet for pregnant women," he explains to me. "When infected, pregnant women are not allowed to take powerful medicine."

"But I am not pregnant," I stammer.

"Precisely. That's why you had to come back here. The medication did contain the disease, but it did not cure you. You should stay here overnight."

"That is out of the question," I protest. "I don't feel as ill as I did the first time."

I manage to convince him, but I am still forced to swallow a very strong medicine. The doctor warns me about the potentially severe side effects, such as loss of balance. It won't come to that, I think to myself. There is no way I am staying here alone. Surely, my team will keep an eye on me.

The following five days are ghastly. I am once again in hell and completely knocked out. The doctor's prophecy comes true, of course, and I need to lean on Emma and the others because my legs keep giving out. I cannot hear a thing, and my balance is gone. It is bad. At times, I am even scared to die. It is several weeks before I am able to recover my strength completely.

"Stephanie, could you imagine staying here for longer? You are doing great work, and we could really use that right now."

I barely dare to believe my ears. I had not seen that coming when I was called into Billy's office. My head is spinning with thoughts.

"What exactly does it involve? And what about Mafia?"

As much as I like my job here, I have been looking forward to the second part of my stay.

"You will be going to Mafia," Billy explains. "But could you imagine staying here until the end of the year to complete a series of studies with us? Free of charge, naturally," he hastens to add. "We will supply food and lodging for free, and we will organize the rebooking of your stay in Mafia."

What an opportunity. I need to let it sink in a bit and request a few days to think about it. My head is racing with thoughts. What speaks against it, I ask myself, answering my silent question at once. Nothing. No one is waiting for me. I have no obligations or jobs that I would need to quit. I don't even have an apartment or any idea about what comes after Tanzania. I could assume more responsibilities in the research we are conducting here and gain more experience so I would be better qualified to apply for real jobs in research programs. I would also be able to improve my Swahili. I felt it in Zimbabwe, and I do feel it here: my heart beats for Africa. I have fallen in love with this continent, the work and the people. This is where I want to be. I shall stay here.

CHAPTER 3

Metumoi iltoiniyak kaake etumoi iltung'anak.

Mountains cannot ever meet, but people can.

For a split second, I forget to breathe. The hair on my arms stands on end. Goosebumps. I am looking at the most handsome man on earth. The world stands still for a moment. My heart is pounding, warm and excited. His eyes, his smile, his body, his posture. Proud and unbelievably handsome. I am fascinated. He is not alone; two other men accompany him, all of them wearing special robes in bold red tones. One of them has braided his hair into many tiny plaits. The most handsome man in the world wears his hair short. His build is broader than the others, not quite as thin. I don't like bony men. The man who makes my heart race is muscular, his shoulders square. The three of them wear eye-catching jewelry of tiny white pearls around their ankles and wrists or on their heads.

"Do you know them?" I asked my colleague Sophie, who I have also just met.

I try to sound as casual as possible and not stare at the men, even though that proves a little difficult.

"Of course!" she replies. "This is Sokoine, his cousin, and another Masai. They work as security guards at the diving station by the beach. They also work for us."

My heart gives a little leap at these words.

The men are Masai. This accounts for their striking clothes. I have not often seen men wearing traditional garments. Most of them wear everyday clothes. These three young men, however, are an exception: my first encounter with Masai warriors. There is no way I am going to miss this opportunity.

"Hey, *habari*, where are you going? What are you doing?"

I am surprised at my boldness that I should address them so easily! I have to talk to them before they turn the corner and disappear. I look into their faces, beaming, trying very hard to appear charming and cool. This has often helped me break the ice, yet it does not seem to work under the present circumstances. The boys do not show the slightest interest in me. Quite the contrary. They do not let it show if they are surprised at my speaking Swahili.

"We don't have time," they answer politely before turning on their heels.

Ouch, that stings. I cannot believe it. Today is not my day. I try to keep my composure as best I can, but the rebuff hurts. Sophie grins.

"Believe me, you're not the only one who finds the boys attractive. Masai men are very popular here. A lot of female tourists are after them," she explains.

"I just wanted to get to know them. I wasn't hitting on them," I protest.

"All right, then. No harm done."

What a start.

I arrived at Mafia one hour ago, my new job site for the Frontier organization, and I am already upset. Wanting to come here was a foolish idea. What is wrong with me? I was adamant about coming here and participating in that extraordinary marine conservation program. But that had been my plan a long time ago. I had not known, back then, how well I would feel in the other camp in Ifakara after having spent an entire year there. I have met people there who have become very dear to me. I have made friends, learned to speak and understand Swahili, and I have come to love life in the wilderness. I have not missed the comfort of European life. Being out in nature with others and doing something useful was very exciting. Yet now I have left all this behind. I feel a sharp pang of longing. The exhaustion I feel after the long, arduous journey to the village of Utende does nothing to improve things. When I arrived at the new camp, I felt very disappointed. It is small, narrow, and located in the middle of the village. There is no comparison with our huge camp in Ifakara, where one could enjoy many places of retreat. Whenever I needed to be on my own for a while, I would run a few laps around the open grounds. Here, however, the buildings stand close to one another. The neighbors can even peep into our open *banda* through the fence, as I notice right away. No privacy here, then.

Lovely. Everybody can gawk into my mouth as I sleep, I think to myself, upset, my mood deteriorating by the minute. Perhaps I have wasted my money here. The volunteer programs were quite expensive, after all. I paid over 2,500 euros to sign up, using part of my great-aunt's inheritance. Perhaps I could have found some more meaningful way to use that money…

"Let us take a walk," I suggest.

My colleague Sophie, who has been here for a few weeks, gives me a quizzical look but does not comment on my curt tone.

"Let me show you our departure dock by the beach. An important place for you in the coming weeks."

Things cannot possibly get worse, I think to myself as I muster up my courage and follow Sophie.

After a 200-meter walk through a palm grove, we find ourselves, very unexpectedly, in paradise. I am speechless in the face of such beauty. A long white sand beach stretches before us, the Indian Ocean a soft, rippling surface of crystal-clear turquoise waters. Beautiful and kitschy. This is my new job site, Mafia Marine National Park, a gigantic marine reserve where I will work for the next few weeks. Not such a gloomy prospect after all. My mood improves a little, and my resentment fades. That is precisely why I wanted to come here in the first place. Mafia is famous for its many areas that are rich in fish, its extensive coral reefs, and its strict regulations for travelers. Only a certain number of tourists are allowed on the island so as not to endanger the delicate flora, fauna, and underwater world.

In the eastern part of the island, not too far from here, sea turtles dig nests in the sand to lay their eggs, having left their familiar surroundings solely for that purpose. What I could only see on TV or read about in magazines until now, I now get to experience up close.

We wade a few meters into the water.

"Just like in a bathtub," I exclaim in surprise, warm water lapping against my legs.

"The ocean is 28 degrees warm at this time of year. Not exactly refreshing when the outside temperature is about 31 degrees," Sophie explains. "But wait until you dive deep underwater. Thirty meters down, things get much cooler."

I swallow. Thirty meters. Until now, I have spent most of my life on dry ground. I am not exactly a mermaid. But that's exactly why this program appealed to me so much, as one is expected to learn how to dive.

"It'll be a while till you get to do so, though. You are going to start slowly," Sophie reassures me. "This kind of depth is for advanced divers."

My one-week-long diving course starts on the next morning. There's nothing much one can do before taking it, and I am looking forward to it with much joy and anticipation. What is it going to be like, I wonder.

Gazing into the water, I can make out the gently sloping seabed opening into an abyss. Tiny, colorful fishes dash around me in the first few meters, and I wonder how it must be deeper down as I carefully avoid stepping on a spiny sea urchin.

Sophie turns around and points towards the beach at a jetty lined with small huts sporting thatched roofs made of all kinds of material.

"This is where we start; the diving school is next to it. That's where Sokoine works, by the way," she adds, grinning.

I grin back.

"Who knows, he might also be responsible for your oxygen."

We both laugh out loud.

"The other colleagues are still out there. We use several boats with various equipment according to the distance and mission we need to fulfill," Sophie explains. "Sometimes, we also sail out to other smaller islands for one or two hours. You might as well get used to spending most of the day far out underwater."

I make out a few patches of land in the distance. These must be the Juani, Chole, and Jibondo islands, which are all part of the Mafia archipelago.

Back at the camp, I meet the other volunteers and the Frontier crew. They all strike me as nice and easygoing and give me a warm welcome.

The next morning, the *banda* no longer seems so small and narrow. Sleep has restored my energy and good mood, and I jump out of the camp bed immediately. Diving lessons are the only thing on the agenda for the next few days. I cannot wait.

I spot Sokoine on our way to the diving school. My heart misses a beat. He looks so damn good, I think to myself, as I watch him manipulate the compressed air bottles with great concentration. Looking up briefly, he stops short, probably recognizing me. Then he leaves. We shall see about that, my dear, I think to myself. For now, though, I have another task at hand.

Over the next few hours, I learn about the basics of diving, the most important hand signals essential for underwater communication, and the technical background on land. My head spins with concepts and potential dangers.

"Slowly and safe" are the keywords for the next few days. I am supposed to learn things slowly and safely. "Check" is the word of the day. Everything must be checked again and again. For the first time in my life, I squeeze into a diving suit that feels at least five sizes too small. Dave, my diving teacher, grins.

"It'll get easier in time."

Oh, and now I know why such a long strap hangs from the zipper in the back. So that one can pull it up when there's no one around to help. We are going to snorkel for our first time in the water. I will not use the mouth-piece to provide me with underwater air until my second diving session. Dave puts the compressed air bottle on my back. Phew. Rather heavy. Next is the weight belt, and then we can finally wade into the water in full gear, swim fins in hand. Today and tomorrow, we shall start from land.

On the third day of the course, we sailed out on one of the smaller boats, and I learned how to enter the water with a backward roll. What always appears so easy when performed by others proves a tad trickier in practice. However, I soon developed a knack for diving and stayed underwater for increasingly extended periods.

"Steph, you're a natural!" Dave exclaims, beaming.

"I know," I reply cheekily.

His compliment does please me a lot, though. I love diving.

I dive into what is to me an entirely new world. Literally. Until then, there had only ever been one perspective – standing on your two feet on firm ground. I never suspected what goes on beneath the surface of the water. It has never played a part in my life until then. Fascinated and overwhelmed, I look into this other world that opens before my eyes underwater. I am not afraid; quite the contrary. I am not really religious, but at the sight of such beauty, I feel overwhelmed with something akin to divine emotion. I can hardly wait to dive even deeper.

Time flies by, and I enjoy every second of it. As I get accustomed to my new job, I can barely believe all the things I discover underwater. Ifakara seems incredibly far away.

"I shut off the ocean, stretch ropes, and count fish." This is how I explain my job in a nutshell after work whenever people in the bar ask me about it. The puzzled look on their faces always makes me smile.

This is the short version, of course, nothing more. As it is, we sail out every day to distant areas, which we mark out with weight lines, thus creating various corridors. Our mission consists of documenting the different species that cross these corridors as precisely as possible and observing their behavior within the designated area. We only ever work in a team. As a beginner, I take over the upper layer of water while my more experienced colleagues dive into the deep. But I feel safer and more confident with every passing day.

I have come to feel like a fish in the water, quite literally. As I slowly sink into the dark blue waters, I can feel myself becoming very calm. I have no fear even on such occasions when the others are momentarily not in sight. Drifting into these silent, bottomless depths is an indescribable feeling, disturbed only by the bubbling sound of my breathing apparatus. Before long, though, I stop hearing that too. The silence underwater and the absence of sound are part of the magic. Watching the fishes and other animals breathe, I cannot get enough of that shimmering, iridescent underwater world. Again and again, I spot new, fascinating fishes in all shapes and sizes.

No words can express what I see and feel during these diving sessions. I am both filled with awe in the face of such unspeakable beauty and poetry and, at the same time, very much aware of the importance of the task at hand. I am not just any volunteer enjoying her time. I am utterly convinced our actions make a difference. I am also able, by now, to defend that notion quite convincingly during our evening visits to the pub. Not everyone, it appears, is willing to fully grasp our program's significance.

"And what's the use of that?" is a question I have become familiar with.

"Destruction of fragile marine habitats by waste and pollutants of all kinds, originating either from the mainland or freighters, overfishing, illegal fishing, temperature variations. Even the smallest variations can have extremely damaging consequences for the perfectly tuned coexistence of countless species," I enumerate. "This is what we attempt to get to the bottom of here. Data collected over a long time gives us a clear overview of the animal population and its changes."

I am always glad whenever I win people over to the cause. I finally feel useful. This is what I would like to do.

I also feel enthusiastic about something else: I get to see Sokoine every day. Every morning, upon arriving at the beach and every evening, on our way back to camp, we pass by him, schlepping our heavy gear. His gaze has become more intense. My heart leaps. And hey, a few days ago, he started to wave back. It soon turns into some kind of daily ritual. I am aware of his growing interest in me as a woman.

I feel so exhausted in the evening that I long to go to bed and sleep, but that won't do. After a little rest, I am always able to recover my spirits.

"We're going for a drink at the pub. Are you coming?" Sophie asks.

With the most handsome man on earth in mind, I nod.

My hope is fulfilled. I spot him as soon as we step through the door, sitting at a table with some friends.

Our little cat-and-mouse game goes on. Let me handle that, my friend, I think to myself. There is definitely something going on between us. I can feel it. Your eyes, filled with open, undisguised interest, tell me as much. We keep scanning the room, searching for one another, sometimes hastily looking away when our eyes meet. Most of the time, you offer me the most wonderful smile. A new tension arises between us. If our looks were light swords, the room would be filled with flashes of light; that is how often we keep looking for each other in the crowd.

I had been under the impression, until now, that my obsession with the Masai-man had gone unnoticed, but as it turned out, I was wrong. My colleagues and Swahili friends tease me about it more and more frequently.

"Here comes your Masai," Mike, a local who knows his way around here quite well, whispers into my ear.

"What do you mean, 'my Masai,'" I protest indignantly.

"Come on, Stephanie, you obviously have a crush on Sokoine. And so does he, by the way."

What did the guy just say? I hardly dare believe my own ears. Mr. Uber-cool has a crush on me? That's quite a new way of showing you're interested.

You want to be conquered? All right, then. With my beer in hand, I stroll towards the table of the Masai and start talking to them.

"Hi guys, *habari*. How are you doing?"

"Hey, your Swahili is not bad. Where did you learn it?"

A breakthrough, at last. His Lordship condescends to exchange a few words with me. I show some interest, yet not too much. Don't you go and get the wrong idea, mister. I want to be conquered, too.

I make a point of speaking with all of them. I want to learn more about them and their culture.

I probably also have had a couple of beers already, admittedly. Either way, I feel brave enough to give it another try. No more hide-and-seek.

"Is the place next to you still free?"

"Yes, please sit."

Something has changed. We talk easily and laugh a lot, sharing the same humor. In short, we match. It feels so nice sitting here right next to him. The longer we talk, the warmer I feel inside. Two small dimples appear on his cheeks whenever he smiles. I try very hard not to stare when there is nothing I would like to do more. Sometimes, our bare arms touch, these small, fleeting moments feeling like tiny sparkles. I want to get to know him and learn what being a Masai is like. In a warm voice, he tells me about his family and his village when he is not working on Mafia. He asked questions about my home, family, and life in Great Britain. I struggle to answer at times. Unlike him, the notion of home raises many interrogations, more often than not. We had a deep and very special conversation, and I definitely feel good in his company. The tension between us grows.

And then I decide to just go for it.

"I was told you like me," I say, bravely standing his gaze and searching his face for a reaction.

"And I was told you like me," he replies, grinning broadly.

We both have to smile. His eyes are so big, and I am caught in their depth.

"Is it true?" I ask softly.

Time stands still. His answer will determine everything. I can feel that. Say yes, please say yes, I pray silently. There is nothing I wish more ardently for.

"Yes," he says in a low voice, slightly embarrassed.

"Really?" I ask again, uncertain.

"Yes, I like you a lot."

I feel warm all over. A glowing joy grows inside me. I want to throw my arms around his neck, but of course, I cannot do that, not in Africa, not with the Masai. I have learned as much from other couples. No public display of affection. I long to touch him. Having to contain oneself so much feels very weird.

We both feel the magic of the moment as we look into each other's eyes, raptured.

"And what does your 'yes' mean?"

"We can spend time together. Be together," he answers awkwardly.

Such a perfect sentence. I don't need any more explanations. Not now, not at the moment, that is. We are here together, and he wants to spend time with me. Nothing else matters.

We are so absorbed in each other's company that we don't notice how fast time flies. Looking up, I notice most of the clients have deserted the pub by now, the loud chatter of the early evening reduced to a low mumble. The band's music is no longer as peppy as before either. It must be late.

"A long day of diving awaits me tomorrow. I have to go to bed," I declare, suddenly feeling really tired after all that tension.

"Let me walk you back," he replies, the five words bearing a promise.

I know we won't part tonight as if nothing had happened.

"I'd like that very much."

We leave the pub and step out into the clear, mild night. I would definitely hold his hand or walk arm in arm with him if he were German. But walking side by side with the most handsome man on earth, on a balmy summer night, on a wonderful island, feels so very romantic. He teases me now and then nudges me. Our bodies touch briefly from time to time, my arm brushing against his as we walk through the silky night neither of us will ever forget. Walking next to that handsome, proud warrior feels nothing short of wonderful. Much too soon, we reach the fence of our *banda* and pause, standing very close to one another, a little embarrassed. Neither of us speaks, yet I am sure we both feel the same. Bending down to me, he kisses me softly. Once, twice. By the third kiss, I fling my arms around his neck, and we kiss passionately, our mouths and tongues carefully exploring each other. Staring into his eyes under the soft moonlight, I cup his face, his skin as soft as silk. He seems a little taken aback by my boldness. It is good that it is dark around us because I doubt a Masai man would be entirely unselfconscious. I can feel his unease, but that does not matter right now. We both come from very different worlds and know nothing about each other. No textbook will tell us how to go from there. And this is exactly what makes the whole thing so intense: the unknown, gaining new experiences, and doing things I know nothing about. Trust. Our mutual liking is the only thing we feel. I give in to the feeling, and looking into his face, I see myself and the love in his eyes. My fingers brush his eyelids, his nose, and his mouth. He has beautiful, harmonious features. I bury my face in his neck and breathe in his spicy, smoky scent that reminds me of something I have no words for. I am bewitched by this man. Sokoine pulls away from me and, taking my hand, leads me towards the beach. Neither of us wants that night to end. Our bodies communicate without words. Our intimacy, however, is also a very dangerous game. No one can see us. Making out or being intimate in public is a total no-go in Tanzania. That is why we hush through the night like thieves, looking for a sheltered place in the thick of a palm grove. The place seems safe enough, but then one can never be certain. We might bump into someone and be caught. As exciting as it might be - we both feel more ardent and passionate about it - it is also quite scary. One part of me remains on the alert. Sokoine is not an experienced lover, but I do not mind that. It tells me that he did not have many women before me. I feel safe in his strong arms.

It all happens really fast, and the beginning of our relationship is magical and intoxicating. Millions of stars twinkle above us as we lie in each other's arms, breathing heavily. This was not quick sex but a confession of our love for one another.

"When a Masai sleeps with a woman, it means they are destined for each other," Sokoine whispers in my ear, gently caressing my hair.

"Destined for each other."

That sounds lovely. And right now, that's exactly how it feels to me.

The next morning, I woke up from a short, deep slumber a new woman. My heart leaps as I think: Sokoine! Lying on my camp bed in the *banda*, I smile to myself.

"Someone is in a very good mood this morning," I hear Sophie say from the bed next to mine.

My smile broadens.

"How was it last night? I didn't hear you come back in here. Must have been late."

"Late and beautiful," I reply, smiling.

This small piece of information will have to do. I want to keep my secret, protect it like a precious treasure. What Sokoine and I share must stay between us.

The next three weeks pass in a sort of daze. I can do what I love during the day and love my boyfriend every night. I happily dive underwater to count my fish, laugh with my colleagues, and enthusiastically tackle whatever task is expected of me. Yet my thoughts revolve around Sokoine alone, every second of every day. It is a magic time in a true paradise. The happiest time of my life. We try to spend every free minute together. After we have returned from one of our boat tours, we usually linger by the diving school, and I watch him go about his work. Later on, we meet with others in the pub. If we were allowed to, we would probably not leave his room, but we have no room for ourselves. Sokoine shares his tiny place with his cousins, and I share mine with my team.

In front of the others, we act as good friends who would happen to get along really well. Our colleagues are no fools, though. They notice the sparks flying between us but leave it at that and make no comment.

When we leave the pub, we become lovers, searching for secluded spots on the beach to kiss and make love. Afterward, I lie in his arms, and we talk till the first light of dawn. I don't feel tired or hungry. On the contrary, I am full of energy. I am just filled with us. I cannot stop myself from touching or looking at him whenever we are alone. This gorgeous man with the silky soft skin. I brush his strong arms and muscular chest. Unlike his cousins or the other Masai, Sokoine does not have long, frizzy hair. His hair is softer, and his body and face are almost completely hairless. I love to brush the smooth surface of his skin and feel his muscles underneath. To think this beautiful person has chosen me. I am not usually plagued with self-doubt and like myself just the way I am, but I confess I cannot but wonder why he would have chosen me.

The time I have spent in Tanzania eases our mutual comprehension. I started learning Swahili early, and now it pays off. Sokoine's family speaks Maa, the tribal language of the Masai. Many of his relatives have no other language of communication.

I want to learn everything about the Masai and their way of life. Sokoine has come to Mafia with his cousin and another relative to earn money for his family. They live in a small cabin right by the beach, where they also sell handmade Masai jewelry. But he longs to return to his home village.

"At 27, I am the oldest of many siblings, and I normally live with my family in Lesoit. It is quite a long journey from here."

Sokoine tells me about life in the *boma*, a settlement community formed by many members of one family, with their huts and herds of cattle. The village of Lesoit consists of several *boma*. Sokoine never went to school, as there was none in their remote part of the wilderness. The closest larger place lies fifteen kilometers away, much too long a school way to undertake every day. There are no cars or buses, no electricity or running water.

I listen to him, spellbound, trying to picture life in such a remote place.

"Where do you buy your supplies?" I ask him.

Sokoine laughs.

"Almost everything we need, Nature supplies. We have our cows for milk, blood, and meat. We also have goats. We pick berries, other fruits, and roots. In Lesoit, the bigger village, we buy sacks of rice and corn, which we use to make *ugali*," he explains.

"Why are you here? What brought you to Mafia?"

Sokoine takes a deep breath.

"I have to provide for my family. We did not have enough food anymore and no money. Rain is scarce, and the cows are dying. We cannot grow a lot of feed because the ground is too dry. Many of my brothers leave their families to go and look for jobs. We return home once we have earned enough money. I was 20 when I left for the first time. At first, I bought a few goats, which I was able to sell at a good price. That was the first money I ever made. Later, I went with my uncle to a large cattle market in Dar es Salaam. My uncle owned a truck, and we were able to make more money."

The memory makes him smile.

"We bought cows at that market, and we were able to sell them at some profit. But after a while, that business became really dangerous, and we would be shot at with machine guns when driving through remote areas."

I gasp, appalled.

"More and more robbers would stop the cattle transports and plunder them. The other Masai also told us as much. We tried to find new routes, but it only became worse. The plunderers would steal the money and the animals and then kill the people. Friends of mine have been murdered."

His voice drops.

"We started traveling in larger groups and even paid a policeman carrying a machine gun to escort us. Soon, we had no choice but to carry weapons ourselves, so we took our spears and machetes. But one day, they got us."

I can feel how difficult it is for him to go on.

"There was something on the road. Big branches barring the way. We had to stop the truck, knowing this was most certainly a trap. When we stopped, the robbers jumped out of the bushes. The fighting was horrible. Men died."

Sokoine does not linger on detail; deep sorrow is etched on his face. He does not need to. Listening to his recollection, I feel terrified, my body covered in goosebumps.

"Is this how you got these scars?" I murmur, daring to ask him about it at such an intimate moment.

Sokoine's body bears several large scars, most of them on his head.

"No, these I got in an accident."

"Tell me about it."

"We had a large transport with 50 cows we had bought together with several other people. The truck was driving much too fast. It overturned on a curve and fell into the ditch. There was blood everywhere, screams, the cows. I was stuck inside the truck but somehow crawled out the window. Two people were dead. One of them was my uncle. Many cows were either wounded or dead. The uninjured animals ran away, and then the plunderers were all over us, driving away the rest of our cows. I could not run after them because I could no longer walk."

"Oh no," I exclaim with my hand over my mouth.

Sokoine tells me that people often get robbed in such helpless circumstances. The news of the accident spreads fast, and the robbers rush to the scene and grab whatever they manage to lay their hands on.

It sounds terrible.

Still, despite that dreadful ordeal, Sokoine was lucky. He survived his injuries. But he suffered a huge loss: his uncle and companion were dead, and his money and cattle were gone. A disaster.

I swallow hard. How different my own upbringing has been. Even though things were not always easy, what with my mother's illness, I was still always cared for. I never had to fight for my life. For Sokoine, fighting for his life was part of his daily routine. There is nothing he would not do for his family.

Once he had recovered from his injuries, he started a business with tobacco plants, which he grew with his cousin and would then sell on the market in Dar es Salaam. One day, his cousin told him about Mafia, where one could get a good job with a nice salary. The two of them set out, not knowing where the island lay or how they could reach it. The only thing they knew was that the journey involved taking a boat.

"I must admit I did not much like the idea," Sokoine confesses. "Like most Masai, I cannot swim. Being on a boat is not safe."

But he would not allow such a small obstacle to deter him, though, having gone through much more horrible ordeals. They packed some Masai jewelry, which they intended to sell, having heard from other family members that the tourists paid good money for it. Many young Masai warriors travel to Zanzibar for that very reason. Being smaller, Mafia does not attract as many tourists and does not require quite as many workers, which also means they will have less competition and thus higher chances of making a profit. The two of them sailed out to the island on an old wooden boat.

"I did not feel safe on that shaky thing," Sokoine recalls with a smile.

They find a small lodge on Mafia, one tiny room really, and share a single bed. After all his previous hardships, Sokoine is finally luckier here and gets employed as a member of the security staff at the diving school, where he is in charge of the equipment from dawn to dusk. He learns how to check and fill the oxygen bottles and inspect the different types of equipment. The irony of a Masai, who cannot swim, working on a diving island, does not escape us. Sokoine works twelve hours a day, every day, and makes about 60 euros a month. I swallow. I made more in one single shift at the fudge shop. I keep this to myself, though. I do not want him to feel bad.

"And that is enough for you and your family?" I ask.

"I don't need much. And I also have the money from the jewelry."

"Why do they need security staff here?"

"So the rest of the staff or the locals won't steal all their things," he replies, laughing. "That is why I got the job. My boss, an Italian, says the Masai are men of their word," he adds, nodding proudly.

With his eyes shining, Sokoine tells me about his family and his life in the village. I can plainly see that is where he feels at home, the place dear to his heart. I love listening to his warm, low voice recounting all sorts of tales and stories. Sokoine can neither read nor write. I have fallen in love with an illiterate man. And yet, he is such a smart, wise man. The school of life has taught him so much - more than what I have achieved with my degrees. He takes on responsibility, fears no danger, and is loyal. His home and family mean everything to him. I learn so much from Sokoine during these nights. We become very close. I love his sense of humor and his calm. He never speaks in a harsh or loud voice. I feel completely safe and accepted for the first time in my life.

That is why the prospect of our time together ending makes me feel increasingly queasy. In just a few days, my job in Mafia will be over. Sokoine will return to his family two weeks after my departure. I would like to travel to Kenya and Uganda for the next two weeks with Sophie, Billy, and Tamara from my team. I am also looking forward to seeing my British friend Eleni again, with whom I plan to spend three weeks in Tanzania. These are my plans, at least for the time being. As it is, fate has something quite different in store for me.

What will become of us? What will become of me? I have not given the future any serious thought. I have tried to enjoy every moment of my stay here. I know I lost my heart to Sokoine and Africa a long time ago. Where am I supposed to go? Germany has long ceased to be my home, and England has never been. I have lovely friends there, of course, but no real home. I also have two siblings, each of us presently seeking our own path. In short, no one is waiting for me anywhere.

But then that is no longer entirely true, I think, looking at my breathtakingly beautiful friend. I have fallen in love.

My throat tightens at the mere thought.

"Sokoine, I cannot be without you," I confess.

"And I cannot be without you," he answers tenderly.

"What can we do?" I ask in despair.

Sokoine can only live in one place: his family's village in Tanzania. He will be the head of the village, providing for everyone. A Masai does not leave his family. What would he do in Europe, honestly? I realize this even before the words leave my mouth. He won't ever be happy there. I am not, either.

"I will come and visit," I say firmly.

"Here, on Mafia?"

"No, I will come to your *boma*."

He gives me a puzzled look.

"You would do that?"

"I would like to meet your family. I would like to see how you live. Then we will decide what is to become of us."

In that moment, I also realize something else. I am no longer on my own. We belong together. It is mid-March; starting in early April, Sokoine will have eight weeks of holiday. Eight weeks during which he will live exactly as he sees fit, with his family and his animals.

"I shall be back from Uganda in two weeks. Then Eleni will come here, and I will try to find a job so I can stay in the country. I could visit you in May," I say, mustering up some courage at the prospect despite the pain of parting.

Sokoine looks at me, beaming.

A Dangerous Mission

"You are going to Juani tomorrow. There is a very rare jellyfish species in the bay there, one that swims backward, along with many other exciting fish species. Carla would like to write about it, which would also be interesting for our documentation."

I stare at Tamara, our head of the camp, aghast.

"But this is my last day. I had other plans."

"Sorry, Stephanie, but I need you there. Everyone's going. It is a very important mission."

Quite a strong statement. I cannot believe it. I don't want to spend my last day with Sokoine on some stupid island. He, too, has to work, but I could have stayed with him on the beach. As long as he does his job, his boss does not mind.

"Come on, Stephanie. No need for such a long face," Tamara says. "It is wonderful out there. And we can leave early, so you will be back by 11:00 or 12:00 am at the latest."

Well, thanks then.

We set out at the crack of dawn on several boats during high tide and docked the boats in a small cove. From there, we walked to a small lagoon that could not be reached by boat to observe the jellyfish. Today, though, I have no eyes for the beauty of the island or the oddly swimming jellyfish. I am far too lovesick. I urge the others to work fast; after only 90 minutes, our job is done. While one of the groups wants to remain on the island longer, Sophie and I decide to head back. But then, I had not exactly expected our boat to be stranded. The ocean has completely receded. Low tide. How silly of me. How could I forget to check the tides? Keeping the tide in mind has been my job every day for the last ten weeks. Yet neither cursing nor praying will do. I cannot magically attract the water that will only return in two hours. I cannot believe it. My precious last hours with Sokoine are drifting away, I think to myself, tears welling up in my eyes. To make things worse, we are almost out of drinking water; after all, we had not planned to stay here for hours. The sun rises higher in the sky and beats down on us hard. I am so upset that I can barely pull myself together.

"Fucking crap! That damn cow knew perfectly well this was my last day!" I scream in frustration, the fury only making me feel the heat more keenly.

"Come now, Stephanie, it is no use. Let us crawl under the sail, in the shade, so we don't get a heat stroke," Sophie starts tentatively to pacify me.

We do as she says, but the longer we stay, the more enraged I become. Suddenly, an idea crosses my mind.

"Sophie, it is too hot to lie around like this. Let's go snorkeling a bit to cool down."

Mafia cannot be that far. It must be possible to swim back to the shore. Quite a daring plan of action, actually, but what with my rage and stubbornness, it makes perfect sense to me at the time. The water has receded many kilometers. Following my logic, we should be able to walk almost half the way. I, for one, am absolutely determined to give it a try. The thought of sharks, jellyfish, underwater currents or any other danger one might expect to encounter in the open sea never crosses my mind.

If I had told my friend about my plan, I doubt she would have agreed to come with me, and for good reason, too. As it is, my ruse convinces her to join me in that adventure. We grab our fins and snorkels and set out in the blazing heat towards the waterfront. For a while, we wade on in knee-deep water.

"It's really tiring and far out," Sophie complains.

This is my cue.

"We're too far out now. Look, Mafia does not seem that far. Let's swim over. Better be in the cool water than fry our brains on the boat."

Sophie ponders this briefly, and in the end, she agrees with my plan.

I am still very much convinced by my plan, even though we have been walking for 45 minutes now. The water now is finally deep enough for us to start swimming. I front-crawl through the water like a swimming machine, focusing solely on Sokoine. I feel such longing. When I think that today is the last day I will see him, at least for the time being, my heart aches with sadness. What is to become of us? The thought of spending even one single day without him is utterly unbearable. How am I supposed to do this? Where can we be together? A thousand thoughts race through my head. Pausing briefly, I realize I have slightly drifted off course. Mafia's main beach no longer lies right in front of me but to the far right. Should we continue to drift in that direction, we would end up on a section of the beach that is covered with mangrove roots. Not such a brilliant idea. I suddenly realized how dangerous my whole plan was. Here we are in the open ocean, unprotected, with countless dangers lurking beneath us. No one knows this better than I do. Did I not spend every day of the past ten weeks underwater? I can feel myself starting to panic. Keep a cool head, I repeat over and over to myself through clenched teeth, trying very hard to banish images of sharks and sting rays.

"Shit, what is that? Something just brushed me!" I scream into my snorkel.

And then I see it. A giant jellyfish, its tentacles several meters long. What a fright!

Next to me, Sophie lets out a yelp, her eyes wide open in fear, indicating all too clearly that she, too, has seen the jellyfish.

"Stephie, I can't go on much longer," I hear her groan.

Even though I know I am a better swimmer than she is, I, too, can feel my arms shake with exhaustion. What on earth was I thinking?

"Let's float on our back to regain some strength."

"Or let us wait for the boat; it must be coming soon," she replies wearily.

At least two hours have passed since we left. I have lost all sense of time and could not say for sure.

"That is out of the question. I am doing this no matter what," I shout in her direction.

Anger and pride wash over me again, boosting my strength. I will not experience such humiliation. I meant to reach Mafia before the boat. There is no way this whole action has been in vain. Again and again, I struggle to stay on course, my arms feeling increasingly heavy. It will be at least another hour before we reach the shore.

After some time, I can make out people standing on the beach. Why on earth are there so many of them, I wonder.

"Stephie, do you see the boat?" Sophie calls. "Hey, over here, we're here!" she yells, waving frantically with her diving mask.

Our colleagues on the boat spot us and head in our direction. I am so mad I could cry. Damn it, I don't want to go on board. But it is no use. It would be ridiculous if I went swimming stubbornly and refused to climb into the boat. Grumpily, I allow my colleagues to help me on board. My pride is hurt.

However, we have not been on the boat for three minutes when something magical occurs. A small school of dolphins, five animals in total, swims by really close and escorts us for a while, their glistening silvery bodies rising out of the water rhythmically. My love for dolphins is the reason why I started studying biology in the first place. In Greek mythology, these animals are regarded as the patron saints of seafarers, protecting them from danger-ous waters and helping the shipwrecked. And now here they are. I feel both very moved and comforted by their presence.

"Have you gone completely mad? We were worried sick!" Tamara cries, very upset.

While still on the boat, we learn that the beach crowd has gathered because of us. Word has gone out about two volunteers missing. Aware of the strong currents surrounding the two islands, a very distressed Tamara has dispatched two search parties to find us.

"Do you mean to get yourselves killed? It is extremely dangerous!" she yells.

But then, so can I.

"This is all your fault! Why did you assign me such a mission on my last day? I am a good swimmer. I would have made it!"

There is no reason why I should keep my voice down and vent all my anger and frustration at her. Despite her fury, her face clearly shows how relieved she is not to have lost two European girls to the Indian Ocean.

Sokoine has heard of the two missing girls. He cannot believe that I should have been one of them.

"Why would you do something that crazy?" he asks me, aghast, when we finally meet after his work.

I feel very moved by the distress on his face.

"I did it for you so we could be together on our last day," I reply, as we sit together with our usual group of volunteers, colleagues, his cousin, and other Masai friends by a small cabin in the village. There is a very special mood in the air. Melancholy.

And then it has finally come, that briefest of moments in a wonderful, sad, snug night. A last embrace and kiss in the darkness shielded from prying eyes. I don't ever want to let him go. I want to feel the touch of his soft lips on mine. Will we ever meet again? Even though I feel devastated, I still try to be brave. I won't make a scene. I promised myself I would not cry in Sokoine's presence. I don't want to make things even harder for us than they already are. And I manage to keep my word, until the next morning.

As I wait with my bag packed and my heart torn next to the other volunteers for the tuk-tuk we have called, something wells up inside me.

"I'll be right back!" I call the others before racing along the small path to the beach.

Sokoine and his two cousins look up in surprise as they see me run towards them, panting heavily.

"I wanted to say one last goodbye."

Salwaya pulls a small wooden Masai statue out of his pocket and hands it to me.

"Here, take this, Stephanie so that you won't forget us."

That does it for me. I am about to break down and sob, all my grief and sadness about to burst forth, even though I know too much emotion will only make them feel very ill-at-ease.

"You'd better go, Stephanie, before you start crying," Salwaya says, perceiving my distress.

One last look before turning around and rushing back to my friends. And on that last note, I leave the island and my sweet lover.

CHAPTER 4

Edoli enkir modooni enkarre

Even a blind sheep may chance upon rainwater.

The vibration of my phone startles me out of my sleep and I need a moment to recover my spirits. It is still pitch-black outside; the sun won't rise before one hour's time. But my bus is leaving very early, at six o'clock in the morning. I instantly feel excited again: I am about to travel to Sokoine's *boma* for the first time. Not only will I get to meet his family, but I will also discover the place where he grew up and normally lives. It is a really big thing, for him as well as for me. As much as I enjoyed traveling with Billy and Tamara, half of my heart was always with Sokoine in thought. Our phone fees rise to alarming heights as we try to talk on the phone as often as possible.

The hustle and bustle of Dar es Salaam echoes outside the window of my modest dwelling. Even at this ungodly hour, there is a lot going on in the megacity, which resembles a restless, teeming anthill. Only the actors change as the hours pass. So as not to waste too much time in the morning, I chose a room in the close vicinity of the bus station. It is still too far to walk, though, and I have booked a taxi. Soon Stella will be waiting for me in front of the door. I feel exhilarated and full of life at the thought of the upcoming adventure. I brush my teeth and put on the clothes that I laid out on the previous evening. Did I choose my outfit wisely? Can I actually meet his family, wearing my old pair of jeans and a simple, slightly faded red T-shirt? I shake my head, laughing at myself. I am not usually one to worry about suitable or unsuitable clothing. I like my clothes to be practical, especially since I spend a lot of time outdoors for my study projects and often live in accommodations where there are no washing machines. My things have to be easy to wash and, above all, airy, as the temperatures often rise above 30 degrees even during the wet season. But then I do not possess a lot of clothes anyway. All my belongings fit into my backpack and one small bag. I also made sure to brush and braid my long hair. That is more bearable in the heat. One last look at the room to check I did not forget anything. Closing the door behind me, I tiptoe along the corridor, still shrouded in darkness, towards the exit door so as not to wake the other guests.

A pleasantly cool morning breeze welcomes me outside, and I breathe in the fresh air. Soon, it will feel hot, like baking inside an oven. The day laborers are up and about long before the shop tenants open their doors, and the offices start to get crowded. Vendors set up their stands, selling snacks, fruit, and beverages to commuters, travelers, and passers-by. The denser the columns of cars threading their way toward the inner city in the morning, the more street vendors can be seen scurrying about between the vehicles, offering their goods or services with little insistence.

Finally, my taxi reached a huge bus station, which I usually find very stressful. Today, with the last remnants of the night lingering in the air, the bustle seems even louder and more confusing. I have to walk some distance to reach the station. A gate seals off the area, and Stella cannot get any closer. Everything feels different today, I think, as I focus on finding the right bus stop.

"Madam, do you want coffee or tea?"

I look up, startled. As a *mzungu*, a white woman, I often get mistaken for a tourist and spoken to in English. People are usually very surprised when I answer back in Swahili. Spotting a young man in front of me, holding two thermos flasks, I decide to buy a cup of coffee. I could do with a hot beverage. Then I go on looking for some food for the journey, another somewhat stressful endeavor.

On the map, the distance between Dar es Salaam and Songe, the final stop of my bus, seems very small indeed. About 350 kilometers separate the megacity on the coast of the Indian Ocean from our destination inland. Sokoine and I agreed I would get off the bus in Handeni, the last big city before

Songe, so he can meet me there. We would then travel together for the last part of the journey. Sokoine tried to prepare me for this trip on the phone, explaining how it would all unfold, what could prove tricky and what I should pay attention to.

"Look out for other Masai," he advises me. "Many travel in the same direction and will help you if anything happens."

With that advice in mind, I finally manage to spot my bus stop at some distance, in the teeming crowd of people belonging to different ethnic groups. A group of Masai waiting right next to it reassures me.

This is the right stop. The only thing missing now is the bus itself. To block out the noise around me, I think about the journey that lies ahead. On German roads, it would be a three-hour drive. But this is not Europe. As it is, African roads fall into several categories: the first kind is well-paved and safe in the bigger cities. The second sort comes with a lot of smaller and not-so-small potholes that can make for quite nasty surprises. The third kind is gravel roads, which are a little bumpy, admittedly requiring people to drive slower, yet most of the time, quite okay. And then there are also the many sand tracks, potholes included, that become dangerously slippery during the wet season or else turn into dusty, rutted dirt roads in the dry season. Every journey is a game of chance or at least of patience as vehicles move on sluggishly. I am quite familiar by now with every version of road or path.

"If everything goes well, you should reach Handeni in six or eight hours," Sokoine estimated.

There are still about 130 kilometers between Handeni and the *boma*, and a muddy dirt road is the only path leading there. It is the middle of the month of May, in other words, the wet season. Sokoine did tell me about a few very adventurous journeys, but I will not worry about that now. We are to meet in Handeni, where we will spend one night before setting out together for the remainder of the journey.

A small blue coach stops by the stop. Much to my surprise, rather few people travel in my direction. I get on the bus and make my way along the narrow corridor, even managing to drop my luggage on the seat next to mine.

The group of Masai sits in the front of the bus. I would not dare go and talk to them. I am not that bold. We set off, hobbling and honking. It takes a while for the bus to pass the throngs of people and other vehicles that crowd the bus station. By now, the streets of the city are packed with long columns of cars. The driver, clearly experienced, steers the bus along the streets effortlessly, and after a while, we finally leave the lively streets of Dar es Salaam behind us. I feel slightly nervous about meeting Sokoine's family, but I also feel very excited at the prospect of seeing him again.

My heart has already made a choice: I will live here, in Tanzania. I can no longer imagine my life without Sokoine. Even though we do not know how to make it all happen, one thing is set in stone: Sokoine belongs in his village with his family. As the eldest son, he is responsible for everyone and will not relinquish his duty.

But then, what kind of future could we have together? Will I, as a European and a white woman, be able to live in a small, remote African village within an indigenous community living by its own rules and rites? I, who had never intended to marry or become a mother? I have no answer to all these questions at the time. First, I need to see this place and meet these people so I can get a feel for it all. Despite the short time we have been together, there has been a lot of stress regarding paperwork. Applying for a residence permit, visa, and work permit are all very time, energy, and financially draining and are granted very rarely. For that reason alone, we have to make far-reaching decisions, as the ambiguous nature of my status in Tanzania will have to be clarified eventually. We thus decided that I would spend three weeks with Sokoine and his family in the *boma*. It's definitely a major challenge for all of us. How will they react to a white woman coming to their village? A woman from another world. Never before has a white woman come to the village, and now that same woman is to be part of the community. Possibly, that is.

I am startled out of my thoughts as the bus unexpectedly leaves the road and heads towards a small village, shortly after coming to a halt in front of a gas station and a small adjoining workshop. Various kinds of goods are sold in the surrounding buildings.

"We need to change a tire!" the driver announces in Swahili before urging us to leave the bus.

Somehow, I find that rather reassuring. The man seems to be cautious, taking good care of his vehicle. As it turns out, I was wrong, but of course, I did not know that at the time. We managed to cover the first 100 kilometers, and I enjoyed the opportunity to stretch my legs for a little while.

Half an hour later, we all got back onto the bus to resume our journey. A lush green landscape, typical for the wet season, rushing past my window. The quiet mumbling of the other passengers, the low droning of the bus traveling 80 kph, and the still air, thick with heat, make me drowsy. Leaning my head against the windowpane, I close my eyes. By the end of the day, I shall be in Sokoine's arms. With that thought in mind, I drift into another world.

The loud bang pulls me out of sleep abruptly, my fingers instinctively digging into the backrest of the seat in front of me. The bus has swerved on the opposite lane and is now so dangerously lopsided. I am almost thrown out of my seat as the vehicle slides down the slope by the side of the road and finally crashes into the ditch with a deafening bang. All this I experience in slow motion: my losing balance, items of luggage flying about, and people's screams seemingly lasting for hours. Then, it all turns black. I dream. A dream so beautiful I have no wish to wake up.

Regaining my senses, my gaze first falls on my feet, a lot of blood and lots and lots of glass shards. Blood and shards of glass buried deep in my feet. An eerie silence fills the bus. Apart from a weird buzzing in my ears, I cannot hear the slightest sound. I feel as if I were shrouded in cotton wool. Everything seems so very distant. I gradually realize we probably just had a very serious accident. I see myself lying in a bed of shards, my body pierced with small pieces of broken glass. My arms, legs, feet, my whole skin, riddled with splinters.

Then a thought occurs to me: will the bus explode? They always do in action movies. That thought slowly brings me to my feet. I have to get out of here. The silence is still unbroken. I feel absolutely no pain and manage to scramble to my feet amidst the chaos of suitcases and unconscious, or possibly even dead people lying around. I am the first passenger who has regained her senses.

I glance around me, panicked. The bus is lying on its side. The rear end of the vehicle merely consists of a large glass window, fortunately, and not a closed wall, as is usually the case. Okay, I need to break through that window somehow, I think to myself. Just as that thought crosses my mind, another passenger straightens up.

"Hey! Help me here. We need to break that window!" I call to him in Swahili.

The man nods, stunned, and starts crawling in my direction. Then he simply kicks the window that shatters at once, and we both scramble out of the bus.

Standing in the ditch, I look down at my bare feet, covered with shards of glass, and very carefully move my arms and legs. My jeans and my T-shirt are torn. Despite the countless shards, I do not seem to have suffered any major injury. My right arm hurts because I fell on it. Very delicately, I brush off the small pieces of glass from my skin. Then, all of a sudden, I start trembling violently, uncontrollably. Even my teeth chatter. More and more people are crawling out of the bus, and for a few minutes, I watch them in a daze, completely unable to react. Something is wrong, though. Shaking my head to clear my thoughts, I suddenly realize what is wrong. People are actually crawling back into the bus, not out of it.

Why? I don't understand this. My head feels fuzzy and I can barely think straight. Still, I keep trying to understand what is going on. I realize with a jolt that the people getting back inside the bus are robbers. Like vultures, the looters always stand ready, using the chaos and people's helplessness to fall over their prey. Our accident must have occurred in the vicinity of a village or at least of some settlement. That's the only reason for the nearly instant presence of such shady people on the scene.

The looters crawl inside the bus, looking for money and bags. I can see that now my brain is slowly but steadily working again and instructing me about how to behave. The bus has not exploded until now. I had better retrieve my luggage before I lose that too, I think with great concentration. Cautiously moving towards the bus like a puppet, I climb back into the chaos and battle my way through to my seat. The air is filled with screams and sobs,

62

harsh, angry words too, as the travelers attempt to protect their possessions whenever possible. Thank God, my things are still there, I think, grabbing my two bags. I am even lucky enough to find my sandals. A quarter of an hour must have passed by now and still some of the passengers around me are only just regaining their senses.

I stagger back to the side of the road on wobbly legs. Pulling my phone out of my small bag, I dial Sokoine's number with trembling fingers.

"We had an accident!" I stammer into the phone.

He is appalled.

"Are you hurt?"

"Not too badly, I think," I hear myself reply.

"Where are you?" he asks.

I cannot answer that question. I don't really know where I am. I can only form a vague conjecture based on where we stopped to change the tire. Probably somewhere close to Mbwewe, a locality between Chalinze and Mkata.

The group of Masai I had noticed at the bus station are sitting under the majestic crown of a tree. They have also been wounded, yet none of them appears badly injured, the older one among them in worse shape than the others, though. I tell Sokoine as much on the phone.

"Let me talk to them."

I listen to the men speaking Maa but cannot quite understand their conversation. Later, I will learn that this particular Masai group comes from Sokoine's neighboring village.

"You need to take another bus, Stephanie. Take the next bus together with the Masai."

"I can't do that!" I shout into the phone.

I cannot believe what he is suggesting, his request sending me into a state of frenzied panic. I feel utterly incapable of riding a bus ever again, let alone here and now.

"Calm down, calm down!" Sokoine implores, managing to soothe me after a little while with his calm and yet firm tone.

Despite my panic, my brain has long concluded that there is no other way. African pragmatism is what is called for now, not German luxury care.

"You have to do this, Stephanie," Sokoine implores me again on the phone.

He knows what he is talking about, after all, having survived numerous horrendous accidents himself, which claimed the lives of some of his relatives, friends, and neighbors. He has crashed against trees with buses, cars, and trucks, ending up in ditches or driving off the road more than once, making it out alive only just. He is also probably traumatized by these events. But he cannot change that situation. Nor can he afford to give up driving.

"What will be, will be," he often tells me, offering me a piece of African wisdom.

And he is right. Except this does not help right now. If we were in England or Germany, I would expect him to jump into his car and rush to the site of the accident. But there are no cars here.

"Stay together, walk up to the road, and stop the next bus," he urgently advises me. "I am waiting for you in Handeni, and we will go to the *boma* as planned!"

His words gradually sink in as I attempt to repress the hot, stinging tears welling up in my eyes. Don't lose it now, I think, even though I feel like sitting by the roadside and crying my eyes out. Instead, I nod, if only to muster up some courage.

"We'll meet in Handeni!" Sokoine assures me once again before we hang up.

The old man has been much more badly injured than I have. His arm is bleeding profusely, and there are deep cuts on his wrists. He gives me an exhausted look. I share my water with him because he really is in very bad shape. He is also still in shock. We speak Swahili and talk with hands and feet. I am in for yet another surprise. Not only does the old man, named Lekomoi, as I will learn later, come from Sokoine's neighboring village, but he is also one of his father's best friends. I feel slightly relieved upon learning about that. We share a connection. A connection that actually lasts to this day. Whenever we meet at the market or at some party, we always talk about the very special way we came to know each other, in a ditch by the side of the road.

Meanwhile, some time passed, and the Masai found out that another bus would be here soon. I take heart as we gather our possessions and wait by the side of the road. One hour later, we are finally able to stop another bus.

I try my best not to check the state of the vehicle too closely. I don't want to know anything about that. Glad that we should finally be able to resume our journey, I get on the bus. I just want to leave the site of the accident. My gaze falls on another white woman, who gives me a kind smile. A familiar face, I think, appeased as I take place next to her. Maren tells me she is also going to Handeni, where her boyfriend awaits her. Little by little, I feel more and more relieved. Meeting someone in a similar situation to yours always feels good. Maren wants to know everything about the accident. While we are chatting, I notice out of the corner of my eye that the road is getting muddier and muddier. It is the wet season; after all, heavy rain is forecast, turning the already bad roads into murky tracks. All of a sudden, there is another loud bang. My heart misses a beat and I scream. Once again, the bus slips and slides, yet this time, the driver manages to regain control of his vehicle and stops by the side of the road. Another punctured tire. A rear tire, luckily. I cannot believe that. Three punctured tires on the same stretch of road! How unlucky can one get? Once again, we all have to leave the bus so the punctured tube can be changed, and we can move on. We have only been driving for about half an hour when the muddy, slippery road suddenly goes steeply downhill. The noise of the engine grows increasingly louder, with odd, gurgling noises. The driver struggles as he tries to maneuver his vehicle as best he can. There is no way this will end well. After about 20 kilometers, the bus stops in a small locality, the driver unceremoniously announcing this would be our last stop. Even though Handeni, where Sokoine is waiting for me, is still 25 kilometers away. I cannot believe this! What is going on here? I don't have time for self-pity. My new acquaintance points to a few motorcycles parked not far away. *Bodabodas* are Tanzania's alternative to taxis and along with bike-taxis, a very popular means of transportation.

"Come, let us rent a *bodaboda*," I say with determination.

But I call Sokoine first.

"Don't let the bodaboda drivers overcharge you. Pick one who does not drive too fast and whom you feel you can trust," he advises me.

Easier said than done. How am I supposed to know whom I can trust?

"Make sure the motorbike is not too old, and look the boys in the eyes before you rent one."

"What do you mean?"

"Their reddened eyes will tell you whether they have been drinking or taking drugs."

Sokoine names a price I should negotiate and adds one last piece of advice: one must say "pole, pole" if one wants the driver to go slowly. And that should definitely be made clear before getting on the motorcycle!

With Sokoine's good advice, we pick two older-looking drivers whose motorbikes seem well-maintained. The negotiations in Swahili are short, and the men soon realize they won't be able to fool us. Even though 25 kilometers is not such a long distance, under the present circumstances, it turns out it is, and we progress through the mud at a snail's pace towards Handeni. I cling to the driver, shaking and addressing quick prayers to heaven. Whenever the puddles on the road are too deep, we have to cut the engine and walk around the giant pools of water while the driver struggles to push his vehicle across the ground heavy with water. After what felt like a hundred hours, we finally reach the city. Glancing at my watch, I'm surprised that it only took us one hour to get there. Maren and I pause briefly to say goodbye, I have enjoyed our short, meeting. Here, at Handeni's bus station, our ways part once again. I can see Sokoine waiting for me at some distance, an anxious look on his face. He has been worried sick about me; I realized as much from the numerous phone calls we exchanged during my journey.

More than anything, I would love to fling my arms around my neck. Right now, I find it very difficult to respect local manners. But Sokoine's eyes are filled with empathy. He worries about me, and that alone feels very good.

"I am so sorry this has happened to you!" he says by way of greeting, taking the two bags from me and giving me a searching look as if to ascertain I have not been badly injured.

Then he hails a red tuk-tuk that takes us to our guesthouse. Once we have reached the safety of our room, I fall into his arms, sobbing with relief and exhaustion.

"I am so glad you're okay, sweetie!"

His tender gaze and the pet name he speaks with such love only make me cry even harder as the tension of the day gradually fades.

"You did well, also looking after Lekomoi."

We talk for a while until exhaustion finally overcomes me.

I lie down and ask him to remove the glass shards from my feet. Then I close my eyes, feeling completely safe for the first time on that day.

For now, that is. I don't want to think about the next morning. His village is about 150 kilometers away. 150 kilometers on ragged, muddy tracks. There I was, bruised and grazed, my skin riddled with shards of glass. Such is the state I will be in when Sokoine's family will first set eyes on me.

My First Visit to Lesoit

The following morning, I woke up early, and every bone in my body was aching. The night on the narrow bed was torture for my battered and bruised body. My restless sleep was haunted by the accident, and the loud honking and rumbling voices outside our window were not helpful. At least the temperature has cooled down a bit during the night. The cuts and grazes sting, and my skin glows with an odd bluish hue in many areas. I carefully rise and stretch. I could use a hot tea, but the sparse room is not equipped with any cooking utensils. Asking Sokoine about it would be pointless. Masai men aren't responsible for such things. I realized as much during the first three months of our relationship. I often need to pull myself together to keep from saying or doing something wrong.

But that does not matter right now. I rummage through my things, searching for a set of clean clothes, and quickly wash in front of the grimy sink top, water trickling from the rusty faucet. Despite the pain, my heart slowly fills with joy and curiosity.

"Sweetie, we're meeting your family today!" I say, gently waking him up.

Sokoine nods thoughtfully, and a smile appears on his face.

"You will see where I grew up. I finally get to show you Lesoit," he replies, his face shining with joy. "Lesoit means stone. The ground is very rocky, hence the name. The waterhole bears the same name, too. But you will soon get to see all this."

He grabs our bags that wait by the door, ready and packed, and we leave the hotel. We don't have breakfast, but then I am not hungry anyway. We intend to buy bottles of water and some food on the way. Morning dusk still hangs over the city, and its streets are already bustling with life. Even though the sun will only be up in one hour, at around 6:30 am, street vendors of all ages line the side of the roads with their stands.

Slowly threading our way through throngs of people and avoiding the market criers, we finally reach the already densely crowded bus station. Today, I find the loud voices and turmoil very difficult to bear. My nerves are on edge.

As the bus approaches, I start trembling uncontrollably, every fiber of my body screaming, "No!" I don't want to get aboard this old, rickety bus, but I know, of course, that I don't have any other choice. I put an unsteady foot on the threshold, and Sokoine nodded encouragingly.

"There is no other way. You can do this!" he calls.

I drop heavily in my seat, catching myself looking for a possible way out. Completely oblivious of my panicked state, the other passengers chatter in many dialects, their voices loud above the din of the driver's screeching radio. Some even manage to drowse despite the noise, while others attempt to keep the chickens that travel with us in check. My heart is still racing madly as we drive off. Every bump in the road, every unexpected commotion strikes terror into my heart. The roads are still very muddy today, just like they were yesterday. The bus keeps lurching and slipping on the slippery ground, and every time I cling to the backrest of the seat in front of me or to Sokoine's arm.

"Don't be afraid," Sokoine whispers to me in a low voice, aware of my anxiety.

Easier said than done, I think to myself. But after a while, my heartbeat slows down a bit.

Deeper and deeper inland we move. The rain stopped at last, and the temperature rose to around 30 degrees, turning the road's mud into red dust. The driving noise, and consequently the driving feeling, changes. Our bus hobbles over the many holes in the rock-strewn sand track, accompanied by an odd "bobobobobob" noise that sounds a little as if we were driving on a flat tire.

My head is pounding, and I have to be careful not to bite my tongue because of the bumpy ride. We drive past the villages of Kwediboma and Kiberashi. Not especially appealing, I think to myself, with their derelict houses, corrugated roofs, holey walls, waste, and litter scattered everywhere. That is not how I had imagined the area would be.

The mountain range of the Eastern Arc Mountains rises in the distance. The rain, of course, is much more beneficial than harmful. Nature has virtually exploded around us, and I gaze into an ocean of wide, green meadows. Majestic acacias stretch to the sky, their large crowns providing some much-appreciated shade.

"There used to be a lot of giraffes here," Sokoine says, pointing out the window. "We used to marvel at the giraffes and the acacias when I was a child. It is their favorite food. They're gone now."

"What do you mean?" I ask, looking at him questioningly.

"There were a lot of big animals here when I was a kid. Elephants, giraffes, rhinos, buffalos. When I roamed the bush with my friends or took the cow herds to the waterhole, we had to be careful. There were animals just about everywhere. Sometimes, bumping into them was okay. Giraffes are not that dangerous. But elephants are pretty dangerous when they feel threatened or when they have babies. It was very dangerous at times. We had to be real fast."

He smiles, but the look in his eyes remains serious.

"All this land we are currently driving through used to be Masai land, the land of my ancestors."

Sokoine tells me how the living space of the Masai and the wild animals has been reduced in the last decades as the land was cleared for farmers. More and more people belonging to the Wanguu settled in the area, cutting down many trees and clearing large sections of forest for farming. This was the end of the nomadic walking route of the Masai. The local wildlife population was decimated by hunting and driven away after the reduction of their living space.

All this sounds very familiar. I encountered the same situation during my first study project in Zimbabwe, which also explains why I did not meet many Masai during my travels. I had not expected that.

"I am the last generation to see all these animals as a child. The children in our village today have not."

I listen to him, spellbound, as he talks about the dramatic changes. Suddenly, I see this land with new eyes. When Sokoine recounts the story of his people, his eyes are filled with pride and endless sorrow. I can feel the deep connection he shares with every inch of this land, with every living being (man or beast), with every plant that grows here, and with his culture: the legacy of the Masai that stretches over so many generations. This is something very different from whatever I might associate with Germany. If I intend to live here, I must learn more about the people and their culture.

The deeper we move into the land, the fewer vehicles we see. Cow and goat herds are led on foot by their shepherds to their grazing spots. Occasionally, a cyclist passes by, struggling on a rattling boneshaker. Motorbikes sputter by, overloaded with people, or man-sized loads that tilt and sway dangerously in the curves. Even goats or chickens are tied up fast, a resigned living cargo. Here, too, families crouch by the side of the road, selling their meager vegetable and fruit crop. Judging by the baffled look they give me, I am most certainly the first white woman many of them have ever seen in this remote region. They smile and wave, and I wave back timidly.

We finally reach Songe, our final stop. Today, though, I have no eyes for the characteristics of this new place. I am completely exhausted and ardently wish to reach the final destination of our journey. But first, we have to accomplish another very important mission. We cannot show up empty-handed in the village. We head toward a small shop to buy some presents, small bags of rice and sugar for the adults, and sweets for the children.

After we are done, it's time for yet another *bodaboda*, as the *boma* still lies twelve kilometers away. Sokoine handles the negotiations with the two drivers, and it feels good to have them taken care of. The trip is very different today. No mud, no sliding, the beauty of Tanzanian nature appearing in all its glory as we travel deeper and deeper into the land. Green hills, lush meadows, and fields pass by, with trees bearing splendid fruits. Some of them are quite funny-looking, with thick, fleshy fruit dangling from small lianas. I don't know all of their names yet. But this will soon change. It is already late in the afternoon, and the landscape is drenched in golden light. The heat of the day gradually diminishes, and a soft, warm breeze caresses my face. I am battered and exhausted, but some of the tension I felt earlier is gone. How beautiful it is here, I think to myself, and my heart expands.

I spot the group of small huts from a distance, some standing in the open, others built under the shade of the trees that line the settlement. Cows graze peacefully in a little clearing between the trees, small goats hopping and leaping among them. I get off the motorbike on somewhat wobbly legs. I am finally here.

The *bodaboda* drivers do not want to linger for long; they must return to Songe immediately. We untie our things, and they drive off at high speed, leaving a cloud of dust behind them. A group of people are standing in front of the small, mud-colored houses: children and women mostly, few men, many of them wearing the red-checkered blankets typical for the Masai wrapped around their bodies. The blankets show many different patterns according to the men's age, group, and status. Masai men go through different stages during the course of their life. The women wear purple-colored clothes. All of them wear beautiful, traditional pearl jewelry around their necks, arms, and ankles. For now, I pay more attention to the faces than to clothes and jewelry.

The people walk up to us, and I look into many friendly, smiling eyes. My heart melts with relief. I do not want to do anything wrong and offend Sokoine's family with inconsiderate behavior. I cannot stop asking myself the question of all questions: is it even possible for them to accept a white woman for their son? What if it is not? Would they drive him away? Or would Sokoine have to leave me? I know too little about them to imagine what could happen at worst. All I know is that I love and want to be with him.

A somewhat older woman breaks away from the group. She has a beautiful round face and kind, shining eyes. A timid smile plays around her lips as she carefully puts a necklace around my neck.

"This is my mother," Sokoine says, introducing us.

A very special moment. My heart leaps into my throat. He does not say her name, but this is not usual among the Masai.

"Names are holy and can only be spoken under very special circumstances by specific persons," Sokoine told me once. "Younger ones cannot ever call the elderly by their name. They use substitute terms instead, creations of their own or nicknames, like Baba for Father, Yayai for Mother, or Enkitok for Wife."

Mama Yayai looks at me gently and nods. She is an important person, and I feel it right away. But we don't have much time to ourselves. The children surround us while the adults wait for Sokoine to introduce us. His five brothers, two sisters, and four half-sisters, the children of his father's second and third wife, form a large group. Sokoine points at several young men.

"My brothers, Lemali, Baraka, Lesimba, Maenge and Nanuyai."

Other names and family relationships rain on me. I won't be able to remember them all; there are far too many, but right now, that does not matter. What is important to me is that they should get a good first impression of me. Sokoine's sister, Yeyolai, stands in front of me. The two siblings' resemblance is obvious at first glance, as is the case with his half-sister Mayani, who also gives me a friendly smile. I can tell from people's attitude who is standing in front of me. Here is Baba, the head of the family and Sokoine's father. He nods at me, yet in a much more reserved manner than the women. I am allowed to use the diminutive 'Baba' to address him.

Then I look into a wrinkled face, alive with two wise, knowing eyes: Baba's mother and Sokoine's grandmother. As I will learn later, she is in her nineties and the oldest person in the village. We will come to spend a lot of time together, but of course, I don't know that at that point. Then I look into yet another very impressive face. Sokoine's father's third wife – as I will learn later on – is a strikingly beautiful woman who goes by the name of Mama Mdogo. She presents me with a gift: a large, lovely bracelet made of red, yellow, and blue pearls. I am surprised and also a little embarrassed. Then it is our turn to hand out our admittedly far less pretty gifts, yet just as precious to the Masai. The children cheer and rejoice about the sweets. Songe is quite distant, and they don't get such treats very often.

Although I no longer remember every detail, I do remember how strongly I felt during my first encounter with Sokoine's family, who welcome me with open arms and seek to make things easy for me. No one shies away from the white woman. I am very relieved about that. If there is anything I have come to value in all my years in Africa, it is people's openness and cheerfulness. No matter which country on that huge continent I find myself in, strangers will always welcome me warmly and without hesitation. Sokoine's family has no reservations about me.

"Shoo, shoo, let her breathe," Sokoine says, pushing aside the giggling group of children surrounding us, touching the legs of my trousers and running their fingers through my hair, straight and oddly long to them.

"Stephanie needs a little rest now," Sokoine declares. "We had a long journey, and Stephanie had an accident."

Sokoine speaks Maa with them. I love listening to him speak his mother tongue. We speak Swahili together, but my Maa is not good enough yet, just like his English.

After Sokoine has gently driven away the children, we walk up to one of the huts, surrounded by a smaller group of people, which is just as well, as not all of us would have fitted inside the small dwelling anyway. We step over the narrow and low threshold, lowering our heads as we do so, and it is a moment before my eyes adjust to the gloom and the smoke inside. A fire is burning in the center of the room, which smells of smoke, wood, and animals, a blend that tickles my nose while the stinging smoke brings tears to my eyes.

Today, having spent ten years with the Masai, that smell has become part of my daily life, but my friends often tell me that my clothes smell of smoke.

We sit down, and after a while, I stop noticing the smoke curling up towards the low ceiling. The women boil some water in a huge cooking pot.

"*Sufria, sufria!*" Yayai says, pointing at the pot and using the Maa word for it.

Then we all sit together and drink tea. Sokoine's relatives listen closely to his story, and I struggle to understand more than a few snatches of Maa.

From what I have gathered, there won't be a feast today. There will be one in the following days.

"They will slaughter a goat just for you," Sokoine tells me.

I am glad there won't be a big celebration today. I feel exhausted by the long journey, the accident, and the excitement of meeting them all for the first time. In lieu of a feast, we will share some rice and spinach with his brothers later. I yearn for a bed.

"Where are we going to sleep?" I ask Sokoine.

"Over there," he replies, pointing towards one of the huts.

I glance at the rectangular, sand-colored clay hut standing a little apart in a quiet corner of the *boma*. This is where I will spend my first night in the village. Sokoine does not possess a house of his own. The huts belong exclusively to the women. Men don't have houses of their own. They are only ever housemates, depending on which stage of life they find themselves in. First, they live in their mothers' houses, and then, once they have become warriors, they move together with other warriors in their grandmothers', aunts' or sisters' homes. Before he gets married, a Masai man may also live in a married friend's house. If we live in the *boma*, I would also build and own a house.

The women are very kind to me, bringing me warm water in a huge cooking pot so I can wash in a special, shielded area outside. I wash away the remaining tension in my body, along with the dust of the journey. How incredible the journey that lies behind me. For now, I am filled with the family's warm welcome. Perhaps Sokoine and I do stand a chance after all. I shall see what the following days will bring, I think to myself as I dry myself, put on a clean set of clothes, and walk up to our guesthouse, where Sokoine is already waiting.

So here we are now. We had dinner, and the other members of the family had left for the night. A low murmur softly drifts into the room from outside; a baby cries somewhere, but apart from that, everything is quiet. The chirping of cicadas is the only sound I hear. Just before I entered the guest hut, I glanced up at the magically starlit sky, peppered with millions and millions of tiny dots of light. It is overwhelming.

"Whose hut is that? Does it stand empty the rest of the time?" I ask Sokoine, cuddling up to him in bed.

"It is Mama Klaudia's. She always helps my mother. She sleeps at my mother's."

That night, I feel grateful for such generosity, naturally. What no one tells me, however, is that Mama Klaudia is Sokoine's first wife, as I shall learn two years later, by sheer coincidence.

"Stephanie, come with us. We are going to collect honey."

Maenge and Lesimba, Sokoine's little brothers, respectively nine and eleven years old, stand before me, an expectant look on their faces.

"How? Where do you find honey?" I ask, being the naïve European I am, having only ever bought honey in a glass.

"We know where to find the bees. We'd like to show it to you."

Sounds exciting. I'll go, no question. But I do tell Sokoine we are going into the bush.

"All right, but be careful because the boys will need to build a fire. And make sure you don't get stung," he says before we set out.

The boys are nimble and fast, like two little wildcats. I, being 24 years old, stagger behind them awkwardly. Twigs and branches keep whipping my face because I failed to stoop in time, or else I bang my toes on rocks scattered along the path. My two companions are totally protective of me:

"Watch out, Stephanie! There is a large rock over here. A hole, watch out!"

They probably could have walked through blindfolded while I stumble helplessly through the wilderness. As it turns out, two Masai boys have far more life experience than I do.

I, a trained biologist, would never manage to find wild bees. I know nothing about life here.

Lesimba builds a small fire. He has brought a piece of glimmering wood, which he now uses to build a fire. Then he climbs up the tree and thrusts the smoldering branch into the hole in the trunk, where the bee nest lies concealed.

"Stephanie, step aside a little, and take care!" he calls, quickly covering his head with a piece of fabric to avoid getting stung.

The bees swarm out as soon as the hole fills with smoke.

These two small boys are doing all the hard and dangerous work. Lesimba climbs up the tree once again, and reaching into the hole, he pulls out the honeycomb, dripping with honey.

In the meantime, Maenge cut some leaves on which the boys carefully placed the honey before giving me some to try.

"How delicious!" I exclaim, leaving aside the part with the bee larvae.

Maenge and Lesimba, on the other hand, happily eat it, honey and larvae alike.

Standing here in this forest, in the middle of nature, with these two little Masai boys is a wonderful feeling. It is one of the most beautiful and intense moments in my life. But it is also a moment that questions my entire worldview. The graduated biologist, who would never survive on her own in the African bush, and the nine-year old Masai child, who can neither read nor write, is one with nature.

Little by little, Sokoine and I fall into a small routine in the *boma*. We have tea first thing in the morning before checking on the cows. The men chat, and I must confess I sometimes get a little bored when hour after hour passes without anything happening. One morning, though, I heard a plaintive sound, like a baby's cry.

"Baaaa."

An obviously pregnant goat seems to be in labor, nervously pacing back and forth before walking away.

"Sokoine, I think that goat needs your help!" I cry excitedly.

"No, Stephanie, she does not need us, and besides, she is not ready yet," Sokoine replies, placidly remaining in the shade.

The goat dashes into the bush, I assume, to find a good spot to give birth. I cannot help myself and rush right after her. But the grin on the men's faces does not escape me. They were right, of course. It will still be some time before the goat is ready. After a while, I retrace my steps and stroll back to the group in a decidedly casual way.

A few days later, though, I get to witness the birth of my first lamb.

It is around five o'clock.

"Stephanie, a lamb is about to be born, do you want to watch?"

Sokoine's brothers have come especially to inform me. I see the mother, a brown ewe, bleating and moving restlessly to and fro.

"How can you tell when the lamb is due?" I ask.

"From the animal's behavior."

We sit quietly, watching the ewe lie down, get up, and turn to its side.

About half an hour later, her water breaks, and two small legs suddenly appear.

"She does need our help after all," Sokoine declares.

His brother Lemali holds the head of the animal, and another brother holds her back as Sokoine carefully pulls at the pair of dangling legs. The little, wet body of the lamb slides out of the vagina in one go. It's done. A very special moment. We all smile at each other. I watch on with fascination as, after a little while, the lamb tries to stand up on shaky legs. It takes a few attempts before it manages to do so, but then the small mouth finds the mother's tit and starts sucking greedily. It does not need to be taught. Nature simply takes its course.

The two and half weeks I spend in the *boma* show me how authentic and difficult, but also how beautiful the Masai's way of life truly is. Everyday I get to know and love Sokoine's family a little more than the previous day. Everybody makes me feel so very welcome, and this fills me with enough courage to take my decision. Sokoine's holiday ends on June 1. He has to return to Mafia to earn money for the family. In my heart, I have made my choice. I want to be with that man. Wherever he will go, I will go too. This is not quite as simple as it sounds, as my right of residence on Mafia has expired by then. By a happy coincidence, as it turns out, Hillary, with whom I have worked in Ifakara, was promoted to the top position in Mafia.

"Are you still in Tanzania, Stephanie?" she asks me in an email.

Hillary manages to secure another three-month job for me on the island. After that, we will see, I think to myself confidently, I will come up with something.

"I am coming with you to Mafia."

Sokoine beams at me as I tell him about my plan.

"But I could also picture myself living here with you," I add, looking into the eyes of a very happy Masai man.

CHAPTER 5

Ore enalotu kelotu ake

Whatever will be, will be.

"You're illegal here in Mafia, Stephanie."

I cannot believe what that guy just said. Not that I would not be aware of the island's strict regulations. My residence permit is conditional based on the fact that I am working for an organization in the Marine National Park. Frontier paid very high fees for this. But my work ended a few weeks ago, and my right to reside here has expired. I have accepted several odd jobs to get by, but it seems I have finally discovered. I also know who told on me, a "friend," as it turns out, namely the cook from our camp, whom I saw talking to that guy in a low voice.

"I can help you, though," the seedy guy continues in a murmur. "I won't tell on you if you come and work for me in my hotel."

"What would be my wages?"

"My silence," he replies, making a dramatic pause. "And, of course, you will be accommodated for free."

"This is what you call a good offer? I call this blackmail!" I retort, aghast.

"Give it a thought, but not for too long."

That is absolutely out of the question. I was so happy when my former colleague Hillary got me a new job with Frontier in Mafia after my first three months ended. It is a precious time for Sokoine and me, as we spend every spare minute together. Unfortunately, that new job only lasted three months, too. Asking for an extension is not possible. This means I now have a problem because there is no way I can stay in Mafia any longer. Under no circumstances, however, will I work for that idiot.

Until now, visa issues have never been a problem for me. The volunteer organizations always taking care of it. But my decision to live in Tanzania and give our love a chance has dealt the cards completely anew. Until now, my status only allows me to reside in the country under very specific professional conditions. But then I no longer work here, nor am I a tourist, so my tourist visa expired after 90 days. I am a lover and would like to stay with my friend, but there is no special status for that. I will have to learn the ropes here. That small blackmail attempt is merely an appetizer of what to expect in the future.

Ultimately, I travel back to England for a few weeks to work and renew my tourist visa.

Sokoine and I racked our brains on the best way to secure a permanent residence permit, leaving out no option. I work my way through the Internet, reading articles about residence rights for foreigners in Tanzania. As it is, there is only one way.

"We need to get married fast," I tell Sokoine on the phone as I call him from Bath.

"Why is that?"

"So I am allowed to stay in the first place."

Never would I have dreamt of actually having such a conversation. I am 25 years old. I never intended to marry to begin with, not after the negative experiences in my family. In my view, a good relationship needs no administrative confirmation. But I have run out of options here; only as a family member will I be allowed to stay longer than three months in Tanzania. There is no other way to organize a romantic relationship involving two different continents. It is a terrible word indeed - organize - but I am dead tired of managing our being together. It takes a lot of strength, nerves, and time to juggle the official aspects of my life in Tanzania, Great Britain, and Germany. By now, my citizenship and my siblings are the only things that still link me to Germany. Even though I know I probably won't be living in my country of birth, I cannot bring myself to relinquish my German passport, and Tanzania does not allow dual citizenship. For now, England is the country I work in when I am not in Africa. It is also the country where my friends live. I am still insured in Bath; my bank account and all of my possessions are also in England.

Getting married sounds really odd to me. Being a wife – and for solely practical reasons, too. There is no romantic proposal, no lover falling to his knees. I would have no use for all that, and Masai men are unfamiliar with such traditions. Marriages are usually arranged by the families, and Masai men traditionally have several wives. These unions, however, are not officially sealed and are only celebrated in the villages in private ceremonies. Masai have their own rules.

"My father has three wedded wives," Sokoine tells me.

All of them get along quite well, and they all live in their own *boma*. By now, I know that the Masai entertain polygamous relationships even though I could not imagine sharing Sokoine with anyone.

I am lucky Sokoine is still available, as he is 28 years old. At least, that is what I believed at the time.

In Germany, I would simply go to the registration office with all my papers. But I want to get married in Tanzania. This is why we both need specific documents issued in two different places, namely the competent district offices in Kibaya and Dar es Salaam. In my future husband's case, we have to start from scratch. He does not know his exact date of birth, let alone possess a birth certificate, which we need to get officially certified marriage documents.

I research all this and learn that every authority in Tanzania may request specific documents such as a matrimony eligibility paper, namely the proof of us not being married yet. "Sounds promising," I think to myself. After some research, I discover that we cannot get married at the German embassy. Damn, that probably would have been the easiest way to go about it. Possibly.

To apply for marriage, we need to get a marriage license. And now the race for documents may begin. No matter how well prepared you think you are, if the person on the other side of the desk turns out to be a desperate idiot, he will make your life a living hell. That is the first lesson I learned. It is all a matter of luck. And that is true for all three countries involved in our case. No exception.

First, we set out to tackle the issue of Sokoine's birth certificate. No church register, no birth register, no midwife. Most of the Masai children are born at home, even today. For the last thirty years, however, it has been mandatory for people to register a baby's birth at the nearest hospital. The child is then given a birth card. Sokoine's mother has lost his, but there are other options available. We need to find someone who could testify to Sokoine's birth so we can apply for a new card. Said guarantor must be over 65. With the precious card in hand, one needs to go to the district office and apply for a real birth certificate. Sokoine asks an old friend of the family, happy enough to earn a little extra cash. We are just as happy that he should agree to testify on our account. After obtaining the new card, we hold it close to the fire and work on it a bit so the paper looks worn. Our village, Lesoit, is part of the Kiteto district and the competent office is located in the city of Kibaya, which is about a hundred kilometers away from Lesoit.

A hundred kilometers is no big deal in Germany, yet here, we plan to travel for a whole day.

"Where are your parents?" the official asks us with a stern look.

"My father is an alcoholic. We cannot take him along," Sokoine replies.

"What about your mother?"

"She is in hospital and just had a stomach surgery. We need these papers urgently. We cannot wait until she is fully recovered."

The official seems to fall for our little lie and bangs an old stamp on the new document. The birth certificate is the first milestone in our paper marathon.

Since January 15, I have returned from England and live full-time with Sokoine in the *boma*. Eleven days later, we apply for marriage at the registry office in Dar es Salaam. At least such was our intention, had it not been for that very peculiar lady.

"You are still so young, child; do you really want to get married?"

I must confess I had not seen that one coming.

"And your husband cannot neither read nor write," she hisses angrily.

I am speechless. I don't understand what the woman wants from me. But I don't intend to play along.

"Come on, Sokoine, let's go."

He gives me a questioning look but follows me anyway.

"What was that all about?" he asks.

"She does not want us to get married. She is not a good person," I reply.

There is another office in a different part of the city. I brace myself for the next rebuff. But the elderly man is quite practical and very helpful.

"Your wedding date is on February 8th. Good luck!" he declares, smiling as he hands us a piece of paper.

After four months, the paper race has finally come to an end. The date for our wedding is finally set. I am getting a little nervous, admittedly.

Poison

"Hey Steph, I am on my way home and still have some time in Dar es Salaam. Shall we meet?"

What a nice surprise. Sophie, my colleague from Mafia is in the city for a stopover. That our paths should cross again here, in this city, now of all times! We are very fond of each other and have always tried to keep in touch.

"Yes, I am getting married in two days here. We have to meet!"

"That's amazing! We have to celebrate this."

We plan to meet for lunch. Seeing Sophie again is wonderful. We buy some food at a small stand by the beach. Sophie goes for chips, while I choose rice with some meat and vegetables. Time passes much too quickly. Unfortunately, Sophie won't be able to attend the wedding because her flight is firmly booked. We hug and say goodbye. Completely exhausted, I go to bed early, feeling dizzy. Too much sun, probably.

I wake up in the dark, feeling miserable like never before, drenched in sweat and teeth chattering. Shaking chills, stomach cramps, rumbling belly, and deadly nausea. What is that? Help! I barely make it to the bathroom before it comes shooting out of me like lava. I am literally puking my guts out. A tearing devil rages inside my stomach, and I hardly know how to handle the disaster. After what feels like an eternity, I crawl back to bed, sore and wiped out. Perhaps I will be able to go back to sleep now. Big mistake. I keep running to the bathroom again and again. I am burning up by now. Clearly, something is very wrong.

"Sokoine, Sokoine, I have to go to the hospital!"

He looks at me with sleepy eyes. He was fast asleep and has not noticed anything.

"Why?" he asks, noticing suddenly how sick I look and straightening up, alarmed. "What is wrong with you?"

"I don't know, but it feels like malaria."

I must look really terrible indeed because he does not even try to dissuade me. Standing on wobbly legs, I shakily put on some clothes, the room around me spinning. Sokoine helps me down the stairs of our hotel and hails a taxi. I can barely walk. The city is awakening - it is around 6:30 in the morning. I can hardly keep my eyes open during the drive and silently pray to heaven that I won't puke inside the cab.

The driver stops in front of the Aga Khan Hospital, a modern clinic. I barely manage to get out of the car. Taking one tiny step at a time, bent double with pain, I drag myself to the front desk.

"I think I may have contracted malaria," I say in a weak voice to the nurse behind the desk.

"Then you need to have your blood tested in the lab. It is on the second floor, up those stairs and then to the left," the nurse explains, gesticulating. "But first, you need to go to the cash desk on the first floor, on the other side of the building."

I give her a horrified look. How on earth am I supposed to make it to all these places? Sokoine cannot go in my place. Being illiterate, he cannot read the signs or the bill or fill in any other documents, for that matter. I have no choice. I have to do this despite the dreadful state I am in. One small step after the other.

"Please don't let me puke here in that corridor," I whimper weakly.

My name is called at once, the early hour the only piece of good luck in that whole situation. That's something.

"Oh my, the shape you're in, girl," the nurse who takes my blood sample says with sympathetic eyes. "Go lie down on the row of chairs over there."

And with that, the long wait begins. I drag myself to the chairs and drop sideways. I am too weak to sit up, and I won't stop trembling and shaking. I only ever felt that miserable when I had contracted malaria, hence my suspicion.

"It's not malaria!"

I cannot believe that result. What the hell is it, then, if not malaria? Hopefully, the doctor they have just sent me to will tell me all about it. But this also means I have to get up and walk, unfortunately. How am I supposed to manage this? I shuffle along seemingly endless corridors with Sokoine's help and collapse on the chairs in front of the doctor's waiting room, freezing and burning up simultaneously. My stomach hurts badly. Please, no. My body longs to let it all out, but shame has me muster up my very last ounce of strength. I stagger to the toilet around the corner. As soon as I enter the tiny room, everything starts spinning. Don't lock the door, I manage to think before dropping to my knees on the floor, about to faint, barely conscious, my head banging hard on the tiles. "Better lie down here," I think confusedly before everything turns black.

"Stephanie, Stephanie!"

Someone is shaking me by the shoulder and I vaguely hear my name. Sokoine has come to check on me, wondering what could take me so long.

"What are you doing? It is really filthy in here!"

As if I had had any choice in the matter, I am too weak to answer him. Luckily, I did not lock the door. With the help of a nurse, Sokoine hoists me into a wheelchair and pushes me into the examination room, where he lays me down on the emergency bed.

"You don't have malaria. It looks like food poisoning to me. What did you have to eat?" the doctor asks, looking at me with kind eyes. "You will have to stay here on a drip. You are severely dehydrated."

Tears well up in my eyes as I recall the happy moments I spent with Sophie. Our lunch...

"But we want to get married tomorrow. We have to get married," I sob.

"You are very ill, child, and you are running a high fever. There is no way I can discharge you in that state."

The three of us talked for a little while and agreed that I would remain on the drip for a while to regain strength. I badly need medication and fluid, and that tube in my arm is the only way. I cannot even keep water down. In a dreamlike state, I see the nurse change the empty fluid bags. Towards evening, I begin to feel a little better. Staying here on my own won't do - and besides, I want to get married tomorrow. At all costs. Supported by Sokoine, I leave the Aga Khan Hospital on rather shaky legs.

Fortunately, the following night was much quieter as far as I am concerned. I manage to keep everything inside. Not that there would be much left inside, though. Eating is absolutely out of the question. The next morning, I feel as if I had just been run over by a truck. Clenching my teeth, I limply drag myself out of bed. The day one gets married should be a happy one, but for me, it is just dreadful.

Masai men are not exactly very romantic; rather, they remind me of cool, reserved Britons. Sokoine is no exception here. Today, just like on any other day, he is as serene and calm as usual. I have never seen him really anxious about anything. What about me then? Am I excited and filled with anticipation? Not quite. I don't feel well enough yet. My plan rather consists of managing to walk straight to the best of my ability and get through the day. Just like yesterday, though, I will need a taxi. The two witnesses we need for the ceremony we collect on the way - Masai from Lesoit, whom we managed to ask a few days earlier. As the taxi takes the last turn before the wedding office, my breath hitches in my throat. It is barely 7:30 in the morning, but a lot of couples already line the street, forming a very long queue.

"I thought we would be the first, so early in the morning," I stammer, aghast at the prospect of such a long wait in my present state. It seems ten other couples were given the exact same time as we have.

"I can't do this! Sokoine, you have to talk to the others and ask them if they would agree to let us go first. There's no way I can wait here in front of that door for one hour."

The other couples cast astonished glances at us. I am a nervous wreck. I am terribly scared of fainting in front of everyone or of soiling myself.

"Don't worry, I'll try."

Sokoine cannot bear to see me in such a desperate state. The Masai never show negative emotions in public, and the whole situation makes him feel very uncomfortable. He also finds it very astonishing that we European women should cry so much.

"Why are you crying, Stephanie?" he always asks me. "There is absolutely no reason to cry. No one has died. Do you see anyone weeping?"

On such occasions, our two different cultures violently clash with one another. Today, though, he realizes there is no way I can wait for a long time in my weak state.

Propping me up against a wall, he leaves me in the care of our two witnesses. A few minutes later, he returns.

"Come, Stephanie, they let us go first!"

I am so relieved that I feel like crying even harder, but I manage to pull myself together. Sokoine takes my arm, and we walk past the line of people, towards the building, and along a corridor where other couples, seated on benches, await the most important moment in their lives. They eye us with sympathy and also a little irritation.

As we walk past them, I realize the other bridal couples look quite different from us, donning beautiful dresses and suits and sporting elaborate hairdos and flowers. They look happy, excited, and relaxed, surrounded by family and friends who take pictures and shoot videos.

I glance down at my own clothes, my faded black skirt and my green T-shirt, plain and frayed. No flowers, no jewelry, nothing that would hint at my actually being a bride. I have tied my matted, curly hair with a rubber tie, just like always. Sokoine wears one of his ordinary Masai robes.

What must all these people be thinking? The look on their faces speak volumes. Some whisper and raise their eyebrows. It did not occur to us to prepare for our wedding. The wretched state I presently find myself in does not entirely account for it. What do we know about weddings anyway? I love Sokoine, and I want to live with him in his homeland. I have no doubt about that. But we are only getting married for practical reasons, so I will be allowed to stay in the country. I am a 25-year-old orphan. No one has prepared me for this moment. I follow my heart, and it feels right. The skeptical glances of the other couples, who perhaps suspect us of entering into a sham marriage, cannot change that.

But I don't have enough time or strength to ponder over this for long. Already we are being called up and step into a tiny room. The official gives us a somewhat puzzled look but puts up a good front.

"May I have your rings?"

What rings? Sokoine and I exchange a puzzled look. Oh shoot, we did not even think of these!

"All right then, no rings," the official mutters under his breath, his eyebrows rising alarmingly high.

Then he proceeds to read a text in Swahili aloud. I don't understand all of it, but Sokoine translates it to me. We reply obediently and sign all the documents. Sokoine scribbles a signature. Masai don't kiss in public, and we are spared that part of the whole procedure. No one is filming anyway to capture the moment. Not that I would be overly keen on having pictures taken, judging by my present state.

"I now pronounce you man and wife!" the official declares.

Our marriage is now officially sealed. The man pushes the marriage certificate across the table, where this is written in black and white. We both keep our family name. For the tiniest moment, I feel a surge of bliss until my rumbling, cramping belly pulls me back to reality.

Let's get out of here fast. Sokoine tucks me up in the hotel bed. I am completely wiped out. Then my husband leaves to celebrate our wedding with the witnesses.

The Masai Ceremony

It is a while, back in the *boma*, before I am finally completely recovered. It has hit me hard. I am now a wife, at least in the eyes of the state. Do I feel any different? Nothing has changed, as far as I am concerned. I only took a huge step forward in the struggle with obtaining a residence permit. The Masai wedding ceremony is to take place eight weeks later, in early April, here in the *boma*. Sokoine and his family are proud and very excited, and they have already started preparing. The civil wedding is far too abstract of a notion for them; no one here has an idea of what this actually is. Only Sokoine's uncle's blessing will turn us into a married couple in their eyes. I feel a little scared at the prospect of the upcoming ceremony. It will be a huge event, with over 200 guests. All strangers to me, just like I am a stranger to them. All eyes will be on me – a white woman from another continent who has found herself a handsome Masai warrior. What does it mean for the family? What does it mean for the unmarried young women, who had perhaps pinned some hope on Sokoine? What does it mean for his father and for the others? Am I an intruder? Am I taking something away from somebody? Is it even possible for them to accept me in the first place without my doing anything in return?

"What will they say when they see you getting married to a white woman?" I ask Sokoine in a moment of despair.

I am suddenly no longer certain they will accept it.

"I am getting married, and that is reason enough to be happy," he answers, before adding, "They don't care what color your skin is."

In truth, I have not had any reason to feel awkward or uneasy until then. A lot of people are open and friendly despite the language barrier. Sokoine's mother in particular, spares no effort to support me through everyday life with great kindness. We communicate in Swahili, and there is a lot of gesturing.

Still the whole prospect terrifies me. I never was a huge fan of big events, and I dislike being the center of attention. When I picture myself hosting all these people I don't know and struggling to do the right thing in a culture that is still very foreign and in a language I cannot properly communicate, I must admit I feel funny. Sokoine and I have only been together for a year, and I have been living here, in the village, for three months.

"What if I do something wrong?" I ask Sokoine anxiously as we lay next to each other in bed.

"Don't worry so much, Stephanie. Let's just enjoy the party," he answers enthusiastically. "Trust me," he adds, beaming.

Easier said than done. I endure several nights of poor sleep, troubled by the most vivid dreams.

I simply follow Sokoine's instructions. The preparations ahead of the feast are huge. Hosting such a great number of people in a place without running water and electricity, without a catering service, means of refrigeration, supermarkets, delivery services, or even hotel beds in the neighborhood is no small matter. The huts are rearranged to accommodate the closest relatives from other *bomas*.

For days on end, we drive to Lengatei on motorbikes to purchase countless sacks of rice, beans, and corn flour used to prepare *ugali*, the traditional corn mush.

"Everybody must eat his fill," Sokoine explains. "That is the most important thing."

Gongo is the name of the local alcohol, which is only served men. Masai women never drink alcohol. Sokoine has already told me as much. Women and children will get soft drinks, juices, and biscuits. On the day before the wedding, the older men will slaughter a goat in the *olpul* – a special place, at some distance from the *boma*, to which they alone have access. During the feast, they will share the animal's meat with the other male guests. Traditionally, men and women do not eat together. Everybody is very busy. Pots are simmering over fireplaces just about everywhere, and the air is pervaded with the tangy scent of spices as the huts are being prepared for the wedding, the clotheslines are heavy with all manners of fine garments fluttering in the wind. Despite my uneasiness, I do feel the cheerful excitement ahead of our wedding. Women sit together in groups, laughing, shaving their heads bald with razor blades. The shinier their skulls, the more beautiful they feel. They make every possible effort to involve me in their group but request nothing of me that I would not be comfortable with.

As the wedding day draws nearer, Sokoine gets more and more excited, and I become more and more nervous. I would much rather deal with the whole thing as matter-of-factly as with our appointment at the registry office. But this, of course, is no option. To Sokoine and his family, the wedding is a huge event - Masai girls are being prepared for their wedding many years in advance. I am 25 years old, and the only family gatherings I know are on a much smaller scale. Now, I am to be a central figure in a mega event.

There will only be one guest on my side: my best friend, Eleni, who will come from England, willingly taking it upon herself to shoulder the strains of the long journey to the bush. I feel very relieved at that prospect. No one from my tiny family will attend. I don't have much contact with my two siblings at present.

"Are you sure you want to get married right away?" they both asked skeptically.

I understand their concern. After the early separation of our parents, my sister and I had always said we would not get married. And I probably would have stuck to that plan had it not been for the particular circumstances of our relationship. I can see how my marrying a stranger from an entirely different culture after such a short time would appear very outlandish and unreasonable to my siblings. I am used to the absence of any family life and am about to marry into a very large family and prepare to live in complete remoteness. The irony of that does not escape me. Will I even be able to? Is my love for Sokoine strong enough to go against my nature?

As it is, a wedding dress has already been chosen for me.

"Stephanie, you don't have any Masai clothes yet. We would like to lend you and your friend some clothes," Sokoine's mom says, giving me a warm look as my husband translates her words.

She holds up a bundle of fabric and carefully unfolds it, revealing a long piece of blue fabric that wraps around the hips with a belt, like a dress. A purple-colored cape, artfully draped over it, completes the bridal attire. Yayai calls this outfit *nangan*. Both pieces of fabric are edged with white block stripes.

"These are festive garments, as the stripes show," Sokoine explains. "Masai women add a colorful cape called *kitenge*, to that outfit."

"We will help you put it on," his mother says.

I am very moved despite feeling so anxious. I would much rather keep my own clothes. But I do see how hard Yayai tries to ease my life in the *boma,* and I feel very grateful to her.

The big day has finally come.

"You are going to meet my large family and my many friends!" Sokoine exclaims cheerfully upon waking up.

There are not so many special customs we need to follow today. We spent the night together in Mama Klaudia's hut, and Sokoine told me what to expect during the ceremony. An elder will give us his blessing, and that will pretty much be the only time we will be together, men and women spending the rest of the day separately. I am glad to have Eleni by my side -she arrived three days ago. While we slowly start the day, the *boma* is already alive and busy, and the first guests are expected to arrive soon.

Eleni and I go to my mother-in-law's house to help her cook.

"Ah, Stephanie," she says, beaming at me. "Today, you will become a part of our family."

The first groups of people start trickling in. Everybody is welcomed and greeted cheerfully or respectfully, depending on their age and status. Women and younger people lower their heads to demonstrate their reverence towards the elderly, who in turn gently touch their heads. The young warriors, called *morani*, stretch out their arms in greeting. Stools are fetched, upon which only the older Masai are allowed to use. Children whoop and jump around all over the place. Standing next to them, Eleni and I feel a little lost as we try to lower our heads at the right moment in silent imitation of the others. It is impossible to make out whose name is spoken and when because of the swarm of people swirling around us. Only the closest relatives of a certain age may be addressed by their name; I have not memorized them yet. People's status is specified, an indication of their age and gender. Warrior or elder, man or woman, circumcised or uncircumcised – all these particularities are revealed by people's clothes, hairdos, postures, and degree of kinship. There are so many occasions for me to commit a faux-pas and thus disrespect somebody, which would put an abrupt end to people's friendly and open attitudes.

Whenever possible, Sokoine tries to stand next to me and translate, but he too has to be a good host for the male guests, many of whom use Maa, the Masai tongue, between them. Now and then, I manage to answer or understand what is being said thanks to my Swahili, yet most of the time, I smile at people timidly, unable to utter a single word, quite unlike my usual self.

Then, the introductions are finally over.

"Stephanie, it is time."

Flanked by Mama Klaudia and Sokoine's mother, I am led to our hut. My heart races. I am not entirely sure what to expect. The two women help me wrap the long pieces of fabric around my body with gentle, expert hands. Eleni and I giggle with embarrassment. For the first time in my adult life, I am being dressed by other women. It feels a little awkward at first, but I also enjoy the attention the two women show us.

Once this little ritual is over, we all look the same, all of us wearing the same color and clothes.

"We have something for you. You cannot go without it," Sokoine's mother says, unfolding the piece of fabric wrapped around a small package. I draw in air sharply as she reveals splendid pieces of Masai jewelry made of smaller and bigger white pearls and silver chains. Both women expertly place the precious jewels around our necks and arms, softly naming each piece of jewelry as they do so. *Enkalash*, the colorful glass pearls above which she places another long necklace, called *olkati*, adorned with countless small silver plates. The golden metal strips called *esankoi*, worn around the ankles by the other Masai women, they wrap around my wrists. Mama Klaudia and my mother-in-law both wear their own, quite different from mine, festive jewelry, *esosi*, broad beaded collars wrapped around their necks. On their large, stretched earlobes, they also wear lots of pearls, dangling from long threads. I had watched a group of women as they sat creating these specific pieces of jewelry, and I know how many hours of manual work each piece requires.

"Ah, what a beautiful bride."

I smile with embarrassment.

The two women take leave to get prepared. The ceremony is to take place in our hut a little later.

"I need to have a smoke. This is so exciting!" Eleni declares, shaking her head with enthusiasm.

"We need to find a hiding place first," I reply.

She looks at me, puzzled.

94

"No one smokes here. The Masai don't approve of it. They only use snuff," I explain.

We leave my hut, situated slightly apart from the other houses, and walk towards the bush. Everybody is very busy at the time, and we manage to steal away unseen. After all the community work, I am quite glad to have ten minutes on my own. If I have learned anything during my short stay in the village, one is never alone. There are always people around who might also walk right into your hut at any moment, which makes it quite tricky to enjoy a little privacy.

"I also brought this for your nerves," Eleni announces, producing a small bottle from her bag.

Konyagi is a popular gin-based liquor. We have bought quite a lot of these small flasks for our male guests. I could use a little of that right now. I take a few hearty sips, the liquor burning my throat and filling me with a nice warmth. I shudder, and we both laugh. My anxiety diminishes a little. We also took a few pictures of both of us.

Then it is time to go back. The ceremony will start in less than half an hour.

My heart races wildly as the crowd surrounds our small hut. There are so many people they cannot all fit inside. Sokoine and I are asked to sit on our bed. Then, his uncle stands in front of us. If not for the noise around us, I am quite certain people would hear the loud beating of my heart. Breathe, Stephanie, it's all right, I keep telling myself inwardly. Sokoine's uncle talks to us. I don't understand a single word and cast a glance at Sokoine to try and guess what it could be all about and also to do as he does. Seeing him lower his head, I promptly do the same. A bit of mumbling ensues. Then the uncle wraps a piece of soft bark around both our wrists, and I can only assume he gives us a blessing of some sort. I am suddenly filled with an irrepressible, hysterical urge to laugh, and it is all I can do not to burst into laughter. Here I am, tens of thousands of miles away from everything I know, in the bush in Tanzania. Someone speaks to me in a language I don't understand, and I nod. Just like that, I become a Masai wife. Madness. The laughing fit is soon over, though, and the celebration begins. In front of the small hut, the men start dancing.

95

Singing was in the air all day, with small groups of people singing and dancing forming here and there. There are no instruments, no songbooks, no music notes, and no selected program. Using their bodies and voices, the Masai create polyphonic songs passed on for many generations, from grand-mothers to daughters and granddaughters, from wise old men to their sons. The men stand in a large half circle, their shepherd's stick in hand. The young women stand in front of them. A singer begins with an announcement, and the crowd responds, jumping rhythmically up in the air and replying with a polyphonic song. Now and then, the men utter a low rumbling sound, inter-rupted by the high-pitched shrieking of the women. They bend their knees to jump up high in the air or shake their upper body rhythmically. Again and again, one of the dancers steps in the middle of the circle to show a particu-larly skillful move as the others cheer and sing. Some use a shepherd's stick to propel themselves even higher up in the air. They don't need to coordinate with the others, and their choreography works much like a perfectly well-or-ganized beehive. Everyone knows his place. The young girls eye the proud warriors with wonder as they dance and sing their own songs, the magnif-icent rows of pearl jewelry around their necks and dangling from their ear-lobes tinkling and clinking, producing a whole array of sounds. Sometimes, the young girls and the warriors engage in singing and dancing competitions, with the older Masai, who no longer take part in the dancing, watching them with proud and benevolent eyes. The warriors take me in their midst, and I make a few hesitant moves, much to the crowd's enjoyment. They urge me on, cheering, but the German, insecure, and introverted Stephanie cannot quite let go. This will have to do for a start I think to myself as I slip back into being a mere observer.

My wedding is the first big celebration I experience in the *boma*, and I suddenly get goosebumps all over my body. Looking into the happy, cheer-ful faces, some old and wise, lined with deep wrinkles, others alive with the impetuosity of youth, I feel for the first time the strength of these people and this community living according to ancient traditions and rituals deeply rooted in nature. And standing among them, the man I have just married, Sokoine, beaming and completely in his element. The other warriors and his own relatives obviously admire him. This is a new side of him, one I have not witnessed before. Experiencing all this is overwhelming. This is my new family, I suddenly realize. Right now, I cannot think of anything more beautiful than being here, in this place, and with these people.

Fleeced Out

We barely get to rest after the two wedding ceremonies. The administration and document marathon goes on. The days I may legally stay in the country are numbered. We set out on the next arduous journey to Dar es Salaam, this time in Eleni's company, who feels very relieved not to have to travel the distance alone. And admittedly, the journey does seem easier with her by our side. I take leave of her at the airport heavy-heartedly after we successfully covered the long distance to the city. If her presence distracted me on our way here, I realize as we head back how deeply traumatized I still am by the bus accident I was involved in. Every noise makes me jump, so much so Sokoine is actually upset.

"Stephanie, what is this?" he asks.

"I cannot help it. I am afraid," I try to explain.

"There is no other way, though, or do you only want to stay inside the *boma*?"

He is right, of course, I know that, but I am unable to keep my panic in check. So my frayed nerves may rest a little, Sokoine and I decide to stay overnight in Handeni on our way back. Before going to the hotel, I withdraw some money at a bank, the city being the only place where I can use my credit cards to procure larger sums of cash. I don't have a bank account yet. I need to get my papers first before being allowed to open one.

We need 550 dollars for the residence permit, plus about one million Tanzanian shillings, roughly 500 euros. We also intend to use some of that money to buy a few cows. I stash away the bills, along with our brand-new passports and my vaccination certificate, in the belt bag I wear around the waist. It feels a little awkward, walking around with such a large sum of money, but there is no other way to go about it.

The hotel we are to stay at is called Sawe.

"*Habari*, hello," I say, greeting the man at the reception.

One look at his face and my smile freezes. He does not reply, staring at me instead with a crooked, ice-cold grin. The hair on the back of my neck stands up. I have got a bad feeling about that guy. We have checked into that hotel several times, but I have never seen him before. One part of the building is newly built, while the other part is older. He gives us a room in the newer part, which strikes me as rather unsafe, that section being located right next to the wall surrounding the hotel premises.

"Everything else is booked," the man says, shrugging, ogling me like a piece of meat.

I could not exactly say why, but that guy looks very suspicious. I gesture to Sokoine to step aside.

"Let's go somewhere else," I whisper to him.

"What? Why?" Sokoine answers, giving me a puzzled look. "Don't you fret now!" he adds, working himself into a state. "You're always upset about nothing. That guy did not do anything. I don't want to go looking for another hotel. We're staying here."

I feel furious and offended that he would talk to me like that. The triumphant look on the greasy guy's face is unmistakable. He has overheard us, of course. I am beside myself with rage, but I still give in. Sokoine and I sit in our room for a while, sulking, but then we make peace and decide to go and grab something to eat. The city of Handeni is not exactly devoid of pickpockets. I hide my belt bag under the large travel backpack that we leave in the room and bury everything under a heap of clothes. Then we lock the door and keep the key.

We return to the room a few hours later, making it an early evening after what definitely was a very tiring day. I still resent the argument we had earlier. Why did I allow him to treat me like a small child? With that unpleasant thought in mind, I fall asleep.

"Hey, what are you doing here? Stop!"

There is a cluttering sound, followed by screaming and panting. The noise has startled me out of sleep. What is going on? I need a second to get my bearings. The room is still plunged into darkness. Sokoine has jumped out of bed, screaming.

"Stephanie, that guy has taken our money!"

I am wide awake now, my heart beating hard inside my chest.

"He's escaping through the window!"

I jump out of bed and catch a glimpse of two men climbing on the opposite roof. They are about to disappear, clutching the bag with our money. A ladder is propped against the wall, right under our window.

"Sokoine! Our money, our passports!"

My husband does not hesitate for long. He grabs his *olkuma*, the warriors' club, and dashes to the door to go after them. Everything happens very fast. I realize two robbers have been in our room, and my husband might have to face them alone. I hastily put on some clothes and rush down the two flights of stairs after him, panting with fear and rage, my heart pounding in my throat. Downstairs, at the hotel gate, I bump into a very sleepy nightwatcher.

"Hey you, stupid, we have just been robbed!"

The man gives me a baffled look, as I run on. But where to? The darkness around me is complete. The lights are off everywhere. I cannot distinguish the two robbers, and I can't hear the slightest sound either. I give up the pursuit, frustrated. Where is Sokoine? I wonder, dead scared. Back at the hotel, I vent my anger on the security man.

"You were asleep while we were being robbed!" I hear myself scream.

The man looks at me and gives a shrug, which only fuels my rage. After a while, my husband reappears, panting and drenched in sweat but otherwise unharmed.

"I did not get them."

We cannot believe it. Our whole future was inside that bag. We have worked so hard to get these passports, that residence permit, and that money. All of it is gone within minutes. We won't be able to go back to sleep now. Back in our room, we try to reconstruct what has happened. How on earth could the two crooks have known about the money? I feel sure the greasy receptionist must have had a hand in the whole business. He had a key to our room. He must have searched the room while we were out and told his two accomplices about the bag, unlocking the window so they would not have any difficulty pushing it up from outside. I did not think of checking the window before going to bed. Why would I? That is how it must have happened. How else could they have known that we kept such a large sum of money in the room? It would have been far too conspicuous for the receptionist to rob us himself. He would never have dared to make such an obvious move.

Very early on the next morning, we leave the hotel and head straight to the next police station, describing last night's events, along with my suspicions, in great detail. The police tell us the receptionist's slate is not exactly blank. The man has already been convicted multiple times and is especially known for targeting white hotel guests. This comes as quite a shock for us, Sawe being considered safe among the Masai. Well, we do know better now. Two policemen escort us back to the hotel.

The receptionist listens to the whole story with an impassive face despite the allegations we make against him.

"I don't know what you are talking about. I've got nothing to do with this," he replies, denying everything.

"Trouble follows you! This is not the first time!" the policeman snaps back.

I cannot stop myself and explode with rage.

"Why would you use a ladder to climb into our room on the second floor? Why our room in particular? That is no coincidence!"

The policemen go through the hotel's booking list and catch him in a lie. He had not given us a room in the older part of the hotel, even though plenty were available. I had been right to be suspicious of him! When the policemen leave the hotel without the man, on the grounds that they did not have enough evidence against him, I burst out in anger again, appalled. Standing behind his desk, the receptionist looks at me, sneering. I could punch the guy in the face.

There is no way I will be defeated that easily.

"I want my money back!" I cry as Sokoine and I discuss the next step.

My husband gives me a questioning look.

"We won't leave here before the hotel has returned the money to us."

And this is exactly what we tell the manager shortly afterward.

"Excuse me, lady, but you cannot do this!"

The manager is neither happy nor does he agree with this plan, yet he fails to offer us some kind of compensation for our loss.

"We have been robbed while under your care and we shall stay here until you take action. I will also inform the German embassy," I hiss back.

The man walks away, shaking his head.

I no longer care about anything anymore. Putting our threat into practice, we return to the police station daily to get reports for every stolen item. We need these documents as proof that our passports and papers have indeed been stolen so we can apply for new ones. Having not contracted any theft insurance, I can forget all about compensation. The German embassy is no help either.

The limit is reached when a policeman asks Sokoine for a bribe so he will be able "to do his job properly." On the fourth day, the hotel manager calls us into his office.

"This is all I can do for you," he says, handing me 400,000 shillings.

A mere fraction of what we have lost. One million shilling, plus 550 US dollars are gone, not to mention the fact we have to pay for the renewal of our papers.

In the end, disgusted and worn out by the whole thing, we accept the deal and return to the village, very much frustrated. I am devastated and very upset. This past year has been a tad too much for me. Confused thoughts race inside my head on our way back to the *boma*. I no longer enjoy nature's beauty and suddenly question everything. What the hell am I doing here? First, the heavy accident, then my illnesses, and now that robbery. All these events have left deeper scars than I have cared to admit. I feel empty and filled with doubts. Will I, as a white woman, always be regarded as a source of money one can easily prey on? People will always notice me and try to take more from me, regardless of whether I possess money or not. Perhaps I cannot live here after all if it means I need to be so damn careful about everything all the time. Will I only ever be safe inside the *boma*? That thought scares me. I need to think this over once I am back in England, where I am to spend the next four months to earn new money. I don't have any source of income here, in Tanzania. The robbery has largely drained my inheritance, and Sokoine and I have plans. We want to expand his farm in the *boma*, purchase new cows, and build a mill to increase his income.

Having paid another 550 US dollars, I finally got my residence permit. While I wait for my passport renewal, the embassy issues a transitional document that is, unfortunately, only valid for one year. When I return from England, the paper business will start again. For now, though, I will spend the next two weeks in Germany and then travel to Bath to work at the fudge shop. Plenty of time to ponder over things.

CHAPTER 6

Meing'ua oloitiko isirat lenyena

A zebra does not shed its stripes.

"Ding, ding, ding... baa... ding, ding, baa."

The sound of the goats' tiny bells softly sneak into my sleep, the lambs' hungry bleating resembling a baby's cry, as their mothers reply reassuringly in deep, low tones. The smell of the day's first smoke lies in the air. Yayai is certainly already up and about to start her daily chores. After spending four months in England, I have returned to the *boma*. I have missed Sokoine and the life here very much, and I really enjoy being back. The first thing I no longer have any use of here is my watch. We live according to daylight. The animals are the first to wake in dawn's early light, followed by our small village community little by little. For now, though, apart from the soft bleating, the village is shrouded in a deep silence I love very much. Sokoine is still fast asleep. I watch my husband for a while, then silently slip out of bed. I step outside the hut so as not to wake him and put a pot of chai tea over a fire. Black tea with lots of fresh milk, cardamom, cinnamon, cloves and lots of sugar. This will be our breakfast. With the first steaming cup in hand, I take a little walk in the bush. I have not been part of this community for a long time, but life here warms my heart.

The place will be bustling and lively two hours later, and it will no longer be possible to be alone, even for five minutes. Intimacy is hard to come by here. Large families live in open houses with open doors. At times, this is nice, but it can also be stressful, sad, and overwhelming at others. I see and hear things I wish I had not seen or heard. Friends and relatives often ask me about the lack of comfort. That is the one thing I handle quite well as I gradually grow accustomed to living here. There are other things I find really difficult to adjust to. On the one hand, I am warmly welcomed here, but on the other hand, there are cultural boundaries, even in love. Masai are extremely reserved when it comes to expressing their feelings or talking about things that are not commonly discussed in public. I often suffer from loneliness. In our remote village, there is no one I can talk to who would get my cultural background. My mother-in-law, Yayai, has become something like a substitute mother to me, and I love her with all my heart. I wish every woman would get as much caring and attention as the Masai women offered me after my son was born. In many other circumstances, though, we quickly reach our limits.

The beginning of my life in the *boma* is thus a very ambivalent time for me. Roles are very strongly predefined: women look after the family, and men look after the animals. Masai are traditionally shepherds, and very soon Sokoine goes about his work, while I remain in the *boma*. There has never been anyone like me here before. There is no model for me within that community. I will have to find my role myself.

I want to adjust. After all, I have decided to live here. In practice, however, I must admit I feel a little helpless. Everything is new to me. I don't even have a kitchen. I know nothing about life here, and I don't understand Maa. The daily life of Masai women is filled with activities revolving around the family. But these various activities are handled very rudimentarily, without the help of the tools and equipment I am used to. It requires skill to cook over an open fire, and in the first weeks, the other women cook for us. I watch them stir the *ugali*, the traditional corn mush, with firm and definite movements. Beans and rice take a long time to cook until soft, which is why people around here eat a lot of corn. But how on earth does one adjust the temperature of an open, flickering fire? Either my eyes sting and water from all the smoke, or else I burn my fingers.

"Stephanie, let me do this for you."

Yayai keeps taking things off my hands and smiles whenever she notices me having some problem with household activities.

At first, the other women even went to the trouble to fetch water for me so I could wash, but I could not accept that. A small battle ensued.

"Stephanie, we get water for you so you can shower everyday," Yayai explained.

"This is very kind of you, but I don't want to shower everyday. Water is too scarce. And I will come with you and get water myself."

Water is a big issue here, as it takes a lot of effort to get the precious commodity. There are several sources of water here. Some require a 45-minute walk away from the *boma*. There is a well with a pump, and its slightly salty water comes from a depth of about twelve meters. To reach it, the women need to walk to the village of Lesoit with the donkeys, following a winding path through a small forest towards the hills of Songe. Unfortunately, there is often a donkey shortage. Animals, just like cars, are expensive and thus very precious. Not every family owns a donkey, far from it. People often borrow one, sometimes from the neighboring *boma*. Woe to you if the animal gets harmed while under your care. A great loss. We strap four 20-liter cans on the pack animals, 80 liters last for about three days.

"Are you going to the waterhole? Wait for me. I'm coming with you!"

Such is the usual morning talk, as we naturally prefer to cover the long distance together. We set out in the small hours; it gets too hot during the day, especially in the dry season.

Brackish water flows out of the pump. It is not exactly ideal to drink, but it is the only available water in the dry season. About fifteen minutes walk away is another big waterhole that is only filled during the wet season. This water we use to wash and cook, just like the water from the well. No animal is supposed to use that waterhole to drink to avoid feces and bacteria contaminating its water. But no one sticks to that rule, and the heat, the animals, and the bacteria soon turn the clean drinking water into fetid manure no longer suitable for cooking or drinking. But then, Masai are definitely much more hardened than I am when it comes to water. They drink about every kind of water available, the concept of "clean water" being quite expandable. Their bodies are accustomed to brackish water. On the other hand, I soon learn, at my expense, that bottled water is the only available option for my stomach. Every attempt to do otherwise ends with dreadful stomach cramps and diarrhea. The bottles in question have to be purchased in the village.

The Masai have also adjusted to the sweltering heat. While I drink at least three liters of water a day, they manage with much less. I have great respect for the way they deal with water shortage.

"How do you shepherds manage to get by without water, or with only a very small amount, an entire day?" I ask Sokoine.

He has just returned home after an exhausting walk in the heat and tells me about the dried-up waterholes on the way.

"Sometimes, when it gets really bad, we drink the cows' urine."

Such statements command respect. What a tough life the Masai lead from early childhood on. Recalling the washbasin and the clean, running water I grew up with, I realize how extremely privileged I am.

Which is why I tried to use as little water as possible from the very start. Half a bucket makes five liters, and this has to be enough for showering. Only when I need to wash my hair do I carry more into our bathroom, which consists of an outhouse with a view to the sky, the birds, and the stars and has a low clay wall for privacy.

Food

"What are you eating in the bush? Do you also drink blood like the Masai?" my friends keep asking me.

Food is a special topic. Having spent two years in Tanzania, I know what to expect, even though I must say the Masai's menu is even more limited. Our usual breakfast is spicy chai tea, which I love so much that I drink almost one liter a day during the cold season (from May to August). Lunch consists of either *ugali* or rice, with some milk in the wet season, but the cows barely give milk during the dry season. Sometimes we buy *maandazi* on the market, a traditional Swahili pastry resembling small donuts. During the harvest season, vegetables are added to the menu, either self-grown or market-bought. They include potatoes, tomatoes, or more rarely, carrots or green chili. The wet season brings different varieties of spinach, like *mchicha* or *matebele,* for instance, sweet potato leaves or, my favorite – pumpkin leaves. All this is served with the same sauce -fried onions, potatoes, and tomatoes with a dash of milk- into which we dip our ugali or our rice dish.

Everything is cooked in one huge pot. The servings are just huge but very one-sided. At dinner, we eat the leftovers from lunch. At first, I enjoyed this food very much, but after a while, I started to get tired of it. Food is not a matter of pleasure or enjoyment here. One eats whatever is available because one has to eat. In the beginning, I would sometimes buy some food in Dar es Salaam, but I quickly stopped. It is actually pointless. Stocked food goes bad very quickly and only triggers the desire for more. This is something I had to learn very quickly here. Things are just the way they are. Either I accept this, or I am bound to be very unhappy. Unlike in Europe or on other continents where so many people struggle with overweight and obesity, food has a completely different value here. Masai are grateful when they have enough food, and they do not ever complain about their meals lacking variety. Things get complicated when the dry season turns to drought and huge parts of the crops are lost. Then the cows cease to give milk, and everything becomes very difficult.

This does not mean I do not enjoy eating different kinds of food outside the *boma*. According to season, there are bananas, papayas, mangoes, pineapples, oranges, or watermelons. Meat is only served during celebrations, births, or after an animal dies. On such occasions, a goat or a sheep is slaughtered.

Masai drink the blood of their animals to strengthen themselves. I did take a careful sip once. But that was not for me. No one has ever required me to. I have never been asked to do anything against my will.

Sokoine

If I had no trouble adjusting to the living conditions in the wilderness, the same cannot be said of the relationship between Sokoine and me. As it is, we did move into his village in the early days of our relationship, when we were still two strangers with two very different personalities. This turned out to be a real challenge. It is not always easy for him to be patient with me. Neither is it easy for me. Our love is boundless, and so is our stubbornness. Not only are we fundamentally different, but we also come from two different cultures, which makes our fighting inevitable. We do not fight over big issues so much but rather over some smaller aspects of daily life.

I, for one, would always like to be part of everything. I would naturally like to spend some time with my husband and participate in building our farm. Yet, day after day, my patience is greatly put to the test. The European pace of dealing with things is deeply ingrained into my mind, and often clashes with African calm and Masai rules.

Twice a month, a market is held in the neighboring village of Lengatei. A welcome change of scenery for me, and perhaps a chance to spend some time together with Sokoine as a couple? Far from it.

No sooner do we set foot in the village than an endless story is repeated.

"Hello, my friend, how are you?"

Sokoine greets a first acquaintance or relative. According to age and rank, heads are lowered or touched. A short greeting won't do. Being just 30 years old, Sokoine meets many older people he cannot leave quickly.

"How are the children doing? Is the family in good health? Are the cows fine?"

Every encounter begins with *"Lomoni, Lomoni* – what's new?" Answering that question may take ten or fifteen minutes, sometimes more, during which I stand next to my husband, smiling foolishly and not understanding a single word as the men chatter on. I did try to be tolerant at first.

After some time, though, it would only upset me, all the more so since I am not even allowed to leave.

"That would be disrespectful, Stephanie. That's not how we do it," Sokoine declares as I sulk.

He tries to explain it to me once again.

"I don't have a choice. It would be very rude of me if I did not talk to people. They would think I have become arrogant and ill-tempered."

I don't want this, of course. Still, I cannot help but feel upset.

"Why can't you speak Swahili? I would at least understand what you're talking about!"

"It's not so easy for a Masai to speak Swahili when he does not need to. Whenever it's just us, we speak Maa. It is our tongue, and we're used to it. Many my friends don't even speak Swahili that well."

It might be difficult, but not impossible, I think to myself stubbornly.

On another occasion, we have once again come to Lengatei to make purchases, and things get really weird. We had just been discussing what we still needed to buy when a group of friends came our way. Sokoine starts talking to them, but instead of pausing, he walks on with them. No one is paying any attention to me. Sokoine does not even bother to turn around and check whether I am following or not.

"Hellooo, what about me?" I shout, irritated.

A few passers-by look up.

"Why don't you just come along?" Sokoine asks, obviously annoyed.

People were staring at us, and his unfriendly tone push me over the brink.

"Why are you just walking away without saying anything? That is not cool; we were talking together. And then these people come along, and you just go with them and leave me standing here! Can't you see it makes me feel kind of stupid, like a fifth wheel?!"

Masai hate fighting in public. I have just committed an unforgivable mistake. My husband's anger is plain to see. He does not want any more attention.

"We'll talk about this later," he hisses. "You are living with the Masai. Either you adjust, or you leave. There is no in-between."

Sokoine puts it quite plainly, and after a few weeks in the *boma*, I realize he is right. That sentence becomes some kind of mantra to me. It is my firm intention to live with the man I love in his village. There is no other option. Sokoine and his family go to great lengths to ease my adjustment to the Masai way of life.

And yet, I yearn for a little privacy, which is just as difficult to come by inside the *boma,* as it is on our various errands. No sooner does someone hear about our plan to go somewhere than his brothers or cousins are part of the journey. It is only ever the men, by the way. The women are too busy and would never ask to come to the village or city. Of course, we always pay for everything. Food is not expensive, that's not the point, but still. We do pay for everything.

"It would be impolite not to take them along and pay for their expenses," Sokoine explains.

I am often bored, especially in the early times of my stay in the boma. I am not close to anyone, nor is there anyone I can really talk to. I don't have anything to do either, and I don't know yet how to go about the women's chores. I thus long for Sokoine to return home after his day's work.

"Where are you? Why don't you come back home?" I ask, as I start pestering him on the phone after 5:00pm.

Understandably, he does not find this funny.

"Why are you calling me? I cannot even be with my friends anymore. You stress me out, Stephanie. What's wrong with you?"

"I feel lonely."

"Then go to the other women."

"I don't understand them that well yet."

"If you would spend more time with them, you'd learn the tongue."

I can understand him in a way. He does not want to be my babysitter.

Sokoine's advice is often practical and calm, not so much emotional. He actually gets me to think, and in the end, overcoming my shyness, I go and seek the company of the other women. Sitting in the shade of the huts, they show me how to make Masai jewelry. Children join us now and then, snuggling up against me and touching my arms and hair, a clear demonstration of their curiosity and affection. I realize how hard these women have to work for food and water to wash the family's clothes, grow vegetables, and so much more. Sokoine is right. Little by little, my Maa also improves.

After the initial difficulties adjusting to life in the *boma*, we need to think of ways to secure our livelihood.

"Let's buy a motorbike," Sokoine suggests one day.

We do not possess many cows yet. Sokoine's family is considered rather poor. Wealth is measured by the number of animals one owns.

"We'll rent the motorbike to a Swahili. He can transport greater amounts of water and other items and run other errands. He'll do all the driving around on our behalf and pay us to use the motorbike." Great idea. Practically the first step to creating a small shipping company in a country where motorbikes are the means of transportation *par excellence*. Impressively large numbers of people, animals and goods are conveyed from A to B on motorbikes every day. Only very few people own a car.

As good as Sokoine's plan might sound, its execution fails due to the driver's unreliability. The man does not pay the lease and keeps standing us up. We take the motorbike back.

"I will learn how to drive," my husband says, looking at me for approval.

I am not convinced, but I try not to let it show. Not only have we just lost a source of income -which is bad enough in itself- but now my inexperienced husband also talks about speeding across the bad roads. I can hardly be expected to be a nice passenger in that state of mind and cannot suppress a nervous yell whenever the back tire skids on the sandy path, sending the motorbike careening off the road. And then I scream in warning once too often. That does it for Sokoine. He has had enough. We are just driving along a hilly dirt road to Songe when the back tire starts juddering again.

"Oh God, this is such a bad road," I scream with fear.

Sokoine jams on the brake, jumps off the motorbike and yells at me:

"What's all this, Stephanie? Why do you always make such a fuss? Your screaming drives me nuts!"

This day, too, ends with a fight.

Nightly Assault

"Took, took, took…" What kind of noise is that? I wonder, startled out of sleep. I listen closely into the darkness. Could it be rain? Or perhaps the roof is leaking? It sounds as if raindrops would platter from the ceiling onto my blanket. I fumble about in search of a flashlight. Of course, tonight, of all nights, Sokoine is not at home. He has gone to seek some help for us. Our constant fighting has left him thinking.

"Stephanie, I will go and seek the advice of a Masai healer. He will tell me how you and I can achieve more peace and also how you can control and manage your anger."

His words move me deeply. I don't know what kind of means this healer possesses, but in all cases, Sokoine's offer is helpful.

My husband usually tries never to leave me alone. Especially in the first years of our life together, when everything is still very new to me. But the witch doctor lives far away from our village, quite close to Handeni. The number of people crowding his place is so great that Sokoine cannot possibly make it there and back on the same day.

"Took, took, took…"

The odd noise does not stop. Half dazed with sleep, I switch on the light, and my heart misses a beat. There are insects all over my bed.

"Help! What is that?" I cry in horror, struggling to contain a feeling of deep repulsion as I point the beam of light at the ceiling.

Insects everywhere, crawling out of every crack and gap in the thatched roof. Ants. Not the tiny, cute black creatures we are used to in Germany. No, the beasts crawling on my bed and all over the room are gigantic, and there are really a lot of them. "*Siafu* ants," I pant, horrified. *Siafu* is the Swahili word for one of the world's largest and most dangerous ant species. I am not a fearful person, and as a biologist, there are very few animals I do fear, one notable exception being this specific ant species I have already encountered during my stay in Ifakara.

They show up in great numbers, devouring everything on their way with their powerful mandibles. They killed two of my chicks back then, cannibals gnawing at the birds' flesh to the bone. When I found them, a cluster of ants was still clinging to the chicks' pitiful remains. *Siafu* ants also bite people. I jump out of bed, half insane with disgust. After the initial shock, I realized there weren't as many as I first thought. Calm down, Stephanie, take a deep breath. You can fix this, I think to myself for courage. Fetching the large can of bug spray from the shelf, I aim it at the ants' trail on the wall. Then I shake out my blanket, and a few minutes later the nightmare seems to be over. A few insects still wriggle in agony, but I seem to have averted any immediate danger.

I go back to bed, still badly shaken. "Took, took, took." Barely half an hour later, the eerie sound resumes. Louder, faster, and more powerful. The beam of my flashlight shows the extent of the disaster. Large clusters of ants drop onto my bed, biting my arms, head, and legs. Crap! A wave of panic washes through me as I shine the light on the room. The insects are everywhere, crawling out of the tiniest cracks in the walls and engulfing my clothes, backpack, the shelves, absolutely everything. I feel as if I was trapped inside a horror movie. The scene before my eyes makes one thing very clear, though: a bug spray won't be of any help here. I need to get out of here and fast. I frantically slip my feet into my slippers, my whole body stiff with repulsion, as I desperately try to shake off the horrid, biting creatures. I throw the door open only to find myself facing a whole battalion of *Siafu* ants. Hectically leaping over the bloody beasts, I turn around and aim the flashlight at the outer wall of the hut. The sight before my eyes makes me sick. The wall, four meters wide and two meters high, is entirely covered with ants.

A ridiculous, mad thought crosses my mind. Do the blasted beasts also devour banknotes? We keep a lot of money inside the house, money we intend to use to buy new cows. I don't have time to ponder this for long, though, as I watch our house being buried under the marching throngs of insects. What will remain of my house? Here I am, standing alone in the dark, clutching my small flashlight. I need a bed. There is nothing I can do to fight off these creatures for now. My phone and my blanket – I need to get these out of the house. Clenching my teeth, I rush back inside, the devilish beasts biting down on me at once. I grab my things with one hand and attempt to fend off the dreadful pests with the other. Then I am outside once again, the wounds on my body stinging and burning but otherwise unscathed. I made it.

"Yayai. Yayai, can you hear me?" I whisper through a tiny gap in my mother-in-law's house.

I don't want to wake the others.

"Yayai!"

A moment later, she opens the door, half asleep.

"What is it, Stephanie?"

"Our house is full of *Siafu* ants."

Yayai's eyes widen in shock.

"That can't be."

She has to see for herself. Only a few minutes have passed, yet our house has turned into a black, crawling and swarming mass in that short time. Yayai's hand flies to her mouth. Before I can even get a chance to stop her, she seizes the blanket she had been holding and starts hitting the throngs of insects.

"Yayai, stop. There are too many of them. We don't stand a chance."

She agrees.

"I can't believe this would happen now of all times when Sokoine is away."

My thought exactly. We go back to her bed and lie down, exhausted, to try and get a little sleep. I wake up a few hours later, completely worn out. Oh no, that wasn't merely a bad dream, I think to myself, scared to go to our house. But I am in for quite a surprise. The ants are gone. I can hardly believe my own eyes. The million-strong army has gone, and our house is still standing. The dead bodies of insects are scattered on the ground, bearing witness to the whole thing, not having been a mere nightmare.

As it is, daylight offers a new insight: we are living in the very heart of nature, and the *Siafu* ants were on the move. Our house was standing in their way. They simply crawled over it. I feel quite humbled by the whole experience. We are part of a whole, and such events clearly show us our own limits. Nothing could have stopped that army.

CHAPTER 7

Eta enkishui enkata

There are seasons in life.

The wound under my little toe is so small that I don't even notice it at first. Perhaps I stumbled over a stone or stepped on a twig. I don't know for sure. The fact is that tiny wound soon turns into a major disaster. On the second day, my toe starts throbbing a little, but I still do not pay much attention to it. On the third day, I am supposed to take the cows to the waterhole - a 45-minute walk. The cows are still drinking when a storm sets in, rain coming down in buckets. We hurry back along the path that rapidly turns into a mud bath. Deeper and deeper, I sink into the soggy clay soil, only just managing to keep my flip-flops on. The cows also have trouble walking along the viscous ground. This walk through the dirt probably did not help my ailing foot.

On the next morning, I wake up at the crack of dawn to excruciating pain. My lower leg is bright red and has swollen to the size of my thigh. I feel hot and nauseous, and I probably run a fever.

"Sokoine, I need your help! Look!"

My husband sits up in bed, still half asleep, with a worried look.

"This doesn't look good!"

I keep antibiotics in my small home pharmacy precisely for such cases, but my body rebels against the medication, and I vomit at once. My temperature rises during the day. Feeling increasingly worse, I browse the Internet to try and find out about this sudden bout of illness. Blood poisoning. All the symptoms fit. I need to watch the red streak on my leg. I have read in an article that blood poisoning can be fatal if the bacteria reach the heart. Even though I understand this rationally, my body is unable to react.

"We have to get you to the hospital in Songe," Sokoine says, seriously alarmed.

"No, let me just rest here. I can't make it," I reply.

But my husband won't be deterred. Early the next morning, after another dreadful night, Sokoine hoists me onto his motorbike. My leg hurts and burns like fire whenever I step on it, and I can barely hold on to my husband. Inside the clinic, I experience a small déjà-vu, recalling that time I had stood at the reception desk, severely ill with food poisoning and nevertheless having to handle everything on my own. Information, payment, treatment. After what feels like an eternity, I finally get to see a doctor.

"You have to stay here. We will put you on IV antibiotics."

My head is spinning. That is out of the question. I cannot stay at the hospital alone. No way. As a man, Sokoine is not allowed to stay in my shared room. We have to find another woman to take care of me. Otherwise, no one will help me if I need to vomit but feel too weak to get up. Every hospital nurse is in charge of at least 50 patients. This is all too much for me. I would much rather return to the *boma*. I would feel much better there, in my current state. I don't want to be stared at all day long as the only white woman.

"Just give us the medication."

The doctor looks at me and shakes his head.

"It is not so easy," he replies.

"They can put it on me in the small clinic back in Lesoit," I suggest.

After a while, the doctor agrees to this plan and I get a first shot before we leave, to relieve the pain and reduce the fever. They also insert an IV cannula into the crook of my left arm, so it won't be necessary to find a new vein every time I have to have a new IV. Somewhat relieved, Sokoine and I make our way home. I am completely exhausted when we reach the *boma*, and I lay down to rest at once. The next day, Sokoine once again hoists me onto the motorbike, half-dead, and drives me to the small village hospital in Lesoit, only five minutes away. A nurse mixes the powder and puts me on the IV, the effect of which begins to show on the third day, with the fever receding a little. Seven days to go. I slowly start to feel a little better, yet my nights are restless, the cannula in my arm hurting and impeding my movements. My leg remains swollen, so much so I can barely bend it, no more than I can move my arm. I cannot even tie up my hair on my own.

"Let me do this for you," Sokoine says, offering, to my surprise, to help me wash my hair.

Never before has he offered to help me in that way. Very carefully he pours some water over my greasy hair, applies a little shampoo, then washes and rinses it thoroughly. Once my hair is dry, he ties it up the way I always do. A rare, precious moment that leaves me deeply moved.

Very slowly, my condition starts to improve. However, my leg is still red and swollen on the tenth day. Damn it. In a few days, my sister is due to visit for the first time, and I am not exactly up and about. Far from it, actually. And yet we have so many plans: we want to go on a safari and travel to Zanzibar, and of course, I want to show her the *boma*. Long hours of walking and sitting on the bus in cramped conditions await me.

"We have to cancel, Stephanie. You are much too ill," Sokoine implores.

But the mere thought of canceling my sister's trip brings tears to my eyes.

"That is absolutely out of the question. I am really looking forward to seeing her again," I reply through clenched teeth.

We extend the antibiotic use, even though I am not sure whether this is the right medicine for me or not. My leg does not really improve. I don't entirely trust our village doctor, and I read on the Internet that I need another kind of antibiotic. My foot, too is still a pitiful sight. And then, on top of it all, yet another problem arises. A fresh wound, the size of a plate, appears suddenly above my ankle, gradually taking on a dark purplish hue, like a bruise. Shortly after, pustules materialize, and a little later, pus oozes out of the wound. Finding this rather scary, I decided to have the secretion analyzed in the Aga Khan Hospital in Dar es Salaam. Perhaps they will advise the use of another medication. I will not cancel my sister's visit, though, and book two seats side by side on the bus to Dar es Salaam so I can at least elevate my leg. Before Sokoine and I go to the airport to pick up my sister, I ask a doctor in the large hospital to take a smear.

My twin sister and I spend three very intense weeks together and have a great time, even though she often worries about the state I am in.

"Stephanie, that wound does not look good at all."

"I'll take care of it after you're gone," I keep answering bravely.

I am in such pain at times that I have to call off some of the strenuous day trips we have planned. All in all, however, the wound seems to dry up and no longer oozes pus. A scab forms and falls off after about two weeks. By then my sister has already returned to Germany. My leg, however, remains just as swollen as before.

"Is it healing?" Sokoine and I wonder.

The hospital sent us a report stating no bacteria were found in the sample they took. And that's it, nothing else. Perhaps they had my sample mixed up with someone else's? Or perhaps they could not find anything because I had been taking antibiotics for quite some time before they took a smear? At a loss for an answer, I decide to leave the matter at that. Big mistake.

Meanwhile, daily life in the *boma* keeps me quite busy. A few weeks after the first bout of infection, a purulent pimple appears on the old wound. Where on earth does this thing come from? Yet, instead of being alarmed, I start worrying and popping the pimple. The effect is immediate. Upon waking up the next morning, my leg is once again red and swollen. I feel hot. The fever has returned. Crap!

Then, something happens that leaves me deeply shaken. My husband looks at my leg and starts crying.

"What is wrong with you? Why are you constantly sick?" he sobs, very upset. "Who would wish us ill?"

Never before have I seen him in such a state. I flare up at once, very upset.

"Why are you yelling at me? This is not my fault!" I shout.

We are both very distraught.

"I need you to be strong right now! I really feel very sick!"

It is a while before we manage to calm down and stop shouting hysterically.

"I want to go to the hospital in Songe. This cannot remain untreated," I declare.

Suspecting they wouldn't let me go home that easily this time, I asked Yayai if she would agree to come with us and stay with me at the hospital.

"This does not look good. You have to stay," the doctor says thoughtfully, shaking his head.

It is all far too much for me. I am tired of being ill. I am exhausted, stressed out, and furious. Perhaps I don't have any other choice. Perhaps staying in that hospital and getting some rest is all it takes for me to get better. I very much hope it is. Without opposing any resistance, I allow them to bring me to a shared six-bed room and take a sample of my blood.

"How much water do I have to add to mix the antibiotic?"

I cannot believe my ears. The nurse does not even know the exact dosage. *Help!*

"You have to add a hundred milliliters of water," I call across the corridor.

"Are you a nurse now?" the woman snaps back.

"No," I retort, "but I can read, and I have been given this medication for weeks now. I know how it is done. And that's exactly how you're going to do it!"

I have raised my voice, my anger about to surge. Shortly afterward, the doctor enters the room with a second syringe.

"What's that one for now?"

"Your malaria."

My face drops.

"I don't have malaria."

"Your blood sample says otherwise."

I am speechless. Why do I have to get a double punishment? No wonder I feel so worn out. My body cannot take such a level of infection. I give up the fight and present my behind to the nurse so that she can give me the pain and malaria medication.

This time, though, much to my comfort, Yayai is here with me; her presence alone is a great source of solace. Given the weak state I find myself in, Yayai proves a great help in all practical matters. We share the same bed, not being able to afford two beds. Neither of us sleeps very well, though, the single bed being quite narrow.

Just as I had feared, I attract quite a lot of attention as a white woman. People keep showing up in the room, pausing at the foot of my bed to see what the *mzungu* – as I am called here – might be up to. Our room is constantly crowded and loud, and Yayai defends me like a mother lion protecting her cub. She too finds all the unwanted attention very bothersome. Yet, as it is, our time together at the hospital proves very precious for our relationship. It is here, in that hospital, that we really start to get closer to each other. Much to my relief, the medication kicks in pretty soon. My leg looks a little better, and five days later we are able to return home.

"We had to slaughter her."

I gaze sadly at the bloodied remains of my favorite cow. I have just walked to a small pasture to see her newly born calf, which will now have to be raised on the bottle. The birth of the calf turned into a disaster, as the baby would not appear, or only under the greatest efforts. Seeing right away the mother did not stand a chance the shepherds chose to put her out of her misery.

"The elderly say she has died for you," Sokoine tells me. "They believe you would perhaps have died otherwise."

But the Masai men will not leave it at that. A few days later, Sokoine leads me to the *olpul*, a special place in the *boma*, normally reserved for men and where many important rituals occur. Animals are slaughtered there, and young men turn into warriors. Just this once, I am allowed to step into the sacred place.

"They worry about your health and wonder why you keep getting sick. They have spoken to their healer and have prepared a Good Luck ceremony for you."

I don't know what to say. Tears well up in my eyes, but I quickly wipe them away so I don't upset Sokoine. To think these wise men have sat together and pondered over me, a white girl! I still feel like a stranger here; after all, I have just arrived in the village. And yet here they are, giving me their full attention and offering their wise advice. I am deeply touched.

"What exactly is a Good Luck ceremony?" I ask Sokoine, who looks at me, beaming.

"They will spit on you."

Sorry, what? I cannot believe my own ears.

"They take the holy milk and spit it on you. To dispel evil spirits."

I am glad Sokoine has told me what to expect because the ceremony I am about to experience is not for the faint-hearted.

"They have also slaughtered a sheep for you. You must sit on the animal's belly so its strength passes on to you."

At twelve o'clock sharp, I thus find myself straddling a soft, bloodied sheep belly while twenty old Masai men stand in a circle around me.

"It has to be at that exact time," Sokoine had explained.

A calabash is passed from hand to hand, the men taking turns sipping the milk. One of them arranges my feet in the right position, my posture apparently being important - my heels and my legs must touch the ground. Being the center of attention feels awkward, yet at the same time, I am oddly moved and excited about the whole procedure. No matter how disgusting it sounds, I would never dream of turning down the offer. The fact these men have actually organized a ceremony, handed down for generations, for my sake alone, shows me that they have truly welcomed me into their midst. It is an overwhelming, heart-warming feeling. Never before in my life has anyone gone to such trouble for my sake. I know nothing about paternal care. My father never had any part in my life. And yet here I am now, looking into the caring faces of these men, all of them fathers, too.

Then it all happens very fast. As on a secret signal, they spit the white fluid on me all at once. My hair, t-shirt, and my entire body is soaked in milk. I resist the urge to wipe it away. Milk drops into my eyes, but it does not matter. It is of utmost importance that I do not disturb this sacred ritual or inadvertently do something inappropriate. The eldest speaks a few words, and the entire choir responds with "Nai." This goes on for several minutes until one of the men signals to me to get up. Two men lift one side of their garment to create a sort of curtain I am supposed to walk through. I am not to speak to anyone and must return to our hut at once, keeping the drenched clothes on for some time to allow the effect of the Good Luck ceremony to unfold. This is not all. The men have prepared something else. Sokoine and my father-in-law join me in our hut.

"Stephanie, you need to regain your strength. You should drink sheep fat."

Oh my... The women of the family have told me about this custom. Yayai says it tastes really awful. She actually fears the whole thing. She speaks from experience, of course, Masai women are made to drink the greasy fluid after having given birth.

"I ask you with all respect," my father-in-law declares, looking at me gravely.

That is the keyword.

"The most important thing you must learn about our culture is respect," Sokoine told me before our wedding. "Always show the others respect, especially the elders."

Even though I rebelled inwardly against the whole thing, under no circumstances did I wish to spoil my relationship with my father-in-law. Meat and a few bones of the slaughtered sheep sizzle over a fireplace. A cup of blood waits next to it. I need to get used to the idea, admittedly, but I actually admire how important and valuable animals are to the Masai. Not only do they eat their flesh, but they also use and process every little bit of their bodies. Nothing is wasted. After about an hour, the fat separated from the meat and the bones and formed a pool of clear liquid, the sight of which made my stomach turn and heave. I very much hope I will manage to keep it down. Throwing up would be doubly unfortunate in my present weakened and medicated state. Not that I have much say in the whole matter - Sokoine's father's request is sacrosanct.

Lemali, Sokoine's brother, hands me the *sufria* containing the warm liquid fat that resembles liquid gold. I have no doubt it tastes awful.

I pour the fat into a cup, filling it only to half. The smell of the fat makes my stomach churn as I put my lips to the edge of the cup. I can feel people staring at me, and I ardently wish to be on my own. But the Masai always drink the fat in the presence of many others. They are apparently not afraid of throwing up and embarrassing themselves. Mustering my courage, I ignore all the onlookers around me, especially Sokoine's father, who is watching me closely.

The first sip makes me gag, but Lemali pats me on the back, saying:

"Drink on. Don't be afraid!"

With his help, I manage to get the half cup down. Not much, as far as Masai are concerned, but nonetheless, a great success in my own eyes. Not only in the hope that it might heal me but mostly because I have managed not to disappoint my Masai family.

As much as I hope for the Masai magic powers to unfold, unfortunately, nothing of the sort occurs. The lengthy, severe infections I have suffered, the accident, and perhaps also the other past challenges of my life have left scars. I am infinitely exhausted, both mentally and physically.

"I think I need to return to England for a while so my body can get some rest. I am still covered by health insurance there."

Sokoine ponders over this for a moment, then nods.

"This sounds like a wise decision!"

One week later, I am on a plane to Great Britain.

New Cows for Our Farm

After the death of my parents, my French grandparents, and my aunt, I inherited quite a large sum of money. Leaving that money in my bank account in Germany seems pointless. I want to use it for something useful.

"Let us build a farm," I suggest to Sokoine upon returning from England a few weeks later, feeling much better and restored. "We'll buy cows and land to grow food. It would benefit the whole family."

Indeed, it would. Having decided to live in the *boma*, we had to think about our livelihood. My husband cannot go on working as a poorly paid security man. As his wife, I naturally want to support him. What better investment for the money I have inherited than this family of ours? No one would have to starve anymore.

A farm. That sounds pompous. It would take at least a million euros to buy a farm in Germany. Here, though only a small fraction of that sum is needed. For most Masai, such money is out of their reach.

Masai don't count the cows or houses within one *boma*, as it is believed to bring bad luck. By and by, Sokoine and his brothers purchase new cows at various markets in Lengatei, Songe, or Sunya. I would like to be part of it all, but the men deter me from doing so.

"It is too dangerous, Stephanie," my father-in-law declares.

"Why?"

"There are a lot of robberies, especially in Sunya. If people notice you have come to buy a lot of animals, you will be in danger," he explains. "They will also ask for a higher price when they see you."

My skin color makes it doubly impossible for me to join the men.

If there is one thing I have come to learn by now, it is to respect an older Masai's wish. If my father-in-law expressly asks me to do something, I cannot refuse him; that would be disrespectful. Every other day, new animals, cows and goats, are bought and brought to the *boma*. Two or three months later, we are the proud owners of quite a stately herd. My family can barely believe its own luck. Until now, they were regarded as rather poor, and now their status has dramatically evolved.

Our next step is to meet the mayor, Mwenye Kiti. We want to buy some land to build our farm. Easy enough – at the end of our meeting, we are allowed to cultivate and harvest fields. The land on which we plan to set up our farm is about one hour and a half walk away from the *boma*, only twenty minutes with the motorbike.

It is the beginning of a busy time for Sokoine: he buys seeds, prepares the land with Swahili people, sows, gets water, provides food for the farm workers, and supervises their work. My part is to provide the money. I am not supposed to lend a hand. I don't know how to ride a motorbike, and my presence impedes negotiations. For many Masai and Swahili men, having a white woman as a "boss" is simply inconceivable. As it is, the whole business is a crucial test for our relationship. I am a strong and proud woman, and I don't want to supply the funds while cooking and waiting in the *boma* for my husband to return. But I also see the delicate balance Sokoine struggles to achieve to do right by me. On the rare exceptions I accompany him to the market to buy cows, I notice people raising their prices simply because they see me standing beside my husband. Sometimes, they ask me to wait for them at the edge of the market, but that, too, proves stressful for Sokoine.

"You're not safe there, Stephanie."

It seems there is no satisfying solution to this dilemma, and thus, I stay in the *boma*, sad and frustrated.

But I won't be easily deterred from participating in the fieldwork. Despite his protest, I accompany him to the farm.

"Stephanie, the work will be too hard for you," Sokoine says.

He fears digging deep holes in the hard soil under the blazing sun will prove too much of a strain for me.

"The men can do the digging. I can sow the corn seeds," I reply with great determination.

It is, after all, also my farm and my investment. I am looking forward to it, and I want to make sure that everything goes well. This stresses my husband, who wonders whether I trust him or not. I do trust him, of course.

"Let me be a part of it. This is our project," I reassure him.

One year later, we harvest our first corn crop - a proud moment for everyone.

"I thank you, my child, for having bought these cows and the farm," Sokoine's father declares warmly, "you are one of us, and I am so glad to have you here. We will never starve again."

His words make me feel proud and very happy. My presence here is truly meaningful. Sometimes, at least. Until I find myself once again plagued by boredom.

I look after the goats in the morning, yet this activity does not fill the entire day. Cooking lunch does not take much time either, especially since I have learned how to deal with an open fire. I feel too young to take a small nap in the afternoon, and my days seem to stretch on endlessly. After some time, I start making Masai jewelry, but I lack the skill and experience, not to mention that making jewelry is not exactly my life's dream. I am basically waiting all day long for my person, Sokoine, to return home.

Not that the women were anything short of wonderful to me. But my unease and insecurity makes me overly careful and stiff. They ensure I don't stay too long in the sun so my skin does not get burned. It takes a long time before I realize how much of her life Sokoine's mother, Yayai, has given up for my sake. She normally enjoys going to church quite regularly, and she also quite often visits relatives in other *bomas*, yet since my arrival, she stays here to take care of me. It is important to her that I should be able to settle in and feel well.

I often take long walks into the bush out of sheer boredom, which is actually quite risky. When I proudly hand the firewood I have collected to Yayai, she exclaims:

"Stephanie, where have you been? We were worried about you. What if something had happened to you?"

She looks at me with alarm, then offers me one of her nice smiles, happy that I should have thought about her.

From time to time, my stubbornness does get me in trouble. In November, Sokoine roams the area on his motorbike in search of pastures made lusher by an early rain in search of a new feeding ground for our cows. It often starts raining earlier in the mountains, and he gets lucky just behind Lengatei, about 15 kilometers away from our *boma*.

"I'm coming with you," I declare, looking forward to a bit of adventure.

My man gives me an irritated look.

"No, you're not. It is much too tiring for you," he replies.

I, in turn, find his answer outrageous, even though he is right. I have just overcome a bad bout of malaria shortly before.

"I cannot look after you; I have to take care of the cows. And it is going to be very hot; you'll get a sunstroke."

But the prospect of leaving the *boma* for a while and actually do something is too tempting. Obstinacy being second nature to me, I choose to brush off his concerns.

"I'll wear a hat, and I'll put on lots of sun cream. And I'm perfectly able to look after myself."

Sokoine shakes his head wearily. He knows when he's lost a battle.

Cows are leisurely creatures, trotting slowly alongside us humans and stopping now and then to graze. A 30-kilometer long journey awaits us, we set out shortly after sunrise. The path is beautiful, even though the heat soon gets very intense. We pause for lunch at Sokoine's relatives, sitting with them in the cool shade, playing with the children and drinking tea.

Our herd is large, which is why our group of shepherds is rather numerous. The path leads us through Swahili villages and alongside other farms. We have to make extra sure that the animals don't run off into the corn fields. On the road, we have to watch out for motorbikes or trucks – a danger for the animals as much as for the vehicles.

Little by little, the scenery changes. We now progress under the gigantic crowns of huge acacia trees, meter-high grass lining each side of the path. This actually comes as a surprise, as everything around our *boma* is withered and bone-dry. As the path gets hillier, it also becomes steeper and narrower. Absolute concentration is required. The animal mustn't come to harm on the sloping ground.

I gradually realize how exhausted I am, and I have to sit down for a while. I have completely underestimated my physical condition, having recovered from malaria so recently. I have just stopped taking the medication, and I can still feel the disease in my bones. I cannot go on anymore. Sokoine was right, of course, and he knows it. He also knows that he chose peace. He calls a motorbiker, who takes me back to the *boma*. I never hear a single word of reproach.

The Vision

"Three young bulls are gone!" Sokoine's little brother exclaims, aghast.

He was watching over the herd with another brother while Sokoine and Lemali were on their way to the farm. Controlling the herd on such hilly ground is no small task, and single animals keep running off in search of tasty plants, inadvertently leaving the rest of the herd. Sometimes they join other herds, and on other occasions weaker animals cannot keep up with the group's pace. With such a large number of animals, one can easily lose track. In the evening, the shepherds check whether all animals are present. On that particular occasion, though, this is not the case: three of them are missing. On the next day and on the day after that, there still is no trace of them.

Damn. I feel more and more worried. Three bulls are extremely valuable; it has cost me great effort to acquire them. I picture them grazing peacefully somewhere, not wishing to imagine them stolen, their bodies roasting over a campfire.

"If I can picture them safely grazing somewhere, perhaps it means they are still alive?" I ask Sokoine in a hopeful voice.

Masai have a deep spiritual connection with their animals, which I have come to share by now.

"If you can still see them, then nothing bad has happened to them yet," Sokoine answers, nodding gravely.

Days pass by and soon it is a week since the three bulls went missing. And then I have a dream. Stomping through a lush meadow in a small clearing, a giant white ox with long horns comes across our three young animals. I wake up, shaking my head. I know this meadow, but it just cannot be. Sokoine will think I am insane if I tell him about it. But then again, perhaps he won't, and I have nothing to lose anyway.

"Sokoine, I have dreamt of the place where our bulls are," I say, telling him the whole story.

Much to my surprise, he does not laugh at me. Quite the opposite.

"Your connection with them is very powerful; this is why you have had this vision."

It is a very intense moment between us. I am very moved that he should take my dream seriously and declare himself fascinated by my powerful vision. I have a second dream. The white ox appears to me once again, yet this time I can see its face and black mouth. I tell Sokoine about this second dream.

Two days later somebody calls him on the phone, his face lighting up as he listens to the other person.

"This sounds like our young bulls," he says, glancing at me. "I am on my way."

I can barely believe my own eyes. A Swahili shepherd has found the three runaways and asked around, wondering whom they might belong to. My husband has gone to check whether the animals actually belong to us.

"Please, look out for a white ox in the herd," I call as he leaves.

Two hours later, he is back and looks at me, beaming. Our bulls are safe and sound and will be back soon.

"And yes, there is an ox in that herd. Not entirely white, and with a black mouth."

I don't believe this. It is magic!

My First Masai Birth

"Stephanie, come with me. I'll take you to my great cousin, Kara. She is having her baby, and she wants you to be there."

Straddling his motorbike, Sokoine gives me a big grin. I cannot believe what he has just said to me. It is about ten o'clock in the morning, and I was in the process of packing our things to go to Kibaya. But this is a very special invitation. I have never witnessed a birth before. On the one hand, I admit to feeling a little awed at the prospect, but on the other hand I also feel flattered. And curious.

Kara lives in the neighboring *boma*. As we arrive, I see other women entering her hut. Every female relative has been informed of the news and have set out to join her. But only women in Kara's age or above are allowed to watch and be with her. According to Masai rules, younger women or young mothers whose own children have not teethed yet are forbidden to watch. Nearly all Masai births are home births, managed by the midwives who live in every village.

It is quite dark inside the small hut and the women crowd the bed, standing before it, some even sitting on it. About 40 persons are present. The air inside the room is stifling.

"Karibu, Stephanie! Welcome."

Greeting me warmly, the women push me forward towards the bed so fast I don't have time to realize what is happening. A woman cradles Kara's head in her lap, caressing it. This must be her mother. The midwife is kneeling between the future mother's legs. Only older women stand in the first row. Not wishing to take anyone's place, I take a few steps back. There is nothing I can do to help anyway. The labor process is in its late stages and Kara moans softly. Then her wailing becomes louder. The painful contractions have started. The atmosphere inside the hut is full of expectation and sympathy. A few women whisper softly to each other: " Oh, she is still so young. The first child is hard." Kara is about 16 years old. Through the gaps between the crowd of women, I catch glimpses of many hands doing helpful things, such as wiping sweat from the young mother's brow or supporting her legs. The women expose Kara's upper body to allow her to get some air.

The energy inside the room is electrifying, and the atmosphere is full of love and solidarity. We move as one to the rhythm of the contractions. Everyone wants this birth to go well. Never before have I experienced such deep-felt women's community. Tears roll down my cheeks. I don't care about the sweltering heat inside the hut. All I see is Kara, a beautiful, cheerful girl, as she is being carried and lifted up in a wave of love. When she gestures to signal she is about to throw up, two women sit her up, and the younger women remove the vomit without a word. Everyone has her own task.

"If she vomits, it means it will soon be over," a woman whispers in my ear. A few minutes later, Kara's panting becomes louder. Masai women try not to scream, regarding this as shameful. My Maa skills are not yet elaborate enough to understand everything the women say, but then what happens here right now does not require any translation. A gap opens in front of me. I don't wish to push forward, but at the same time, I feel magically attracted. The midwife sprinkles a few drops of oil on her fingers and rubs Kara's vagina with it. And then, all of a sudden, a tiny head appears, pushing forward and out to the rhythm of the contractions. Filled with respect for Kara, I hold my breath. Then everything goes very fast. The tiny body slips out of her, followed by a last, long moaning. The baby is here! The energy inside the room changes at once, a wave of joy and relief washing over all of us as the midwife presents the child to the women. We laugh and cry and fall into each other's arms.

Men are nothing in this world. We women make it all happen. This thought comes to my mind as I leave the hut, overwhelmed with emotion. So many thoughts race through my mind. Here we are, in the middle of the bush, apart from civilization. No ultrasound machine, no anesthesia, and no hospital close by, but the endless wisdom and experience of the 40 women present, almost all of them having given birth themselves. The midwife is the mother of eight children and has decades of experience; she has brought thousands of babies into this world. How different things are in Europe. The fear, the uncertainty, the stress, and the belief in conventional medicine. In Germany, women usually give birth to their first child when they are in their thirties, and the average number of children is about 1.5. European women would definitely benefit from a supportive group of women. Here, with the Masai, I experience a deep connection with nature, and I also witness the innate trust of Masai women, who believe in their own strength and in the natural processes of life. This experience has been completely overwhelming, and for a long time afterward I did feel awed and very moved.

The Unspoken Secret

Sokoine has another wife. Our whole relationship is based on a lie, or rather on silence. It is a few years after our wedding before I learn about this. It may be due to the fact that they did not consummate the marriage, but it does not hurt any less for all that.

"This hut was built so my brothers and I would have a place to sleep," is the first version Sokoine gave me. "This hut belongs to Mama Klaudia," is the second version.

I did not suspect anything wrong at first. We had slept in that hut on my first visit to the *boma*. I was still traumatized by the bus accident and very much excited at the prospect of meeting Sokoine's family for the first time. There were also quite a few language difficulties, and I was not yet familiar with the Masai rules. Unmarried men do not own houses. With this in mind, the explanation of Mama Klaudia's living in the hut seemed perfectly fine to me at first. I did not give a thought as to what her role or status in the family might be. Everything was new and exciting. We struggled a lot to get our papers and, therefore, only stayed for one or two weeks at a time in the hut in the *boma*.

But then I learn, quite by chance, that Mama Klaudia actually owns the hut, yet always willingly lets us live in it while she moves to my mother-in-law's hut to sleep. How terribly inconvenient. After staying in the *boma* over a longer period of time, I feel I need to change this.

"Let us build our own house. We cannot keep using Mama Klaudia's house," I suggest.

My Maa has improved a lot by now, and I understand people much better. The women tell each other stories while they work and as it happens, they mention two women who gave birth to children despite being unmarried, which is quite unusual. One of them is Mama Klaudia. She has two children but no husband, and I wonder whether she could be involved in a polygamous relationship, which is quite a common situation for older Masai. I also keep wondering why Sokoine was still single when we met despite having long since reached the marriageable age. Was it perhaps me being lucky, or was he simply too poor?

Bit by bit, via many detours, I learn about the truth.

While Sokoine was trying to provide for his family in many different ways, his father arranged his marriage. Against Sokoine's will, he made all necessary preparations and paid for twelve cows before presenting his son with a fait accompli. While his first-born son was toiling on Mafia, Mama Klaudia was brought to the *boma*.

"Who is this woman?" Sokoine asked his mother on one of his visits.

"Oh, she helps me in the house and kitchen. She can also take care of the water for your shower and help you."

When Sokoine realized what was really going on, he was shocked.

"I don't want to marry yet. And when I get married, I want to choose my wife myself!"

A huge argument ensued.

"Send her away. I don't want to have anything to do with her."

Sokoine's father became very angry.

"Are you stupid? You have to marry a wife and father children."

"But I want to choose my wife myself."

"It has all been arranged. There is no way back."

The fight escalated. Sokoine's father was about to curse his son, which is the worst thing that could possibly happen to a Masai. Sokoine does not want to live with that. Everybody must be able to save his face.

"I don't want her, but you have already paid. For this reason, she may stay. But I won't have anything to do with her."

And this is how this unusual arrangement came to be. Mama Klaudia is officially Sokoine's wife. But she bore the children of another man. I suspect one of Sokoine's brothers, who for a long time was unable to marry out of poverty, to be the actual father of her children. Sokoine is responsible for Mama Klaudia and her children, and so am I. It is a while before I fully understand and process the whole story. As it is, this is my only condition to Sokoine: no second wife. I cannot agree to that. Very soon, I can plainly see that Sokoine's and Mama Klaudia's marriage is really nothing more than a relationship of convenience. The longer I get to live in the *boma*, the clearer the traditional network of relationships, with all its rules and principles, appears to me. Mama Klaudia and her children are very dear to my heart.

"How is it for you, being one of three wives?" I dare to ask Yayai one day after we have gotten to know each other better.

Naturally, I do have a very Western view as far as polygamy is concerned. Even though it is difficult to conceive, what I do witness here, in practice, is actually much less dreadful.

"How do you perceive us?" she replies in turn. "I like our community. We are a large family. We watch out for one another. I was happy when the other women joined us because we all get along very well. We share a lot, and we have found a good way to live together."

Yes, I do see the harmony between the three women. They really like each other. If I did not witness this everyday with my own eyes, in such a positive way, I probably would have harbored quite a few doubts as to this way of life. Arranged marriages, such as Yayai's, or the older generations', are becoming less and less common. Polygamy is no longer as obvious as it used to be. Many young Masai men do not possess enough cows, and thus wealth, to provide for several wives. As Yayai puts it quite wisely:

"Stephanie, whatever you grew up with becomes your truth."

She just happened to grow up that way.

The Falling-Out

There is a young woman in the *boma*, who feels a special connection with me. Ngallande, the wife of Sokoine's brother, Lemali, is about 13 years old. Masai men who own many cows are very coveted, and Lemali can only marry after we have acquired cows.

When the marriage is agreed upon, the woman moves to the man's village, leaving her own family behind, which often proves very hard on the young girls, who are afraid and homesick. Our mother-in-law, Yayai, goes to great lengths to make her daughters-in-law feel welcome, but she is only responsible for us to a certain extent.

As it is, Ngallande chooses me as her attachment figure, perhaps because I too am different and new here. She follows me everywhere and is always by my side – whether we take the goats out, during work or during our free time. If I lie down to rest in the afternoon, she just lies down next to me. She is like a younger sister to me, so fascinated by me that she actually has to touch me to check what white skin really feels like. I let her do all these things, even though I have to admit her constant presence can be annoying at times. We probably share what one could call a community of fate, both of us having lost something. Very soon, I learn about her arguments with Lemali.

"He often comes to me and wants something from me, but I don't want that," she tells me, a frightened look on her face.

Her confession moves me. It is very understandable that she should be afraid of sex and keeps running away – back home to her mother, who lives in another *boma*, half an hour away from ours. Sokoine and Lemali go and take her back to us. Her story offers me a deeper insight into Masai culture. Of course, the fact that girls should be married at such a young age and be made to engage in sexual activity, which they fear, feels very strange to me.

Lemali and I had a good relationship before he was married. He often took the cows to graze, and I would accompany him because I too love our herd very much. Not only did we spend time together tending to the animals, but we would also go out for a drink together from time to time. It took a while, but gradually, I came to understand him better and better. Until I heard about him beating his wife, that is. This knowledge affected me deeply, and it also made me very angry.

One night, we got into an argument.

Ngallande was milking the cows, an important task assigned to women alone.

"Where is the water for my shower? Come here this instant and get my water ready."

I cannot pretend I did not hear that. Lemali is drunk and clearly wants to show his wife who the boss is.

"I'm almost done milking, and then I'll get your water," she replies.

Standing between the two of them, I can tell right away he does not like her answer.

"Go get the water right now!" he orders, striding up to her and pushing her.

"Let her finish what she's doing. She's coming. Don't make such a fuss," I say, trying to placate him.

Yayai also witnesses the nasty scene and tries to help Ngallande milk the cows so she can do it faster. The atmosphere is tense. Lemali storms away from the fence, casting angry looks at me over his shoulder. For the first time, I witness how badly Masai men really treat their wives. Even though I feel that to do so would be a mistake, my protective instinct compels me to take action.

Later that day, Lemali comes to see me.

"Tell me, Stephanie: is Ngallande my wife or yours?" he asks.

"What kind of question is that?" I reply skeptically.

"I don't want you to get involved. Is that clear?"

His tone is harsh. I nod. No point arguing. I seem to have overstepped some boundary. In the evening, I tell Sokoine about the whole thing, fearing he will be mad at me.

"Stephanie, don't get involved in other people's marriages," he declares in a firm tone of voice.

Since that day, my relationship with Lemali has noticeably cooled, a fact I very much deplore. I have lost his trust. It is a hard lesson to learn, especially since I do feel that I am in the right to protect another woman. But I also see that my western values are of no help under the present circumstances. Or else I can just pack my things and leave. It is easy to judge from the outside, when you're living very far away. I am the last person who would readily accept the fact that women should be beaten by their husbands. Witnessing this is really difficult, which is why I make myself a promise. I must find another way to show my support and solidarity.

Emuratare

"I am now an *olpaiyan*, a man who is no longer a warrior," Sokoine explains to me.

It is a while before I am able to fully grasp the complex structure of Masai men's social status. Circumcision and excision are two entirely different things at the Masai. The removal of part of the foreskin is one of the most important rituals for young Masai boys, symbolizing their transition from boyhood to warrior. Never would a Masai boy willingly renounce it. The act of circumcision itself, called *emuratare,* is a carefully defined procedure followed by a huge celebration.

"First you are an *olaiyoni*, a boy. The *emuratare* ceremony makes you an *olmorani*, a warrior. When the time has come, you leave the ranks of the warriors to become an *olpaiyan*, like I have now."

The "knife is opened," as the saying goes, every 13 to 14 years, which means the village elders assess the group of eligible boys between 14 and 18 from the neighboring *bomas*, deciding who will be part of the next *emuratare* ceremony, a fact that depends on each boy's personal maturity.

"I was circumcised in 2000, when I was 17 years old. Our age group is called *ildieki*. The last boys of our group had their *emuratare* in 2005. Then the *oloiboni*, a wise man, put his knife away. The knife was drawn once again for my younger brother in 2013 and then put away in 2018."

In 2016, I take part in the preparations for the *emuratare* ceremony for the first time, having been away in England in 2013, when Sokoine's brothers were circumcised. Women are forbidden to attend the ceremony itself. They are only responsible for organizing the feast and tending to the boys. Hosting dozens of guests, who come to the *boma* for the occasion proves a huge logistical achievement, and Yayai and the other women work and toil to the point of exhaustion. I try to help them wherever I can, but I have to admit I do feel a little out of place. To the Masai, the ceremony is a highly emotional event, a mix of pride to see your son becoming a warrior and sorrow to witness a shared stage of life come to an end. What mother does not worry? The women bravely conceal their anguish, as their sons must undergo the whole procedure without expressing any pain - a fact that is supposed to show the boy's strength and a way for him to honor his parents. No newly made warrior would like people to say that he has shown weakness, thus dishonoring his parents. The *emuratare* ceremony is held in a specially assigned and secluded place. After the circumcision, the warriors rest in their mothers' houses so the wound can heal while the other men celebrate their courage and the ritual coming of age of the new generation of warriors, called *ilmoran*.

Excision, on the other hand, is forbidden in Tanzania since 1998. Parents violating this interdiction face a prison sentence. But it is almost impossible to make sure the law is enforced in the many remote villages. In the past twenty years, numerous anti-excision campaigns have been run, and more and more shelters have been built to protect the girls who run away from home because their parents want to subject them to excision. The one huge drawback of these public policies lies in the fact that the excisions now happen in secret and most probably under even more adverse circumstances, at the hands of certain excisors.

During my first years in the *boma*, however, I never hear about all this. I don't understand the language yet, and I am too busy finding my place in the community.

"What about excision?" I ask Sokoine much later after he has just explained to me the various stages in a Masai man's life.

"We don't perform this here anymore," he replies shortly.

Actually, there is not much he can say about it. Being a man, he plays no part in the process. The *emuratare* ceremony is strictly separated according to gender, and thus, excision is exclusively a women's business. Before the interdict, girls would usually be excised between the ages of 15 and 18, the same age as the boys. I believe Sokoine suspects that excision is still performed in the *boma*, but would rather keep the fact from me, just like the rest of the family. They probably fear my reaction, especially during my first time with them. They don't know for sure whether they can trust me or not - they don't know whether I will denounce them or not.

The more proficient I get in Maa, though, and the closer our relationship becomes, the more I come to notice and see.

I hear people talk about their daughters, yet most of the time, whenever I venture to ask them about it, they wave aside my cautious questions.

In the meantime, though, our trust and confidence in one another has grown. Today, the women speak openly about this subject in my presence, yet only because I have assured them that I accept their culture.

A ceremony quite like the one held for boys was organized on the occasion of their own excision, which symbolizes their passage from girlhood to womanhood. The ban on excision did not lead the Masai to stop performing the act altogether - they simply continued to do so in secret. This led to yet another ghastly side effect: so the girls would not be completely aware of what is being done to them, and also possibly heal faster, they are now being excised at a much younger age, when they are five or six years old.

The view of women on that subject varies depending on the generation. Not all girls are excised nowadays, far from it. I witness the women's inner struggle: on the one hand, they wish to keep their culture alive, but on the other hand they are afraid to be arrested or lose their daughters.

This might actually be the most difficult lesson I have had to learn here. Even though I was brought up in an entirely different social environment, I don't have the right to demand a change in the cultural ceremonies of the Masai. This also goes for the custom of burning the children's cheeks with a red-hot iron to show their belonging to a certain tribe or the removal of the front middle teeth without anesthesia using a knife. All these things are also performed in our *boma*, yet not to all children. Should I try to change these customs or oppose them openly, I would lose my place in this community.

I keep thinking about what Sokoine once told me: "You are living with the Masai. Either you adjust, or you leave. There is nothing in between!"

CHAPTER 8

Esuji ewang'an enkiwalie

Light will follow the darkest night.

I am startled out of sleep abruptly. The room around me is shrouded in darkness and silence. There is a pounding in my ears and my heart is racing. Very slowly, I recover my senses, but my brain is fuzzy. My throat is sore and aching. I am hot and parched. I am about to sit up in bed when a sharp pain shoots through my body. Wait, I have just remembered where I am and what I am doing in this place. I am in the Aga Khan Hospital. Yet this time, I am not seriously ill. I have just had a baby. They have cut me open and taken the baby out. My eyes wander across the dark room. The curtains separating me from the other beds are drawn. I can hear the slow, deep breathing of the woman lying next to me. The two of us share one room. There is something missing, though: the baby cot! I am suddenly seized with a new, a terrible fear: where is my baby?

I can catch small sounds, a whining and whimpering, snoring too, soft steps, the clicking of a light switch and the rattling of doors, in short, the sub-dued bustle of a large hospital at night. My head gets clearer.

"We don't ever want children!" Such was the almost sacred pact my sister and I had concluded in our teenage years, our family life and the divorce of our parents serving as a quite powerful deterrent example. In Tanzania, however, my view on the matter evolved, and soon I feel the growing wish to become a mother. There are lots of babies around me and I get to see how lovingly families welcome their new babies. No doubt this triggers something inside me. But patience is required.

"Why doesn't Stephanie get pregnant? What about having a baby?" my mother-in-law asks her son after Sokoine and I have been married for two years.

In her eyes, a baby is long overdue. She would never broach the subject with me directly; she is much too sensitive for that. But the entire village is probably whispering about my still not being blessed with a child. I, too, feel more and more ready, but I had not expected my husband's surprising reluctance.

"Shouldn't we try to have a baby?" I ask him.

"Are you sure? Don't you think it will be difficult for you out here, in the bush?"

What? He cannot seriously come up with medical arguments. Not when he himself was born in the *boma*; not when he has seen his mother and other female relatives give birth to so many children here over the years.

Perhaps he does not believe I am actually capable of that, being a white woman? His doubts affect me greatly. What difference can it possibly make whether a young Masai woman or a 27-year-old European woman gives birth at home? I am starting to have doubts about the whole thing. But these are not his sole arguments.

"Let's wait a bit longer before we get children. Until we have everything under control and a steady income."

"What do you want to wait for? Are you a millionaire?" I reply sarcastically.

We have just harvested our first crop. We are still in the early stages of setting up the farm, but our situation is more stable than ever before.

"It is never the right time to have a baby," I hear myself say, puzzled that I should find myself resorting to such ancient wisdom.

Perhaps the scars left by all the effort and struggle we had to put into our relationship to make it work run deeper than I would have thought. Be it as it may, Sokoine is as far from an easygoing African family planning as one could possibly be.

"Not now, let's wait a bit longer," he says over and over again, repeating these very words like a mantra.

Three years pass by. This drives me mad to tell the truth; I will soon turn 30 and my biological clock is ticking loudly.

Enough is enough. I am not going with this any longer. I decide to go off the pill in secret and start noting on a small calendar the days we are having sex and the days I get my period. Before long, my period stops, and I secretly buy a pregnancy test in the village on a market day. I already know that I am pregnant, but I need to be absolutely sure. I open the small package, shake hands, and pee on the strip. Two pink stripes appear even before the waiting time has passed. Unbelievable. I am actually pregnant! What I feel right now is overwhelming. I want to shout out loud, but I manage to keep it to myself and decide to remain silent for now. It is my secret. It's not exactly an easy burden to bear. After four weeks, I start to feel the first signs of pregnancy. I feel nauseous. Very much so, actually. The feel of my toothbrush alone makes me want to throw up. Eating is absolutely out of the question. Meals in the *boma* make my stomach churn. If I were living in a city, I would be desperate for pizza and pasta. As it is, *ugali* and rice just make me sick. In search of an alternative, I manage to make some kind of fried sandwich using old bread and eggs, over the small stove in my hut. A tube of mayonnaise sends me into a childish frenzy. The smallest dollop feels like a delicacy. I laugh at myself. But my stomach is not the only thing rumbling and churning. A storm rages in my head and heart, too. I am ecstatic, anxious, confused, and a thousand different thoughts constantly swirl around in my head - in short, the whole emotional shebang. My breasts are hurting, and my body is changing. I still have not spoken about the pregnancy to anyone. I want to be certain that everything is ok. At times, I am overcome with weariness, and my blood circulation goes haywire. Keeping my present state from the family and community, and especially from my husband, is not exactly easy. But I do not wish to give them any false hopes. Yet, apart from feeling very sick all the time, I also start to panic. What if this is malaria, once again? Would it endanger the baby?

I need to have this checked and go to Dar es Salaam with Sokoine, who only knows about the malaria part.

"Madam, malaria is not your problem. You are pregnant! Everything is fine. Congratulations!"

The doctor beams at me. I feel very relieved and ready to tell Sokoine the good news, as I join him outside the hospital.

"Are you insane? We said we would wait!"

He is really furious, rage distorting his beautiful features. I cannot believe this. Everything inside me tightens, each of his words as sharp as blows. Tears well up in my eyes. Here I am, telling my husband about my pregnancy, and instead of taking me in his arms, he yells at me.

"That's so stupid of you, Stephanie! What were you thinking?" Sokoine cries, unable to calm down.

What is happening? I had not expected such a violent and negative reaction. Hearing us, passers-by turn their heads in our direction. Sokoine lowers his voice but does not stop cursing and swearing. This is too much for me. I turn on my heels and leave him. We do not spend the next few hours together. I need to let it all sink in. I feel so desperately sad and abandoned as I aimlessly wander the streets of Dar es Salaam.

"I am telling you such good news, and you are not even remotely happy!"

It is all I can do not to start crying again. But I manage to pull myself together. We have returned to the hostel and are trying to make peace, having wandered about the city for hours on our own.

"I'm sorry, that was wrong of me. But you did give me a huge fright," Sokoine begins in an attempt to convey his state of mind.

I can see he regrets his previous outburst, even though he does not expressly say so. I also see how worried he is for us and our relationship.

"I *am* happy, sweetie," he adds after we have talked for quite some time.

We feel calmer and more at peace after returning to the *boma*. But the whole thing has left me hurt and wounded.

"Why doesn't your wife get pregnant?" Sokoine's grandmother asks.

Despite being in her mid-nineties, she does not mince matters with her grandson. That she should ask him about that now of all times is actually quite baffling. As if he had been waiting for her to say the word, my husband replies, beaming:

"Why do you ask? She is expecting a baby!"

He can no longer conceal his pride. Telling me about it later on, I can see this quite plainly.

There are no congratulations or cheering, no one addresses the subject of my pregnancy openly. We don't make a common announcement either, Masai being far too reserved for that. Yet I do notice Yayai beaming at me more often, even though I do not dare to directly broach the subject. I am not well assured enough. Nothing is ever discussed openly. In the evening, when people gather around a campfire, gossip is a favored subject of conversation.

I am very surprised to learn that the sister-in-law, the wife of Sokoine's half-brother, is eight months pregnant, her baby belly undetectable under her wide clothes. The older women did suspect something, but they only broach the subject now.

"Nine months, I would say. The baby will come soon," Yayai says, touching the young woman's belly as we all stand together, talking.

"No, I think she still has two more months to go," Sokoine's aunt declares.

A small competition follows to determine which one of these smart, wise women will better assess the progress of the pregnancy. From then on, I decide to listen closely to any conversation or piece of advice about pregnancy the women share with one another.

After the twelfth week of pregnancy, the nausea I had been experiencing until then disappears all of a sudden. I'm blown away, so to speak. My British friends, Eleni and Claire visit us in the *boma*. We go on a safari together and travel to Zanzibar. I am as fit as a flea; I can uproot trees, and my belly is growing nicely. Sometimes, I have to look at it to remind myself that I am indeed pregnant. I am so confident I even fail to make an appointment with a midwife. But then, I have never felt that good.

"Stephanie, you have to conceal your belly better," Yayai says to me, looking at me kindly and also a tad embarrassed. "You cannot show yourself like this here."

I startle and look down at my belly.

"But why?" I ask, slightly annoyed.

What did I do wrong? I don't usually give much thought to what I am going to wear in the morning, and anyway, it has never been a problem in the boma until now. I wear rather practical clothes, but my belly has grown so much that my top does not fit anymore, and my baby belly shows a little.

"It is fine with us women, but one does not show one's belly in the presence of men."

Now that she is addressing the subject, I realize that pregnant mothers are often indistinguishable from other women. Clearly, my behavior has caused no little embarrassment. This makes me feel sad and awkward, but I do not wish to offend anyone, and first conceal my belly with a scarf. Then I buy wider clothes, but my easiness is gone.

I have trouble breathing now when chasing after the small goats. This does not feel good, obviously, and I stop doing so altogether. Will I get fat from now on and unable to move, I think to myself sadly.

In the fourth month of pregnancy, I go to the small clinic in Lesoit for an examination. They feel my belly and take a sample of my blood.

"Ouch!"

The nurse presses so hard on my belly that I let out a cry, alarmed. This is the last time I shall allow that rough lady to touch my belly! I take it upon myself to make the long journey to Dar es Salaam to get ultrasound examinations.

I will travel to England one last time before the baby is due, trying to push aside my concerns about pregnant women traveling on a plane. We could really use every last cent of the money I can make, and who knows if I can still work after delivery.

I still have health insurance in England and can have all the necessary examinations there. Not to mention that I would like to work for two more months.

"Stephanie, can you come and help me over Christmas?" my friend Vicky, whom I did also help the year before, asks me.

We met in the fudge shop, and she started her own business, selling dog biscuits. Her shop is buzzing, actually, and we prepare for the Christmas market in Bath.

By the middle of December I am back in Tanzania. It is high time now to make some crucial decisions. *Boma* or hospital? Home birth or clinic?

Giving birth in the clinic is an expensive option. I have attended many Masai births and never witnessed any problems. One or two children were born dead, sadly, but then a hospital delivery would not have changed that either. I have not yet seen a single problematic birth here. Shouldn't that encourage me? And yet, I cannot seem to take any definite decision on the matter. Indeed, I trust Masai women more than I trust myself and my body. I hesitate a lot. My stay in England has made me unsure.

Too many friends in England have given me questioning looks and put forward many arguments when I told them about my intentions.

"I would consider this carefully if I were you. Why would you want to take this kind of risk?" the gynecologist examining me asks.

I cannot quite shake off the effect that the word 'risk' has on me, and I also recall my mother saying: "Your brother did not want to come out, and they had to do a C-section to deliver the baby."

My twin sister and I were also born through C-section. Does this not show how dangerous delivery can be? I picture the baby getting stuck in the birth canal and no one there to help us in the wilderness while the women shuffle around my bed, unable to do anything. No one will cut my belly open in the *boma*, should that prove necessary.

In Germany or Great Britain, home birth makes up only a very small part of all deliveries. We are being told that women can only give birth safely at the hospital, and this is deeply ingrained in my mind.

Time presses, though. My delivery date is due in four weeks, and I have to decide before Nature robs me of options.

Sokoine's opinion on the matter is very clear: he is absolutely against a home birth.

"There's no way you'll get our baby here. Let us go to the hospital," he says as we talk about the subject.

He is probably afraid to lose me. After all, I have been gravely ill very often in the past few years.

I feel moved, but his concern does not alleviate my hesitation. Not even my husband believes I could give birth at home, not to mention the fact that he gives me very little attention lately.

I have come to realize more and more that my husband may very well be the most reserved and private man in the world. Pregnancy makes me soft, wistful, and affectionate. But there is no one I can actually lean on. Sokoine and I are drifting apart. It is natural, in his culture, to become more and more distant as my baby belly grows. Between the lines, I hear from other pregnant Masai women that husband and wife stop having sex in the second or third month of pregnancy. How much I crave for a warm and tender embrace, especially now! I don't hold it against him, though. I know how deeply rooted in his culture it is not to touch during that period, but I must admit that it hurts and saddens me a lot, particularly at this stage.

In the end, my fear wins, and my decision is made. I will give birth in the Aga Khan Hospital in Dar es Salaam. I can at least choose the most modern clinic around. I am already quite familiar with it, having been hospitalized there for sepsis and food poisoning. The die is cast.

The delivery, however, must be scheduled. I don't wish labor contractions to set in while we are in the middle of the endless, bumpy way to the city. I don't even want to picture that scenario. Should I get a C-section, I won't be able to take a jerky, juddering bus back to the *boma* before the wound has healed. After some hesitation, we decide to spend a few weeks in the megacity before and after delivery. This could actually prove quite expensive. It also means we will need help, as Sokoine won't be able to stay for six weeks. He has to return home from time to time to look after the farm. He will come and get us once the baby and I are fine.

"Can we take Yayai along? I'd like her to be with me," I ask Sokoine after having given the matter some thought.

"No, that is out of the question. That is far too stressful," Sokoine replies in a definite tone.

"Why is that? I would definitely prefer to have her with me."

"Stephanie, Yayai has never been to Dar es Salaam. She won't be able to make purchases there or take care of anything for you. Let alone find her bearings in that ghastly traffic. It will be much too stressful for me if I have to look after my pregnant wife *and* my mother."

I understand his arguments, even though the prospect does not make me happy. Yayai is the one person I feel the closest to.

"My mother will take care of you when we are back in the *boma*," Sokoine promises.

That thought comforts me. If I am not to give birth to my child in the traditional Masai way, I can at least benefit from the many good rituals in the time afterward. These include Sokoine moving out of our hut for a while, and his mother moving in to look after me.

"How will we manage in Dar, then? Who can we ask?" I ask at a loss.

A few days later, my husband comes up with a solution.

"Paulina will come with us."

My heart drops. Paulina is a Swahili, seven years younger than I am. She works at a bar in Lengatei where Sokoine and his friends often hang out. A bar acquaintance is supposed to be with me during the most important weeks of my life. Not that I have anything against Paulina, mind you. I know her. She has two children and is thus experienced, besides being sweet and calm. But I want Yayai to be with me, someone I feel close to in these private moments. My mood darkens, but I still comply.

Sokoine and I set off in the last week of January. Paulina is to join us after the baby is born. According to the doctors, the baby is due on February 10, but then what baby respects these deadlines? We set out on the long journey to Dar es Salaam, along with my huge belly, excitement, and shortness of breath. I have not been very comfortable on a bus since the accident, but today is even worse, with every jerk on the road going straight to my belly. Please, please, let us make it out of that bus alive, I think, sending a silent prayer to my inner demons.

Two persons - three after the birth - living and eating together for three weeks costs a lot of money. Money we don't even have in the first place. For weeks now, we have been looking for affordable accommodation.

"These are perfectly fine flats," Sokoine declares, showing me what he found on the Internet.

"That one's not bad," I reply, "but it is located a little outside of town. I don't want to live in an unfamiliar neighborhood with a newborn."

Once again, we book a room in the rather shabby, almost derelict YMCA we have stayed at several times over the years. The building and furniture date back to the seventies, but the place is centrally located, close to the clinic, and affordable. The rooms are small, equipped with two simple beds and a small table, and the shared toilet is in the corridor. The whole place is extremely stark. There are not many guests. Yet what some people might consider not good enough is a small luxury to me, with a fan humming over the bed and running water from the faucet. A restaurant serving delicious Swahili food is just down the stairs. Our double room, breakfast included, only costs 20,000 shillings, approximately eight euros.

The place is ideal for me. I enjoy spending time in the city, having more variety on the menu, sitting at tables, and the busyness of life here, even though I feel increasingly slow and heavy. Stretched out on my bed, I mentally prepare myself for what will come.

It Starts

Something is not right. Hot waves have been washing through me for quite some time now. I toss and turn in my bed restlessly. Oh no, what is this dreadful stinging? Ouch, that really hurts! I cannot identify the pain at first, but then I realize labor has started. It is February 13th. I don't like that date. I remember thinking rather foolishly that February 14th, Valentine's Day, would be much better, but then I would have to endure this for quite some time. I realized afterward that only a woman who has never given birth before could ever think that way.

"How do contractions feel? How do I know it has started?" I remember asking an English friend on the phone who had just become a mother when I was seven months pregnant.

"It is similar to the cramps during the period, only much more painful," she told me.

All right then. My lower abdomen hardens. The room is pitch-dark. My mobile phone shows four o'clock. Lying next to me, Sokoine snores lightly, fast asleep. No need to wake him now. I shall wait for the pain to get stronger. For a while, I lie in the dark, waiting, listening closely to my body. The contractions come and go, but they are still spaced out, so much so that I occasionally fall asleep between two contractions. As daylight gradually seeps into the room, I am still rather calm. It looks like I am to become a mother today. I nudge my sleeping husband.

"Sokoine, I think the baby is coming!"

"What, now?" he asks, opening a sleepy eye, a faint smile on his face.

During my studies in Bath, 2009.

Holding an elephant's thighbone.

I discover my love for Africa in Zimbabwe.

Sokoine and I, 2011. For me, it was love at first sight.

Mama Klaudia holding baby Klaudia in her arms, 2011.

Sokoine and I marry in April 2012 according to Masai tradition.

Sokoine and I receive the marital blessing.

Yayai, Mama Klaudia and I sew anklets for my sister who has come to visit. Traces of sepsis are visible on my leg.

Fighting spiders inside our house.

Cows are the Masai's livelihood.

Yayai and I. I am grateful to be part of her family.

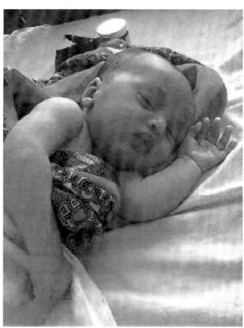

Yannik, one week after his birth, in February 2016.

Sokoine first needs to adjust to his role as a father.

Yannik enjoys the view on Lesoit while we watch the cows.

Our cows in the light of the fading sun.

Surrounded by young Masai women who are fascinated by my tablet.

Mlari, one of my brothers-in-law, and I.

The women in our boma.

It is very important to me that Yannik should grow up a Masai.

Yannik and I riding our bikes in the fields of Lesoit.

The Masai's future is threatened. I fight to preserve it for my son.

Our little family.

Warriors tap the vein of a cow to drink blood.

Yayai, the most important woman in my life, sitting by the fire in her house.

During Cate Butcher's visit to our Massai Women Enterprise.

Left: With Kaja and Mateusz of the Globstory YouTube channel, during the shooting of the YouTube video.

Right and Below: I love spending a lot of time with our goats, especially with the baby goats.

Masai warriors during a ceremony.

"No, I don't think so," I grin back.

I am no expert, but the contractions are still irregular and not very painful. We decide to remain calm and wait a little longer. The room is filled with an odd, somewhat tense atmosphere. At one o'clock in the afternoon, we leave the room for lunch, the contractions now noticeably stronger.

"Shouldn't we head to the hospital now?" I ask Sokoine, realizing as I speak that he cannot answer that question accurately.

"Are there other signs? Bleeding perhaps?" the Aga Khan doctor asks me over the phone.

"Yes, a little."

"In that case, you'd better come."

Around four o'clock, we hail a taxi that takes us to the hospital. I no longer trust myself to take the fifteen-minute walk to the clinic.

"The cervix is only three centimeters open."

"What does that mean?" I ask the doctor.

"It means there's still time. You can go back to the hotel for a while."

I am taken aback. Twelve hours have passed since the first contractions. So many hours for only three centimeters. How long is this supposed to last? I try to remain calm, but I can feel my exhaustion and frustration grow. But then what can you do? We leave the hospital and return to the hostel.

I buy a snack at a stand on the way, yet halfway through the food, I suddenly feel weird and leave the rest untouched. I lie down on the bed, exhausted, and doze off right away. It is nine o'clock in the evening when I awake, and I feel like vomiting. My stomach rebels, and the contractions are definitely stronger.

At eleven o'clock, I can no longer bear it.

"We should go now!"

Another taxi drive to the hospital. Sokoine and I are very excited, growing more frantic with every contraction. I, for one, because I am more and more aware that labor is about to start, and Sokoine, because he is sitting next to his wife bent double in pain, panting, unable to understand what the nurses at the reception want him to do with all the paper stuff. In between two waves of pain, I try to explain things to my husband and sign in at the hospital. Deep breath, I keep thinking to myself as I focus on the tearing pain in my body.

"It is five centimeters open now."

"What?" I cry, aghast. "But that's impossible!"

The nurse attempts to placate me.

"Let me show you to your room. Everything is going to be fine."

She leads me to a large room on the fourth floor, with two beds and a view of the sea. Today, though, I have no interest in the mighty waves of the Indian Ocean, being in the process of fighting waves of my own that come crashing over me every two minutes.

"The staircase is at the end of the corridor; you can go up and down the stairs; it'll help push the baby downwards," the nurse says before leaving me.

I spend an uneasy night. Sokoine and I share one bed, and sleep is out of the question, although we are both exhausted. The pain gets even stronger when I lie on the side. It is a tad better when I lie on the back, but then my husband has to squeeze himself next to me. He keeps looking at me worried-ly, and I keep trying to reassure him in between contractions. But I am still glad to have him here with me; otherwise, I would be all alone.

Various doctors pop in to check the opening of the cervix, which makes me feel powerless and very awkward. Where is the doctor who accompanied me through pregnancy? Why isn't a woman checking on me? These examina-tions are exceedingly embarrassing for Sokoine, too. But I am in no condition to protest. Things are not going forward, though, and after 24 hours, I am still not any closer to giving birth. Just much more exhausted.

As dusk falls, I send Sokoine back to the hotel. There is not much he can do for me here anyway, so he might as well get some rest. He leaves with a look of relief mingled with fear on his face. Five hours later, at around ten o'clock, he is back.

"We'll transfer you to the delivery room when your cervix is seven centimeters open," one of the doctors had told me. Seven is the magic number I need to reach before things can get started. At eleven o'clock in the evening, I finally seem to be ready, and they wheel me into the delivery room. Much to my relief, a Masai woman now looks after and examines me.

"You're not open that well down there," she says, giving me a skeptical look.

I don't want to hear that. This is all too much for me. I feel so sick I cannot even keep water down. I vomit again. Weirdly enough, it helps me gather up my courage for a short while. Masai women say that birth follows soon after one has vomited. However, this does not seem to be the case for me. Hours pass, and my cervix does not open more. The faces around me grow increasingly worried.

"Nothing changes, and you are clearly exhausted. We can only recommend a C-section."

My mind is whirling. I would love to give birth to my child naturally, but at the same time, I remember my mother had two C-sections herself. How long will I be able to stand the pain? I am completely worn out and ardently wish for this to be over. The small sensor fastened to my belly is the final straw. Not only does it monitor the contractions, but it also shows the baby's heartbeat. During a particularly violent contraction, the fast pounding goes suddenly silent. I panic. Is my baby in danger?

"I don't care what happens to me! Please help my baby!" I cry as everything around me gets hectic and confused. Everybody sees and hears what happens on the monitor.

They hoist me upon a stretcher. And in that moment, as if by magic, the pain stops. Obstructed labor. I am probably in such shock that my body freezes. Beside himself with worry, Sokoine runs along the stretcher as they push me towards the operation room, even grabbing my hand. That is how I know he is really scared. He barely understands what is happening to me. Despite my panic, I realize the situation reminds him of all the people he has lost. He is terribly worried about me and utterly traumatized by his past experiences of surgery. Masai are often treated in small, poorly equipped clinics, and the surgery itself does not always end well. It is no wonder he does not like all this at all. If he were married to a Masai woman, he would have no contact whatsoever with the delivery process, which is strictly a woman's business in the boma. Neither of us is prepared for this.

"Fear not, we will take good care of your wife," a nurse says to him soothingly.

She fails to get through to him, though. The last thing I see as I am being pushed through the door is my proud Masai husband, utterly distraught. His desperation moves me deeply.

Everything happens very fast afterward, so much so it almost seems unreal. Out of the corner of my eye, I catch a glimpse of a chubby Indian child playing with a tablet.

"The things you're doing, Mrs. Fuchs!"

The voice sounds familiar, and so does the face appearing over me. My Indian gynecologist, Mohammed Shafik, who has seen me through the pregnancy, smiles down at me. I am very relieved. Apparently they paged him while he was on call, enjoying some time with his family. The boy sitting outside must be his son.

"Let us get your baby out."

I glance at the room, which is not different from any room in a German hospital. After all, the Aga Khan is one of the best clinics in Tanzania. One of the most expensive, too. The local poor cannot afford it. White tiles, gleaming chrome, fearsome medical equipment. Soothing, kind eyes behind a mask. I am already tied to the operation table, arms outstretched and cannulas inserted, surrounded by the calm bustle of people wearing surgery clothing. A part of me becomes very calm. In a few hours, I will finally get to see my child for the first time. But I also feel excited and afraid of the whole procedure.

The anesthetic mask is placed over my face.

"See you later, Mrs. Stephanie, sweet dreams!" I hear the nurse calling before it all turns dark.

"I did not know if I would ever see you again!"

My husband sits by my bedside, sobbing. I have never seen him like this before. The effect of the anesthetic is still so strong that everything feels blurred and foggy.

"Everything is all right!" I whisper, reaching out to him just before drifting off to sleep.

The next time I wake up, quite surprisingly, Paulina is standing by my bed. Is this a dream? Sokoine must have called her. I give her a faint smile and wave at her. But the anesthetic and my exhaustion get the better of me, and I fall asleep again.

I awake to darkness. I am alone in the room. No more pain. It is finally over. I am a mother. It is an unfamiliar, unreal feeling. How long has it been since my child was born? I have no idea. What time could it be? I cannot read the darkness outside.

Very carefully, I roll over onto my side and straighten up in bed. If I move very slowly, the pain is more or less bearable. A brief moment of dizziness as I take a few deep breaths, trying to pull myself together. I put my bare feet on the cool tiled floor. Grounding. Where is my baby? Is it alive? Is everything all right? I only have a vague recollection of having been briefly awake. I could just press the button next to me to call a nurse, but I don't want to. I cannot stay in bed. Very carefully, I place one foot before the other. It works! Now I need to go and find my child. I slowly make my way along the corridor, dimly lit for the night.

"What are you doing here?" a voice hisses suddenly, making me jump.

The nurse looks at me, aghast.

"How did you manage to get out of bed on your own? What are you doing here? You can't get up without us!"

Her raised eyebrows and puzzled expression almost make me laugh. For a moment, I feel like a student caught red-handed. Apparently, not too many C-section mothers wander about the corridors a few hours after the intervention.

"I am looking for my baby!"

Her face softens, and she gently takes me by the arm.

"Come, I'll take you to your child. It is lying in the room over there."

The two of us walk down the long corridor together. A clock on the wall ticks softly. It is a little before midnight. Eight hours have passed since the intervention. I have been out all that time. Several rows of baby beds are lined up in a faintly lit, darkened room at the far end of the corridor.

"Look, here he is," the nurse says, heading towards the second row and stopping in front of a bed.

I hold my breath. Here he is, my son. My heart warms at his sight. He is perfect and just wonderful; I can see Sokoine and myself in his tiny face. It feels so familiar as if we had always known each other.

We had not known the baby would be a boy. I had secretly wished for it, though, as giving birth to a son meant I would not be expected to get pregnant again right away. When I was in the seventh month, I dreamt the baby would be a boy. I recall waking up and ardently wishing that it would come true.

And here he is now, exactly like in my dreams. A boy with golden hair and a round head like his father and grandfather. The nurse has brought in a chair for me. My scar hurts, but I could not care less. Very gently, she takes the baby and puts him in my arms. As I feel the small, warm body, all tension falls from me. I press my nose to the golden down on his head and take a deep breath.

"Hello, my little son, hello, Yannik, Mommy is here now."

It is the first time I call my son by his name. It feels both unreal and very familiar.

Having wished for the baby to be a boy for such a long time, I had already found a name for him. I had actually given it a lot of thought. I wanted a name that could easily be pronounced and understood just about everywhere. I liked the softness of the sound "Ya." And so it came that with Sokoine's blessing, our son's name became Yannik.

"Your husband has been here already," the nurse tells me, smiling.

Sokoine has already seen his son then.

"We had a little fun with him," she continues mischievously. "Pick a child, that's what we told him."

But he could not be fooled and found Yannik immediately because our son's skin is lighter than the other babies.

"Of course, I would recognize my son," he had exclaimed proudly.

I cannot take my eyes off our baby. Right now, everything is just perfect.

"Come, I'll take him to your room. Get some rest while you still can."

The nurse allowed us a very special moment, but I didn't seem to catch the last part of her sentence for some reason. For the time being, I am just overjoyed. Yannik is placed back in his small cot, and we shuffle slowly back to my room along the corridor.

Exhausted but ecstatic, I sink back into my bed. I have a son now, and he is sleeping next to me. What will Sokoine say? I am so happy about my small family; tomorrow, we can start our family life, I think to myself as I drift off to sleep. It seems to me that I have just fallen asleep when I hear a baby crying. Yannik. The room is still dark, and it is a little while before I manage to regain my senses. My job as a mother begins now. The nurse told me Yannik had had a bottle while I was still sedated. But several hours have passed since, precious hours because a baby is usually put on his mother's chest right after birth to induce lactation. A mother's brain needs the message: the baby is here; release the milk! But nothing has happened so far. No swollen, hurting breasts, full of milk.

The baby looks at me with his big brown eyes, his small fists clenched and pressed to his face. Then he starts wailing again. His cries break my heart. He is hungry, but his mommy's breasts are empty. I had not given much thought to breastfeeding before giving birth, regarding it as a natural process I would manage without any problem. Which is actually the case when everything goes right. In my case, though, problems start with the nipples, which are much too soft and smooth, with nothing there for Yannik to cling to. His small mouth tries to find a hold on the smooth surface to get to the warm milk. Much like a fish out of water, he tries to latch on the breast and suck, but nothing happens, and he cries. It breaks my heart.

Here I am, all sweaty and sad and desperate, holding my tiny, hungry bundle. The adrenaline surge I felt during birth has long gone, and I suddenly seem to notice everything at the same time: the stinging C-section scar, the hungry, crying child. No one can get any rest. Not Yannik, being much too hungry, and not I, out of worry. Could this harm him? Does he need to be close to me right now? When will my milk finally come in?

After a while, the nurse came into the room and put him on my chest again.

"Grant yourself a little time; it is all very new to you. Everything will be fine."

I try to relax and calm down. Some kind of odd interplay follows. I put Yannik to my breast every hour, and he sucks on the nipple and tries to drink while I bite my lip. I want to endure the pain so my son can get something to eat. The same scene is repeated throughout the night, and for the next few days, Yannik and I fall into short, restless sleep in between. I want to breastfeed him more than anything, but the lack of sleep, his crying, and my own distress are utterly overwhelming.

Two days later, something finally changes. My breasts have become heavier, and when I put Yannik on my chest, I can feel the milk coming in. What a relief! I do have milk, after all, and I can breastfeed my child. A wave of gratitude washes over me. I feel more confident now: my body can feed Yannik. Everything will be fine. I even endure breastfeeding pain much better than I used to.

In that moment, the door is pushed open, and my husband pokes his head into the room. Then he walks up to my bed with careful steps and gleaming eyes. It is a magical moment. We are both very moved by our son, our creation, and the atmosphere around us is very tender and quiet.

Before long though, the magic is gone. Yannik starts crying, and I get nervous and frantic. This proves too much for a proud shepherd accustomed to having everything under control back in his village. Sokoine quickly leaves, while I remain with our son and my hurting nipples, feeling infinitely lonely.

When does one start to feel happy? I ask myself. When does motherhood take over? None of these things happen while I am at the clinic.

Once the painful first moments of breastfeeding are over, I look down at my little son. He is so sweet, warm, and cute. Yet something within me is oddly detached. It is not his fault. But I do feel guilty, and that makes me very, very sad. I have no words to convey the sorrow I feel. This peculiar state of mind will weigh upon me in the coming weeks like a heavy, dark blanket. I love my son more than anything, yet I cannot but question myself constantly. Not to mention the fact that there is no one I can really talk to about this.

Alone

After three days, I leave the hospital with Yannik. Despite the C-section scar, I am in astonishing shape. Back at the YMCA, we adjust the rooms to our new circumstances. I share a room with Paulina while Sokoine sleeps in the other room. Two women and a crying baby are too much for my husband. He no longer seeks to be close to me and even wants nothing more than to leave.

"I have to go back home and look after the farm," he says, three days after Yannik's birth.

On the one hand, I can understand him: now is the time to prepare for the harvest. But on the other hand, as a new mom, I am desperate. Paulina is a kind woman, but we are not familiar with each other. Sokoine is the only person I feel close to in the city. I want us to turn into parents together.

"Do you have to? Please come back soon," I implore him.

"But you will stay here for quite some time, won't you?" he replies.

I look at him, puzzled. What does he mean, exactly?

"You cannot travel for twelve hours on a stifling bus with a newborn baby," he explains.

I know that. Just as I know that my scar has to heal a little more. But the thought of us being apart makes me infinitely sad all the same.

Paulina looks after us devotedly, taking care of Yannik so I can go and grab something to eat in the city. Besides using the bathroom and toilet in the corridor, these are the only occasions I actually leave the room. During the postnatal period, Masai women don't leave their hut. I am no Masai, but I still wish to follow the same rules.

In Dar es Salaam, I feel the full force of my isolation. I have no family here who could come to visit and protect me. Although this is nothing but an illusion, having only two siblings in Germany. As it is, the thought is not comforting. I have no one. No one asks me how I am doing. Paulina is so shy that she barely dares to speak. The only sound echoing in the room comes from my little son. Even though Sokoine does not show any physical affection in public, I am used to the closeness of his warm body in the privacy of our home. I miss him very much. I don't get enough sleep, attention, or exchanges. I am literally going crazy.

Sokoine Lets Me Down

We are finally to go home. Sokoine used to make 60 euros a month on Mafia, as a security man, the same price we have to pay to rent a car with a chauffeur to drive us from Handeni to the *boma*. A fortune by Tanzanian standards.

"You cannot be on a stifling bus with Yannik, not when it stops every 200 meters on that slippery sand track," Sokoine said. This also means I certainly won't attempt to take my newborn son, along with a healing scar, on a motorbike. For once we agree upon this. Sokoine has organized it all over the phone, particularly impressing on the chauffeur the necessity to drive extremely carefully.

Our arrival in the village causes quite a sensation. No one ever gets here in a car, not to mention the fact that new mothers never ever show themselves in the presence of men. They don't need to, as a matter of fact, giving birth in their homes. I had to break this unspoken rule, unfortunately. I soon find myself surrounded by a group of women, Yayai first. She beams at me and takes Yannik in her arms.

"I cannot believe that you made it back here safe and sound. We were so worried about you when we heard that you had to have surgery."

A wave of love wraps around me, a balm for my bruised soul.

Everyone chatters on lively and wants to hold the baby. The usually so reserved Masai cannot but melt inside in the presence of a baby. It is a while before Yayai notices my exhaustion and puts an end to the welcome party.

"You'll be able to visit Stephanie and Yannik in the morning," she declares, as I take leave of the group, feeling very grateful to her.

Yayai has already prepared everything for me.

"Come, dear Stephanie, go inside the house."

Sokoine has already moved out, as is customary for Masai fathers, two to three months after a baby is born. They have heated the shower water for me over the fire, and I can freshen it up with clean water. So much motherly care feels very good, and I gratefully let it all happen.

"Make yourself comfortable," Yayai advises. I saw new mothers lying down on their beds almost completely naked, the advantage being that one does not need to constantly fumble around with one's clothes whenever the baby is hungry. They simply cover themselves with pieces of fabric, which is exactly what I do now. I bought two washable and waterproof mats in England for Yannik, along with two cloth diapers. I would not use disposable diapers here since Masai women do not use them either.

For the next weeks, there is a hustle and bustle inside my hut, which is pretty much like Grand Central Station. So many women come to visit, even distant cousins from neighboring *bomas*. No one shies away from the long way. Everyone wants to welcome the newborn child. Despite possessing very little themselves, they always bring presents, small blankets, baby clothes, or a piece of soap.

"Should we give Yannik a bath?" Yayai asks me, demonstrating once again her wonderful thoughtfulness.

The both of us wash Yannik in a small basin right next to our hut, a little hidden from view. My son looks so cute, obviously enjoying the warm water dripping off his skin. My heart swells as I watch my son and his loving grandmother holding him in her expert hands. She does so much for me. Wishing to spare her some trouble, I try to wash the two diapers myself in secret.

"Let me do this, Stephanie," she says, to my surprise.

"But Yayai, this is no hard work," I reply, attempting to convince her.

But all resistance proves useless, of course, and she takes the two diapers from me.

The first moments of breastfeeding are still incredibly painful, but I clench my teeth bravely. I don't want to fail my son. Breastfeeding offers us such closeness. It is also as practical as can be, with warm milk always at hand. Bottles, sterilizers and baby formula would be completely unthinkable out here in the wilderness. Yayai gives me oil she has gained herself from a plant to apply on my sore nipples. The C-section scar heals well on its own, luckily.

Yayai is here, and the other women are here. The only one I barely get to see is Sokoine, who only briefly shows up in the hut now and then, his body language clearly signaling rejection, his presence a mere question of duty. These moments are cold, distant, indifferent. Even his sweet baby son does not change anything about it. He does not even take him in his arms. It pierces my heart like a sword. Sokoine is always on the run, hanging out with his friends in the bar for hours on end. What is happening here, and why? I don't understand it.

Days pass by, and my heart gets heavier, sadness lying over me like a thick, black fog. Sometimes, even my wonderful son does not manage to blow this dreadful darkness away.

The women look after me lovingly, Yayai always making sure that I have everything I need and cares for Yannik while I wash. She also makes tea and prepares mush and other food for me so I can recover my strength.

Yet inside me, there is only this gaping emptiness and infinite sadness. Postnatal depression is the medical term used to describe that condition. But as a young woman who just had a child, I do not know this.

I feel increasingly like a prisoner, isolated inside a small, dark hut without daylight. And without exercise. This alone is a capital punishment for me. I am to stay inside the hut for at least the next eight weeks, this being the period of time Masai women who have just given birth traditionally remain in isolation. It is actually supposed to unburden them and help them adjust to their new role as mothers - as well as allow the healing of any potential birth injuries and focus on breastfeeding. This time can prove very useful, but in my case, these measures are far too drastic. Perhaps walking in nature, with the cows, would have done me good. Everything I used to enjoy, apart from Yannik, has been taken from me. Daily chores are done on my behalf: Mama Klaudia cooks for me every day, and Yayai, despite being so busy herself, does our laundry. Other women also come to help. This is nice in the first two weeks, but then things change. The fitter I become, the more isolated and useless I feel. Other than the time I spend with Yannik, there is nothing for me but a dark, endless void. I lie listless on the bed in the dark or pace to and fro in the small room, feeling as if I was about to dissolve into thin air. My postnatal depression, added to my husband's behavior, makes for quite an explosive mix. I feel close and, at the same time, distant from the other women, as we do not speak about our emotions and feelings. The dark hole inside me becomes larger and wider. I start to lose myself. No one notices, and no one asks how I feel. It is as if I would be alone in the world. I need human contact to survive.

In addition to this, something happens to my husband during these weeks. Something massive and threatening, as if a switch had been pulled inside him. Until now, we used to be companions despite our often diverging views. But now we slowly turn to enemies as he becomes increasingly the typical Masai father. It is as if, with me being a mother, we were no longer equals. I don't know what is more painful: his indifference towards me or the fact that he does not seem to be interested in his son. I miss the long conversations we used to have, the closeness and the warmth. But that is not all: Sokoine has also started to drink a lot, all the time. Whenever I smell alcohol on his breath, I feel a surge of rage. How could our whole life and happiness shatter over only eight weeks? And I cannot even leave now. I have no way out.

"What is wrong with you?" I ask him one day, finally deciding to confront him.

"What do you mean?" he replies, these words alone utterly exasperating to me.

"Why are you never here? Why are you not with your son? Why do you prefer hanging out with your friends in the bar instead of spending time with your family?"

"We don't do this around here. I cannot sit here and hold your hand."

"Why not?" I exclaim, not believing the words coming out of his mouth.

"The others will think I'm stupid or mad."

That is his excuse, then. That is the reason why he leaves us night after night without even glancing at his son. That is what hurts me most.

There is a new enemy in my life: alcohol. I no longer recognize my husband.

Yayai, of course, notices a lot of this, as I often cry in her presence.

"Yayai, your son is once again dead drunk and only talks bullshit," I tell my clearly concerned mother-in-law.

The normally gentle and kind woman gets really furious and decides to confront her son, too:

"Why do you treat Stephanie that way? What are you thinking? Are you drunk?" she asks him as he returns to our hut later on.

"No, I'm not."

He often simply denies the fact. There is not much his mother can do. Sokoine's father, an alcoholic for many years now, used to beat the living daylight out of his wife in his younger years. This is Sokoine's role model. There was not much Yayai could do about him either.

"Stephanie, that's the way men are," she often says to me with resignation.

But I won't accept that.

During the next few weeks, not a single day goes by without us fighting. I try to pull myself together at first and avoid insulting him, but it feels increasingly difficult not to. He always returns to the hut in the evening, unfortunately exactly around Yannik's bedtime, wishing to talk to me about his day. And also about utterly trivial matters. Like all babies, Yannik is cranky and irritable at this time of night, and I am tense. Instead of helping me with our son and spending time with him, Sokoine only gets on my nerves and does not understand why I would not listen to his tittle-tattle.

"You're so full of crap! Why don't you come home earlier? We would be able to talk then, but not at this time of night."

One evening, at 6:30 pm, Yayai brings me the usual liter bottle of hot Masai mush, just like she always does, the warm food giving me strength and consolation. It also makes me sweat profusely, but Yayai reasons with me, saying, "This is good for your body." This bottle of food has become a very important ritual for me. Yannik is restless, but his grandmother rocks him in her arms, wishing to give me some peace, as Sokoine steps into the hut.

"Ah, my dear son, here you are. I need to milk the cows. Take your son," Yayai says, placing the small bundle in the arms of his baffled father.

There is a defensive look on his face. He had not planned for this, obviously.

I keep silent, slowly sipping the warm mush.

"I am so tired," Sokoine begins, complaining.

He clearly has no wish to take care of his son. His friends are probably already waiting for him.

I do not reply and continue to swallow my food.

"I had a very bad night last night. I did not sleep well."

There is a silence, then after a couple of minutes, he adds:

"I need to take a shower. You take Yannik."

"You cannot be serious, can you? You cannot even hold your son for ten minutes so I can eat my mush in peace? So I can gather new strength and produce new milk for your son?"

I can hear my voice becoming louder.

"I am tired and need to shower," he repeats stubbornly.

"Do you realize how tired I am, breastfeeding Yannik three times a night? And you don't even have ten minutes to spare for your son?" My anger swells. "You poor, tired man, you're such an egoist! Go!"

He does not need to be told twice. Undaunted by my outburst, he puts Yannik in my lap and turns to the door.

"Get the hell out of here!"

Then something happens that changes everything.

His gait alone shows me he has had too much to drink. I feel enraged right away. I don't want this now.

"What are you doing here? Stay with your drunken friends."

"I have a right to be here," he says, his speech heavy and slurred. "I am your husband and would like to see my son."

"You have no right at all, not the way you behave. Right now, your son needs to sleep."

Our voices become louder, and Yannik starts to cry. The situation escalates. I won't have any of this. I grab a piece of cloth and tie Yannik to my back.

"Where are you going?!" he asks aggressively.

"Out of here," I snap back.

"You're not going anywhere!" he cries, pushing me violently backward with both hands.

I stumble, lose balance, and hit hard against the wall. Yannik's head bangs against it first.

At once, the baby starts howling in pain. For the briefest of moments, I am motionless, stunned. Then, I feel a surge of frenzied anger.

"Are you going to hit us now? Just like your father used to do? Are you this kind of man? How can you dare to hurt our son? I won't accept this! I despise you!"

I yell and scream, spitting my words in his face. There is no fear inside me, only rage. This has visible results. Sokoine stands motionless in the dark with his arms hanging down. I can see it in his face: he knows he has crossed a line.

A bump appears on Yannik's head, and my heart tightens. I caress his head gently and hold him tight. This is too much.

"Get out of here, and don't you dare touch us ever again!" I cry, storming out of the hut, our crying child in my arms.

Once outside the house, I tie him to my back again. I am not staying here one more day. The evening bustle echoes from the other houses, but no one would come and help me right now. They did hear us fight, though; nothing ever stays private within the community. But then, every woman has to go through this. Every woman, but not me. I won't. Beside myself with rage, I set off to the neighboring *boma*. I will find a safe place for Yannik and me at Sokoine's cousin's.

"I have come to get Stephanie," Sokoine says the next day, standing on the threshold as if nothing had happened.

"What is wrong, Steph?" he asks innocently as I glare at him.

No apologies, no regrets, no concern about Yannik's state. I follow him without a word, not wishing to embarrass his family.

A loveless marriage is painful enough as it is. But I also grieve the loss of my best friend, the person I felt the closest to. Most of all, I grieve the loss of the respect I once felt for him. How am I supposed to love a person I no longer respect?

To top it off, we also have financial worries, as our farm is not productive yet. I have invested all my money in this project. I did not go back to England for fun but to work and make money. Money that helped us make ends meet. We do miss this source of income now. I have become the breadwinner of the family, a very large family. That is a lot of responsibility. But my bank account is empty. I have paid for the emergency C-section with the last remaining savings I had - 2,000 euros. I even had to ask my aunt to lend us some money.

"*Rehlein*, can you help me?" I asked my aunt Renate on the phone, when Yannik was only five days old.

Renate is not exactly wealthy, but there is no one else I could borrow money from.

"How much do you need?"

My heart leaps with gratitude.

"The hospital wants 2,000 euros," I whisper meekly into the phone.

"No problem, I'll make the transfer."

What am I supposed to do? My marriage is over, and my relationship with my husband is shattered. But this is still my new family and my new home. Our son was born here. I live in the *boma* with the Masai. This life has become a very important part of me. I am happy here. If I ever return to Germany, how would I fare there as a biologist and a single mother? Not to mention the fact that I don't even have the money to buy a plane ticket. For the moment, I am utterly at a loss.

170

CHAPTER 9

Osina likiyaa nodoo

Trouble will lead you to many places.

I hear them roar, the sound echoing across the unrelenting heat. The sun fries our brains all day long, preventing any kind of activity, and it is often in vain that we wait for the evening to bring a much-longed-for cooling. It is constantly sweltering hot, day and night. Not to forget the animals roaring on top of it. After some time, the sound becomes lower and lower until it stops entirely. Then I know for sure another cow has died. The spectacle of the emaciated animals breaks my heart. Some still manage to stand on thin, frail legs, while others are too weak to get to their feet. The young are too feeble to suck on their mothers' tits, sagging udders dangling, wrinkled and flaccid, under their bellies, like old balloons from which all air has escaped. We have to watch on as one animal after the other slowly dies before our very eyes. Our village is like a graveyard. We have turned into a large group of mourners. The children's cheerful smile has long vanished. They can feel the seriousness of the situation.

Never in all these years have I seen my husband in such a state: helpless, discouraged, and sad. He feels responsible for his people. What now?

Not long ago, I had cursed and fought with him because he would let me down in such a despicable way, yet now all I feel is boundless compassion. During this drama, I can see clearly what needs to be done. I will not leave. Choosing to stay suddenly comes very easily to me. I must act, I must do something...

"Can I come back to our house?" Sokoine asks, his big round eyes looking sheepishly at me.

I have not forgotten the pain. It still hurts very badly that he should have treated me that way, but I have not yet found an escape or come up with a solution, and I cannot leave the *boma* in my current state. I have no strength to forge new plans.

"You may come back, but only if you never ever hit me again!"

He flinches.

"And if you show up here every night dead drunk, our ways will part, do you hear me?"

Shall I welcome my husband back with open arms? No. But this is my home, a home our son will grow up in as a Masai. And so I declare some kind of truce.

Several months have passed and Yannik has become a sweet, quiet baby. If anything has the power to move my sorrowful heart, it is my son, his big round eyes gazing at me as I breastfeed him. Sometimes, when his tiny hand grabs a strand of my hair or brushes the skin of my throat, it fills my heart with indescribable warmth. This is how I know I am starting to feel again, slowly crawling out of the dark place I had been locked up in. Yannik and Yayai most certainly saved me.

Now that Sokoine is back in the house, I also regain my freedom, the return of the men putting an end to the mother's period of isolation. Standing outside the hut, I take deep breaths, overjoyed to leave my secluded time behind. I tie my son to my back with a piece of cloth, and we take long walks through the bush together. I greedily take in everything around me as the love of a large African family surrounds Yannik. His many cousins, aunts, and grandmother caress, cuddle, and laugh with him.

"Give him to me, Stephanie," Sokoine's grandmother requests.

The old lady is about 95 years old and no longer very steady on her legs. I place Yannik on her lap, and she rocks him at once, humming a song.

I return sometime later to the two of them taking a small nap. I still spend much time with Yayai and the other women. My Maa continues to get better.

A truce does not mean peace. Sokoine and I fight every single day. His alcohol consumption, his absence, and his lack of interest in our son still hurt me deeply. Yet, the better I feel, the easier it is for me to make decisions. Not that he would not love his son, but just like all Masai men, he has no business with crying babies. Our son is still an infant, but I don't want him to grow up around constantly fighting parents. What is it that still connects us? Most certainly being responsible for a large family and our farm. We both share a deep connection with our animals. As it is, they slowly help us find a way back to each other.

I have realized something very important: I cannot allow my happiness to depend entirely and exclusively on our relationship. This cannot be, as it would mean I could never be happy again should the relationship end. Are these the only two options? Leave or stay? And if I stay, then only if I am in a romantic relationship? I have been living here with the Masai for four years now. I have long since taken root here, building close relationships within the family. Yayai has become like a substitute mother to me; no one has ever cared for me as much as she has, especially in my deepest need. Being part of their community, I experience the Masai's wonderful and precious connection with Nature through their many traditions and rituals. They are the true keepers of this tiny corner of the world they can still call their own. If anyone lives and farms in a sustainable way, without producing any garbage or wasting any resources, it is them. Yet precisely, this precious knowledge and way of life are in danger. There is less and less land available less and less income. It has become increasingly difficult for cowherd men to provide for their families.

Five months later, it is already September. Yannik has turned from a helpless newborn to a splendid baby, chuckling and laughing a lot, turning to his side and even sitting up. Even Sokoine cannot escape his charm, and very slowly, father and son get closer to each other, which soothes my bruised soul a little. By now, our hut is much too small; perhaps a new house will offer more space and allow us to make a new start as a family. It seems there are only bad memories in our old hut.

"Our hut is much too small. Let's build a new one," I tell Sokoine. He readily agrees, no doubt grateful for every step I take in his direction.

There is only a single place to sleep in our old hut, along with a small alcove I use for cooking. The bedroom in the new house needs to be larger, and we also want a space to take our meals. Sokoine persuades me not to build the new house exclusively according to Masai design. Instead of walls of clay and cow manure topped with a sand roof, he uses a mixture of clay and cement and a corrugated iron roof.

As good a prospect as it sounds, this decision is nonetheless exactly what I will get mad about later on, as quite unlike the other houses, our new home turns out to be much too cold in the cold season. The other houses in the village manage to keep a fairly warm temperature inside, even when the thermometer drops below ten degrees during the cold months of May, June, and July. We find ourselves freezing within the walls of our "modern" house.

"Let us build the house before the wet season starts," I suggest.

Once the rain has started, our village will soon change to a muddy construction site, and the walls will have enough time to dry properly in the current heat.

"We will need help. We won't be able to make it on our own," Sokoine says.

For 200,000 Tanzanian shillings, about 80 euros, we hire a few Swahili people to help us with the construction.

Upon the arrival of the construction crew, all the children of the *boma* dash out of their huts, not wanting to miss the spectacle.

The workers dig the foundations and set up the "blocks of stone." Other than the cement, a few wooden beams, and the corrugated iron roof all the construction material is at hand in the village. Water, sand, and cement are mixed together and formed into large blocks. Being busy at the farm, Sokoine is practically never around, which leaves the construction supervision to me. I am quite busy myself as it is, what with Yannik, the goats, and all my other daily chores, but if I don't drive things forward, the building will proceed very sluggishly. I don't want a badly built house, and thus, I keep a vigilant eye on the construction workers. This displeases them understandably and leads them to complain to Sokoine. Swahili men do not like being ordered around by women.

One day of building is in full gear, and the site is deserted at a standstill.

"Where are the men?" I ask Sokoine.

"No idea," he replies, puzzled, starting to make phone calls.

After a while, he has discovered why the men are absent.

"They want more money," he explains to me.

"This is insane! A deal is a deal," I reply.

Two days later, the workers return to the construction site, sulky and dragging their feet, to resume work. It is upsetting and weighs heavily on the general mood.

In the end, the house is finished in time. I am extremely relieved when the grumpy construction gentlemen finally leave the *boma*. I bought some paint in Songe, which I will use to paint the inner walls of our new rooms a vibrant orange and fresh green. We shall be happier in this new home. Our few belongings are quickly gathered and packed, and with the help of a few people, our move is swiftly done.

The wet season may start now. Yet, week after week, we wait for it to start.

"Where is the rain?" Sokoine asks, glancing worriedly at the sky.

Twice a year, with clockwork precision, rain follows the hot season. Such is the course of the seasons in Tanzania. Men plant crops and care for animals during these two wet seasons, the longer from March to May and the shorter from mid-November to mid-January. Yet this year, nothing happens. Such a thing has never occurred before. Days pass by without the smallest cloud in the sky as we all wait for the rain.

Instead of rain, though, there is plenty of dust. All-pervading dust that clings to the skin and tickles the nose, crawling under people's clothes and seeping into every crack in the house as if someone had sprinkled powdered sugar over our world. Except that this specific powdered sugar, far from being sweet, truly desiccates everything: the grass under our feet disappears as large cracks tear through the leathery soil. Unless one plows through the sub-soil, littered with rustling withered leaves that fall from the trees like snow-flakes and drift away with the wind. A hundred shades of brown and grey, peppered here and there with the pinkish-red clothes of the shepherds. The countless hues of lush green are long gone. Never in all these years have I witnessed such a terrible drought. It is truly different.

"I don't see any change," Sokoine repeats every night as he stands motionless in the darkness and stares into the starry night sky.

Anyone but us would be awed by such a spectacle, the stars glistening pure and sharp in the dark. There is no light pollution in the bush. The Masai have always read the sky and the stars, and to my husband, the disaster is plainly written up there. The location of the Milky Way tells him when the weather is about to change. I often join him outside when the night is balmy and listen to him telling me about the signification of the shifting constellations in the firmament.

"The rain won't come. We will need to take the cows to the waterhole every day."

Yet this is a difficult enterprise. A lot of waterholes in the area have dried up because of the ongoing drought, and long queues have formed in front of the water pump, which is a 45-minute walk from our *boma*. Patience is required. We have to pump longer and longer to coax the water out of the ground as the groundwater level sinks rapidly.

There is another problem we have to face. For weeks now, our animals have barely been able to find anything to eat, becoming thinner and weaker with each passing day, hipbones sticking out sharply under their wrinkled skin as wordless reminders. They drop their heads, increasingly apathetic.

The cows and goats usually only drink every other day, gaining enough fluid from grass and leaves. However, as the bare trees no longer offer any shade to protect them from the intense heat, their milk production also recedes. It is a critical point, as cows are our main food source.

"We need to give them supplementary feed," the men advise. "Otherwise, they won't make it."

It is an absurd situation. Under normal circumstances, the lush nature around the *boma* provides more than enough food for our herd. The part of the corn plant that remains once the grains have been separated from the pistons is called *pumba*. This is what we feed our animals now: one sack of *pumba* costing ten euros. A preposterously high price when considering the huge amount of *pumba* 60 cows will need. Every day, we empty one whole sack into their trough, which costs us a fortune as prices soar with increased demand.

"Let us buy enough *pumba* now," I decide.

As it is, we are doubly lucky, possessing both a motorbike and money. Lots of families do not. Sokoine drives tirelessly back and forth between our village and Lengatei, transporting the heavy sacks on his motorbike. We help each other out, of course, but the need is too great for us to be able to share with everybody.

Sokoine is not the only one staring at the sky. Every Masai, our entire village, keeps looking up, hoping for clouds to appear. November goes by, then December, and still no rain in sight. Fewer and fewer cows manage to get up and move about. They are all much too weak.

"We have to watch them around the clock and help them to their feet," Sokoine explains. Our Tanzanian breed of cows is significantly smaller than their European counterparts. The ruminants spend the chief part of the day ingesting and digesting feed. They don't sleep for hours at a time as humans do but for much shorter periods throughout the day and the night. When the large animals lie down for too long, potentially harmful processes are set in motion. Very often, the animals find themselves incapable of getting up on their own, with poor circulation causing their legs to become numb.

"I'll help with the night watches," I offer Sokoine.

The two of us work out a schedule. At about two o'clock in the morning, my phone rouses me from deep sleep, and I trudge to the enclosure with half-closed eyes. I can hear the animals snorting from a distance and sweep the darkness with my flashlight. Sokoine and three of his brothers are trying to help a cow to her feet. One grabs her by the horns while the others push against the animal.

"Hey-ho!" they call, cheering for the cow as much as for themselves.

Sometimes, they manage on the first try. Other animals need a little more help. Sweat runs down the men's faces. They look exhausted. I build a campfire to make some chai tea, its aromatic fragrance soon drifting through the night. Hopefully, the sweet tea will somewhat restore the men's energy. Everyone lends a hand, and everyone is exhausted. The night watches, the lack of sleep, and the worry are taking their toll. The women build fires to cook tasty dishes out of the few ingredients they have at hand.

The sky cannot be trusted anymore. In January, the Masai even ask me for advice in their despair.

"Stephanie, we have heard that you white people can predict the weather. Could you look it up on the Internet?"

I have been doing little else for quite a while, and my hopes for rain in the coming weeks are not very high.

"The rain won't come now," I prophesy somberly. "Perhaps in March."

That is the harsh truth, unfortunately. The wet season does not happen this year – with harrowing consequences for us, the animals, and nature.

Death has taken charge all around us in the past few weeks. I have witnessed the occasional death of a cow in the past four years, but this is absolutely devastating. Namelok, one of my favorite animals, is lying on her side, breathing heavily, legs stretched out.

"Come on, sweetie, don't give up! Please don't give up!" I keep whispering like a mantra in the animal's fluffy ear, even though I know that imploring won't be much use.

I have learned so much about cattle during the years I have spent here, and with Sokoine's help, I managed to save a few animals in critical situations. But Namelok is far too emaciated and weak. Her strength and resistance shattered, just like my heart. As I gently stroke her fur, the soft nostrils flare to the rhythm of her ever-weakening breathing.

The calf she has just given birth to won't make it either. Still wet from the amniotic fluid and blood, it lies next to her, trembling. We tried rubbing the much too-light body with straw to stimulate blood circulation, but in vain. For weeks now, I have been watching my cow becoming increasingly thin, her pregnant belly the only salient part of her body. How could the small being she was expecting possibly be sufficiently nourished? Giving birth finished her off. Now, mother and daughter lie side by side, their bellies barely rising and falling. The calf that will die too soon to be given a name would have sucked its mother's milk in vain. Most of the cows now provide only very little milk or none at all. In our distress, we test all kinds of alternatives. The goats don't suffer as much from the drought because, unlike the cows, they eat other plants and fruits. We make makeshift bottles from leather straps or hollow pumpkins and feed goat milk to the calves. Other Masai, who don't have goats, even fill the small vessels with warm corn mush to get the calves through. Yet most of these attempts end badly, and many animals do not survive.

Pesa's young does not survive either. I have a special connection to her. When I moved to the *boma,* Sokoine did not possess many cows, yet he offered one to me in a very moving gesture. Unfortunately, Pesa is quite moody; one must watch out for her pointed horns. Yayai is the only one who may milk her. Precisely because of her strong will and because she was a gift, I like Pesa. But her small bull does not make it either. One single calf manages to survive the disastrous drought. Mama Samedi, the third wife of Sokoine's father, was able to get the newborn calf through on corn mush.

All our money - my inheritance, which I have invested in this herd so we would be safe - is vanishing before our very eyes. With every cow that dies, a piece of our livelihood disappears.

Horrendous stories reach us from the neighboring *bomas*. Masai are usually very tough, but the situation here now discourages some of them.

"Sereyani has taken his own life. With a piece of rope," Yayai tells us one day, returning from a visit to another *boma*.

We exchange horrified glances.

"All their animals died. No cows, no money, no food."

She does not need to add anything. Having to witness the animals' agony and wretched death is simply terrible.

Our hearts bleed. We could not feel more sad. Corpses of animals are scattered everywhere on the way to Lengatei, the stench of death pervading the air. Desperate news from our region also reaches our *boma*.

"We will find a way," I tell Sokoine.

Perhaps I need to speak this out aloud once and for all so we won't lose hope, including me. If life did teach me anything, it is that somehow, things always go on. No matter how difficult the situation.

My husband, the man I almost felt only hatred for a few months ago, sits before me, looking miserable. I cannot bear it. The distress and the grief we feel for our cows has brought us closer. We talk about this ordeal for hours on end, consulting with each other about what to do.

Every day, I go into the withered bush with a couple of young boys with a machete in hand. Together we roam the area for hours, searching for a small tree or a few bushes that still bear some leaves.

"Mama Yannik, there is an *olmaroroi* here."

I have been called "Mama Yannik" since after my son was born. I glance in the direction of Lengai's voice, one of the boys from our *boma*.

Indeed, we had been looking for that particular toilet tree that usually bears smooth leaves, covered with a soft down and as large as a man's hand, which we use for hygienic purposes. I wipe Yannik's baby bottom with them. Apart from the leaves, which the animals love, the toilet tree also bears magnificent blooms that usually blossom right before the wet season. As it is, the tree we have found does not have many leaves yet, but we rejoice over even the tiniest of them as if it were pure gold.

Something is different. I wake up and listen closely into the silence. What is it that woke me? Some sound. There is a rustling in front of the door; the wind perhaps, or the withered leaves?

"Plop." Pause. "Plop, pling, plop."

The sound comes from the roof. That cannot be true. I dare not believe my own ears. Could this be raindrops tapping softly on our iron roof?

"Sokoine, psst, can you hear that?" I say, nudging him gently.

He blinks at me with sleepy eyes.

"Rain!"

The magic word has an immediate effect. We jump out of bed and thrust the door open, the raindrops leaving tiny, dark patches on the dry ground, like beads of fat on the surface of soup. The water cannot yet sink deep into the parched soil, but the rain is coming down harder and harder. What a wonderful sound. Rain at last! This sound, which we have all longed to hear for months, also rouses the others.

It is March 3, 2017. This date is burned into my memory. A date to celebrate. Our worst fear has not come true after all, and the second wet season has finally arrived, thank God.

It takes a while for the first green stems to sprout from the earth, for the trees to be covered with lush green leaves, and for the waterholes to fill with water. We are all still very much in shock. We have been warned. What happened once can happen again. As it is, the all-clear is short-lived. The drought has greatly affected our animals. Very slowly, they recover from the exhausting months of famine. Three months later, the rain stops.

The fight continues as the heat takes over again. We decide on a new tactic and new feeding grounds.

"We will take the cows to the Gugwi Mountains behind Lengatei," Sokoine says, nodding with great determination. "There is more food there and more shade."

Together with a small party, we set out with our animals. Ten kilometers at least await us as we lead the herd. We need to find the proper path for man and animal, not too steep and not too narrow. It is dangerous to lead the cattle into the mountain; the animals are not used to it.

Even though two of Sokoine's younger brothers always stay with the cows to watch over them, we are still not entirely protected against loss. Three animals wander too close to the path's edge to graze softer grass and fall into the void. They were injured so badly that we had to put them out of their misery. Some animals are permanently lost, having drifted too far away from the rest of the herd in pursuit of food, unable to find their way back. One of the cows twists a leg and limps.

"We cannot leave her behind, but she can no longer go on either. What should we do?" Sokoine says, pausing to think. "Iyarre will stay with her until her leg has healed."

We leave his younger brother behind in the mountains, with enough food for him and the animal. In the end, we lose three bulls and one cow. That is the price we pay for the rest of our herd to survive.

One day, Sokoine and I are on our way back from the village. He drops me off shortly before our *boma*, having some other errand to run. After about 300 meters, I glimpse a small rise in the distance. Drawing nearer, I make out the shape of a heavily panting cow. Probably one of our deserters, as no herd or shepherd is in sight. Diseases have been circulating among animals lately, which they are very prone to in their current poor condition. The cow's neck is extremely swollen. She is obviously in mortal danger, her emaciated body rising and falling rapidly. She stares at me with her big eyes, tongue lolling. I cannot leave her here to die.

Sokoine answers his phone right away.

"What should I do?" I ask him, desperate.

The Masai treat their cows themselves, including antibiotic shots for certain specific diseases.

"We still have a little penicillin left. Inject it directly in her throat."

Every animal is so precious to us that we make every effort to try and save it. I rush to the *boma*, grab the medical bag in our house, and ask Mayani, my sister-in-law, for her help. The two of us dash back to the brown wheezing heap on the road. Kneeling down next to the animal, I open the bag and pull the syringe while Mayani holds the cow's horns. She is very weak but still, perhaps, strong enough to hurt us in her panic. As it is, though, the cow barely moves at all, softly mooing as I push the needle into the leathery skin of her neck. Her brand tells us which herd she belongs to. We stay with her for a little while, and her breathing gradually becomes easier and calmer. There is not much more we can do for her now. Back in our *boma*, I send one of my little nephews to the neighboring *boma* where the cow's owner lives.

As it turns out, our efforts have paid off. The cow survives. The whole thing shows me how deeply connected we all are here in the bush. Every action is crucial, and we can only ever hope to survive as part of a larger community. But what if the rain stops altogether? Then all of us will die...

It would mean the end of the Masai culture; that much is certain. Without cows and land, they cannot generate any income. They need very little as it is, yet if even the little they need falls out... When I imagine Yayai, Mama Klaudia, my father-in-law, my brother-in-law, Sokoine's brothers, everyone in the *boma* having to leave the place and look for a low-paying job... I just cannot get this into my head.

Would it be more worthwhile? In their view, certainly not.

The life of the Masai follows deeply rooted rules and traditions that might appear strange and outlandish to outsiders. Colonization, soon followed by corruption and now climate change, has made the living conditions of the indigenous people increasingly difficult. Still, they are a perfect example of how living in harmony with nature without destroying it is possible. Giving up on the Masai would be so easy. But such thinking would prove very short-sighted, as it will be our turn sooner or later.

Something invaluable is disappearing forever. Something no one will ever be able to restore. I don't want to stand by and witness it without doing anything.

I cannot dwell on such thoughts, though. I cannot allow fear to take hold of me. I need to become active; I need to come up with solutions. There has to be something I can do, damn it. I will not sit here in the bush and watch the people and the culture I have come to love so much perish.

CHAPTER 10

Iyelo enijo kake miyolo enekishukokini

You know what you say, but you don't know what will be said to you.

A Voice for the Masai

"DRY SEASON" - this is what I read on the screen, my finger hovering in the air. To heck with it, let's do this. I press the "submit" button determinedly and take a deep breath. My hands shook, and I was so excited that my heartbeats hurt. It feels good. I have just now published my first online blog, the subject of which came quite naturally to me. What could make more sense than writing about what has threatened the very basis of our existence? Last year's terrible events triggered something inside me.

I have been given this a lot of thought for quite some time, and now, on an impulse, I have just decided to put it into practice. Since I was a student, I have always loved writing. Finding words was never a problem. With my friends and colleagues worldwide in mind, I have chosen to write in English. Should other people be interested in what I have to say, it also probably makes more sense to address them in English, not to mention the fact that apart from Swahili and Maa, I feel much more comfortable with the English language than I do with my mother tongue, having lived and studied in England for a long time.

I have been using the Facebook app for years on my mobile phone, mainly to keep in touch with friends and family, as well as volunteers all around the world. I have 120 followers who have not heard from me for quite some time.

I like to follow inspiring people, which is why I first became interested in bloggers. What sort of different dimension is that? And what an opportunity! Being able to inform the entire world about anything without anyone's help! For many years now, I have banished TV sets, computers, and smartphones from my life. Life offers, in my opinion, quite enough excitement. Until now, my mobile phone has mainly been a practical tool given the secluded life we lead out here, yet as I scroll through the Internet, I discover endless possibilities. Three things motivate my research: I need an outlet for my emotions and experiences. I also need a task. I am not a very talented jewelry maker, and being a housewife is not nearly enough for me.

I don't have any specific task here in the boma, and there is no one to really talk to and exchange views with. I have come to recognize this very clearly since I recovered from my depression. What talent could I use to help my family, the Masai? Well, I can speak up. I can write and invite many people to learn about their way of life, their skills, and their troubles. It feels true and coherent to me.

The horror of the drought still runs deep. One could not possibly experience climate change at a closer range. Even though we live in the wilderness at the far end of the world, people must know what is happening here. I want to shout out to the entire world and write about what moves me, my feelings and experiences, what I have learned here, and the Masai's difficulties in protecting their culture. I would also like to write about my deep love and respect for these wonderful people. This is why I choose to call my blog *Masai Life*. I deliberately write Masai with one a, the spelling of the word being different in many countries: in England, one would write Masai and in Germany Massai. However, as Masai is the local pronunciation, I chose to use this variation.

I quickly realize that my old mobile phone will not be of much use. Building a blog on such a small display screen is impossible, and the phone does not have enough storage space. The phone signal is not very good either, and I want to take good pictures and shoot videos.

"Could you get a tablet for me?" I ask my friend Olivia from England, who plans to visit me in Tanzania.

"What do you need a tablet for?" she replies.

"I would like to start a blog!"

Silence on the line. Talking about my plan feels good.

"Steph, this is wonderful! Sure, tell me what I should buy," she answers readily.

I can literally feel her enthusiasm.

I transfer the required sum to her and asked her to purchase a few accessories. And since a larger storage space requires more power, I built a small solar charging station. Oddly enough, getting a good phone signal in Africa is sometimes easier than in Europe. Despite the fact the display screen of my old phone often shows "E" for "Edge" – which is about the lowest possible service – I am still able to watch YouTube videos, admittedly with lots of patience. The network operator is called Halotel, and I book as much as six gigabytes for 10,000 Tanzanian shillings - about four euros - a week. I love the technical know-how, and before long, I managed to set up my blog on a platform. It feels so good to start a new project.

It seems something inside me had broken loose; I cannot wait to write more. I share my blog article on Facebook, and notifications start coming in soon after. I'm thrilled. It is so exciting!

"Hey Stephanie, your blog is great! Do you remember me?"

Of course, I remember July. After all, we worked together in Ifakara. She is the first to leave a comment and even share my posts.

"This is Stephanie. We used to work together. She has married a Masai and now writes this cool blog."

Her words move me deeply, and I gratefully answer her right away. It has been so long since I have heard from her. Before long, other long-lost colleagues also reappear.

I reply to messages and answer new questions. Nice "conversations" ensue. A sudden change occurs in the number of my followers. As more and more people read my article, some of them are complete strangers. I am boosted by the friendly comments and touched by the kindness and interest they demonstrate. My confidence grows, and I apply myself to the next article.

Visibility

"Join the Faces-2-Heart contest. Show us your video of why we should follow your blog!" The blogger contest keeps popping up on the video platform. I have only just written a couple of articles. Wouldn't signing up for a contest be a tad too bold? But then this sort of contest is not joined by any of the big influencers but rather by anonymous people from around the world, sharing matters close to their hearts. Just like me.

I have been watching inspiring videos on YouTube, studying them closely for some time now. How do people tell their stories? Why did they choose to do so, and what subjects move them? Would they also listen to me and watch my videos? I would like to find this out, and Faces-2-Heart offers me exactly such an opportunity. You can win a six-month trip through East Africa and then write about it on your blog. What interests me most is the possibility of gaining more visibility. The other participants do not have vast crowds of followers yet either, but I do not have a YouTube channel, nor have I ever shot a video. Besides, I am not the kind of person who loves to step in front of the camera. I want the Masai to be in the foreground. Seriously, Stephanie? Will you allow such a small matter to put you off? I chuckle to myself. I have learned so much over the past few years and had many new experiences, including ones far more dangerous than video production. I set to work with determination, and Sokoine becomes my cameraman.

The mooing of the cows echoes around me. I stand within the fenced enclosure for our animals in the middle of the *boma*. After all, the cows are why I am doing all this. I only have two minutes to tell our story; the application video cannot be any longer. The first attempts come out a little too stiff and too lengthy. Come now, Stephanie, that's not the way to go about it, I tell myself. Be cool and tell things with your heart. An overly orchestrated script would come across as staged and inauthentic. The whole thing works better when I think about my core message and then tell things the way they are. In the end, Sokoine hands the tablet to our sister-in-law so he can stand next to me in front of the camera. A few takes later, I am much more satisfied with the result. Better done than perfect, I think to myself, an attitude that has always worked out well for me in life. All I need to do now is set up my own channel. One deep breath, and here I am, downloading my first video. One thing leads to another, and I might as well ask about other interests.

"Might I interest you in our story? I'm a German woman and have been living here in Lesoit for six years with my Masai family."

Africa Geographic is a successful online magazine and a platform for photographers and safaris. Will they even consider giving a beginner such as myself a chance? My audacity is quickly rewarded. Before long, I receive a reply.

"Hey Stephanie, sounds interesting! Please send us a writing sample."

The subject I chose resonates with them. After two more emails and one conversation on the phone, the deal is done, and a perfect deal, too. I am allowed to write for the website.

I learned many new things during those weeks, including some about myself. This occupation pulled me out of my lethargy after the personal crisis and the great drought. Becoming active definitely makes me feel better.

A Beneficial Visit

The trauma runs deep. Too much has happened over the last few years. Sometimes, I feel very strong, yet at other times, an iron blanket seems to weigh heavily upon my shoulders. I miss the closeness to my husband and the intimacy we had at the beginning of our relationship. The constant worry over our livelihood takes a heavy toll on me. Until one day, a ray of hope comes to me over the phone.

"Stephanie, I am coming to Tanzania. I want to finally meet my nephew. And we'll travel to Zanzibar for a few days."

What a lovely surprise! My sister would be the first of my German family to meet my nineteen-month-old son. I don't want to break all ties. It is important to me. Yet, about Zanzibar…

"I'd love to, but I cannot afford it," I explain to her, heavy-hearted.

"I'd love to invite you…"

Even before she finishes her sentence, tears well up in my eyes, threatening to break loose like a bursting dam. Her words hold a promise, a hope that might be able to break through the dark veil of my melancholy. I have not left the *boma* for over a year and a half, and so many terrible things have happened during that time. Perhaps a change of scenery is precisely what I need. I would never have ventured to take the road on my own. I am far too broke and not yet strong enough. My self-esteem is still below zero, or so it feels to me, despite the budding reassurance the writing of my blog conveys. My sister plans to stay in Tanzania for 14 days. I will meet her in Dar es Salaam, and she will spend five days with us in the *boma*. Then, the two of us will travel to Zanzibar.

This also means I have to start weaning Yannik. Severing our intimate bond makes me very sad, even though I know there is no other way. What use is a breast full of milk to my son if I cannot stop crying as a result? If I can no longer laugh? My son needs me to be the happy mother I would like to be. And if that means I first have to let go, then I am more than willing to do so. Nothing will ever sever the unbreakable bond between me and my son.

My sister saves me. We live in two very different worlds, 10,000 kilometers away from each other. As twins, we enjoyed a very close relationship when we were kids, but our diverging lives have kept us apart.

"It is so good to see you!" I exclaim as we hug at the airport in Dar es Salaam.

The long ride on the bus and the few days in the *boma,* pass by in a flash. My sister is delighted with Yannik. We talk for hours on end and finally set out for the second part of the journey. Something inside me shifts, and I start to feel lighter. Leaving the worries and responsibilities behind for a while is nice. There are no concerns here: fresh food, set tables, and nicely made beds. I don't complain about my simple life in the bush, but I can feel how malnutrition undermines me, especially when I am unwell.

Zanzibar heals me. I can find no other word for it. It is not only because of the conversations with my sister, but I also spend long hours walking along the white beach, meeting other people, other Masai. I love talking with them about their culture and the future of our planet. I have missed human interaction so much. This journey reminds me of the Stephanie I used to be and shows me what truly makes me happy - before I became a mother. People, travels, meaningful conversations, thinking outside the box.

Cracks appear in the iron armor around my heart, falling off piece by piece, revealing my true self once again. It is not only about my years in the *boma*. Looking back on my life, I see now that I did carry quite a lot of emotional baggage early on – the premature loss of my parents, too much loneliness and too many responsibilities, Sokoine's betrayal, all the worries. All this has added up and now bursts out as I allow all thoughts and emotions to rise to the surface. I feel endless grief at first, and yet, at the same time, a certain lightness returns to my heart. It is not a miracle cure, but little by little, I can feel my wounds start to heal.

We even go dancing in the evening. Music flows through my body and I gather new strength. My sister and I talk about everything or nearly everything. I don't tell her about Sokoine's outburst of violence. Something inside me still wishes to protect him despite the severe psychological injury and the fact that I will never condone violence. But it would be unfair to depict him solely in this bad light. There is so much more to our relationship; we both fight very hard for our family in Lesoit.

So many answers come to mind to questions I used to struggle with. Can I stay in the *boma*? Yes, I can and I will. Leaving is no longer an option for me. I want Yannik to grow up with the Masai. My inheritance is spent, but then I will manage to make new money. I owe it to these people I feel responsible for. Two questions haunt me, though: first, what can we do to live through the drought? Our cows might die. This is a fact we had to learn the hard way. Not necessarily a safe bet, then. And secondly, how can we diversify our income?

I already have a potential solution in mind. Could I perhaps make some money with my blog? I have seen lots of successful bloggers and You-tubers who seem to have done so. What would our specific situation call for? I scroll through online pages enthusiastically, gathering all kind of information, and come across an extraordinary project: "How can pasture land be preserved despite water shortage? How can traditional knowledge be used for sustainable agriculture?" I am mesmerized. These are exactly the issues we are dealing with. The desperately needed answers are written clearly on the Mara Training Center homepage, education tailored for the Masai. I read through the page feverishly. Bingo. The program matches our problems perfectly. The main thing is to let the animals graze only on a quarter of the village's surface to allow the grass to grow tall in other places and thus make sure the cows have enough feed even during the dry season. This particular method is called rotational grazing.

There is however a major catch to this plan: the courses are taught in Kenya and cost a fortune by our standards. I mentally convert the costs to euros. A three-day boot camp for five participants would cost at least 5,000 dollars. How on earth am I supposed to come up with that kind of money? My head is spinning, but I know that much: that program offers new ideas and insights.

"Why don't you launch a crowdfunding campaign?" an acquaintance asked below one of my posts about the drought.

Back then I was not familiar with the term. Taking other people's money? Why? To buy food and new cows? It did not make sense at the time. A concrete project, however, that would bring us forward in a sustainable way, now that would be something entirely different.

The island of Zanzibar has healed and inspired me in so many ways. Filled with new energy, I return to the *boma*, a million projects in mind. I will never forget what my sister did for me, the gift this trip really turned out to be.

Masai Story

"Do you believe this could be the right program for us?" I ask Sokoine upon his return.

My being enthusiastic about the project is one thing, but I still need to gain the Masai men's trust. And to achieve this, I need Sokoine by my side. As much as the villagers like me, I am still a woman. I cannot walk up to the village's elder, bypassing everyone else in doing so. I have to comply with certain rules and procedures. If not, I might as well forget about the whole thing right away.

My husband listens attentively as I describe to him the content of the training.

"That sounds good, precisely what we need. Let us try! We've got nothing to lose anyway."

This is not exactly the reaction I had hoped for. We discuss how to proceed from here.

"I will ask the Elder if he can receive us so you can present the project to him."

Sokoine takes care of that particular aspect of things while I look into the next steps to collect money, which will require all my time and energy, as it turns out.

"I will support you," Sokoine declares, nodding.

Tackling a positive project together, as a team, feels good after the difficult period we went through.

There is still so much that needs to be done. Even though I have gained followers in the three months since I have started my blog, I am still practically invisible on the net when it comes to raising a crowdfunding campaign.

"Your campaign must be actively promoted for several weeks if you want to have any success." I read this on the crowdfunding platform Indiegogo, where I intend to launch my campaign. But I don't have this kind of time, unfortunately. The wet season will start in three months' time. What if there is no rain? We would not financially survive another famine. I will have to give it a go right now.

Choosing Instagram as the social media channel I shall use for my campaign, I set up my "@masai_story" account. Even though I am the one speaking up, I only do so on behalf of the Masai. It must be about them. My romantic relationship with Sokoine may be part of it, yet above all I want people to get a genuine and undistorted insight into the daily life of the Masai, not as a tourist attraction, but with all its facets and difficulties. I want people to understand what we can learn from the Masai and also tell them that climate change has reached us a long time ago.

Crowdfunding

Things are getting serious. My Instagram account is set up and I diligently write the next blog posts, linking them with my other channels. I have written several articles for the online magazine *Africa Geographic* and we are both also linked, which increases my visibility. How did I fare in the blogger contest? When I see the number of hits I can barely believe my own eyes: over 50,000 people all around the world have already watched my somewhat wobbly debut work. That is incredible! But I must not think about how people may react, or whether anyone is going to read what I am currently writing, otherwise I will lose courage. As it turns out, though, my fear of negative comments proves unfounded. Nearly all comments are positive.

"Thank you, Stephanie, for the insight you offer us."

"You are brave."

"Why are you doing this?"

"Thanks for the inspiration!"

"Love knows no color."

"Your story is wonderful, and the place and people there are wonderful too. I was born in Uganda, but I have spent most of my time overseas. I can relate to your story."

All this stimulates me and supports me in my efforts.

Before creating my account on the Indiegogo platform, I have to shoot more videos so that people could see why we needed the money and what it was for.

I come up with some kind of storyboard for my introduction video. Two minutes are not a long time and it cannot be too boring, otherwise people will not watch it till the end. How does one squeeze one's life and the hardships one has encountered into 150 seconds? First of all, people have to get to know us, which is why I start with Sokoine giving Yannik a little milk. It is nice to witness the intimate relationship these two have developed. Since Yannik has learned to walk and talk, his father shows much more interest in him, a fact that in turn also contributed to our reconciliation.

I shoot different scenes, showing our cows and explaining the whole system. I have downloaded a video-editing app to make it appear more professional. Simply speaking into the camera won't do. People have to be able to get a picture of what it is exactly I am talking about. I show them the nature and the land around our *boma*, especially the dried-up ground, explaining the various connections and the purpose of the money we hope to raise. At the end of the video, I show the children of our *boma* and then add some background music.

Now all I need to do is write a good article to go with it. I make a list of the different cost items so the potential funders will know what the money will be used for. By now I have 500 followers on Instagram. Not so much if one's aims at collecting 5,000 dollars. I am assailed by doubts at times, but there is no way back. On December 21, I press the button and activate my first ever crowdfunding campaign. Such an exciting moment! I share the link with all my other channels, and then the waiting starts, along with shaking hands and a racing heart.

"Pling!"

The tension is almost unbearable. The first ten dollars have reached the donation account. Someone has just transferred money to me. It is a very special feeling.

"Pling!"

The next donation arrives.

"Stephanie, this is so cool! I remember our time in Ifakara. You were always so kind to me, you would always show me everything. What you do, and the way you live, is just great, I will support you!"

Jane and I had worked together as volunteers. We had not heard from each other in a very long time. Five years! Even though we are both on Facebook, I did not really post much before starting the blog and we had lost touch.

"Pling!"

"Pling!"

"Pling!"

Jane is not the only one who remembers me. More and more former colleagues from Ifakara and Mafia send me messages and support my campaign. This is completely overwhelming.

"That's great Stephanie, you two have married! Lots of luck for your project!"

"A really good project I shall gladly support!"

"It's crazy, you living in Tanzania for so long now. You're both great!"

"I admire your courage!"

Apart from the financial aspect, the campaign makes me realize something else, something very precious: I may not have much time or many followers, but it seems I have started preparing for that campaign much earlier in life. Without my noticing, I have gained my former colleagues' trust, their comments showing their appreciation of my actions and the choices I have made, and how brave a woman they think I am. Never before have I felt or seen myself that way.

The money and the messages are a blessing. What a wonderful feeling after the terrible time I went through. In the morning, I keep looking at my phone. "Pling, pling." The campaign is to last for two months and my doubts gradually vanish. People actually see us, it is just unbelievable! So many donate money. Despite being still a student, a former colleague of ours on Mafia makes a 500 dollars donation - a fortune for her as much as for us. I am speechless.

But there is not only cause for celebration. I am also in for some disappointment. Precisely the people I thought would definitely help me respond only briefly or not at all, even though they could help by simply sharing my action and making it known. Seeing former friends or colleagues donate 50, 100 or 500 dollars is very painful when supposedly closer persons, in possession of sufficient funds, only give ten dollars, if anything. It leaves a thorn in my heart. For some people, ten dollars is a very large sum of money, for others, though, it is simply an act of denigration - of me and of my campaign. This is a sad lesson to learn, but I won't allow it to unsettle me. I pursue my efforts, spurred on by the large numbers of supporters encouraging me to go on and do the right thing.

We pass the 2,000 mark, then the 3,000. The 4,000 after some time. I can barely hold back my tears. Are we actually going to make it?

The donations reach 4,311 dollars when they suddenly come to a halt. No matter how long or how often I stare at it, the figure remains unchanged. It is truly an amazing result, achieved by 84 generous contributors. But it won't be enough.

Just as I start to think it has all been in vain, I receive an email that reads as follows: "Dear Mrs. Fuchs, we do not know each other personally yet, but I supervise a rain water tank action in Lesoit on behalf of our community, the Crailsheim Work Group. Your campaign is admirable and we would like to donate 1,000 dollars in support of your project. I have discussed this with our employer, Hugo Boss, and they are happy to put this sum at your disposal. Let us talk on the phone very soon. Warm regards, Anita."

This last large sum seems to have been dropped into our lap miraculously. It is precisely the amount we needed to complete the campaign. Fate is on my side! I feel immensely grateful.

"Campaign ended!"

It is done. I stare at the sum, unable to believe it quite yet. Did I actually do this? I, an orphan living on a foreign continent, entirely without any help? Something that a few months ago seemed so utterly unattainable?

"Sokoine, we made it! We will go to Kenya!" I exclaim, bringing my husband the good news.

As we celebrate our success, I feel something shift and change between us, then fall back into place.

Money is a big issue, that is true, but what I value the most is the recognition and understanding of our supporters. These people believe in me. What I do is actually valuable and right. People support and admire me for it. I have never felt this myself. But then, it is high time, perhaps, that I too should recognize my own value and learn to believe in myself.

CHAPTER 11

Kiyo nisioiyo inno ope'ng, Kiyo nilo nodoo injom tenebo

If you want to go fast, go alone.
If you want to go far, go together.

"The *olaigwenani* is coming to see us today."

I nod thoughtfully. The traditional leader coming to your house is indeed a very special occasion. Each Masai age group elects its own top representative so to speak for all matters regarding the cows and the care of the herd. We would like to talk about the land management project with him. Sokoine and I have discussed the matter extensively between us beforehand, not wishing to bypass anyone.

"You can tell him about the Mara Training Center and the boot camp first," I suggest, "then I'll add a few things and explain to him how we got by the money."

The program seems indeed perfect and precisely tailored to our needs. Or rather to the Masai's needs, as it is intended for cow herders struggling with climate change and who do not want to give up their own culture and traditions. Two instructors supervise us, Richard and Mussa; the latter, being a Masai himself, plays a very important part.

During my exchanges with Mara, I learn that we will be taught theory in the morning, and then work in the field in the afternoon. Apart from acquiring agricultural knowledge, learning how to deal with apparently un-avoidable cultural change is also a very substantial element of the program. I am curious to hear what my fellow participants will have to say about this.

"What if someone cannot read and write?" I ask just to be on the safe side.

"That is no problem for us. We use panels and pictures."

This answer, along with the fact a Masai will actually be leading the program, reassures me. The men I shall be traveling with will certainly trust him, as he knows what he is talking about. After several extensive conversations, I have gathered all the information I need. We are now able to present the *olaigwenani* the full picture - and hopefully get him on board.

I wish to go about this with great care and respect. A Masai will always trust and listen to another Masai first. This is not about imposing my own view as such, but I do believe the whole village might benefit from this project. What options and chances do the Masai have in fighting the consequences of climate change? How can our family hope to be better prepared for the next drought?

We need a lot of open ears and minds; such a step can only ever be taken by the entire community, and as many shepherds as possible need to agree to the plan.

"What do think they'll say?" I ask my husband.

"They will think it is a good plan. They know you have been living here with us for the past five years, showing everyone respect and doing so many good things for the village. You have never once done something wrong."

My work, and my mission, are being put to the test here. Without the recognition of my fellow villagers, I will not be able to achieve anything. I very much hope they will acknowledge and recognize my efforts, as well as my love and respect for their culture.

The *olaigwenani's* appearance is very impressive. Surrounded by an aura of wisdom, the grave and quiet man of about 40 years of age - only slightly older than Sokoine - embodies the Masai traditions both inwardly and outwardly. The hardships of life have left deep marks on his handsome face.

I can see why the other men chose him as their representative. He listens to people, showing interest for the issues and problems of the villagers, who clearly trust him, and he reflects and weighs things up wisely before making a decision. It is thus very important to me that he should be on board our project.

His checkered, deep-red cloak wrapped tightly around his body all, he strides up to our hut, tall, almost majestic. Several silver earrings dangle from the upper and lower part of his ears.

Having a private conversation, undisturbed, is not exactly an easy matter in our *boma*, with children and adults constantly popping in and out for all manner of purposes. Today, though, we want to be able to talk in peace and have taken place on small stools.

The men exchange a few polite words at first, before getting to the point. In great detail, Sokoine proceeds to explain what the project is about and how it could benefit us. Our guest listens attentively, asks questions and nods thoughtfully.

"This sounds like a great plan we could all gain from."

I hear the leader's words of assent with great relief. We can go on with our plan.

"Who is to go to Kenya, then?" the *olaigwenani* asks.

Names are suggested and rejected, our heads spinning until we have finally chosen the participants. Apart from us three, we will ask our mayor, Mwenye Kiti, and his predecessor, Kaipai, to join us. Indeed this combination is most likely to prove successful, every man holding a leadership position of sorts and thus able to convince the local village community and its many *bomas*: the mayor on an administrative level, the traditional leader on the Masai community level and Sokoine as the leader of our *boma*.

We would have loved to invite more participants, but unfortunately only five spots are available. This will have to be enough for us to accomplish our goal. During the following days, Sokoine and the *olaigwenani* will talk further with the other men.

My mission is to provide the money and see to the general organization of the travel.

This trip could not take place without me. Two of the participants have never left the village before and barely know how to read. I am invested with the honorable mission of safely taking the proud Masai delegation to Kenya and escort them back, just as safely.

Not an easy prospect. We will travel for three days to the neighboring country and back, riding different buses. It's practically a world tour for someone who never set foot outside his own region.

Three of us already hold passports that enable us to cross national borders. Kaipai has even traveled as far as America – quite an extraordinary fact for a Masai – after a foundation took notice of him, in his capacity of mayor, and offered him a grant to come and learn English in the US. The *olaigwenani* and Mwenye Kiti, on the other hand, need to apply for official papers for the first time in their lives. Fortunately it is only a matter of obtaining a travel permit, the simple document being sufficient within the East African Community. Actual passports would put a strain on our budget and delay our travel plans unnecessarily. I am to travel to Arusha with the two men to apply for their papers.

A Special Mission

Being the tour leader for two respectable Masai men, both a good head taller than I am, does feel a little odd. The *olaigwenani* exudes this incredible calm, and despite leaving his familiar surroundings, he does not exhibit the slightest sign of anxiety. He carries only a tiny satchel, which cannot possibly hold a change of clothes for our ten-day journey. My head starts rattling. How is someone who has never traveled in his entire life supposed to know what he must pack up? On the other hand, I can hardly broach the subject with the leader of our community, especially not now. I decide to talk about it with Sokoine later. It is five o'clock in the morning, the air on this particular day in March, one of the hottest months of the year, still moderately cool. A long ride with many stages awaits us. We will need over six hours to cover the 330 kilometers to Arusha. Sokoine having provided two more motorbikes, we set off towards the bus station in Songe. From there we will travel to Arusha via Handeni. This part of the journey is already a big adventure for the two men, their eyes darting about as they take in the passing landscape.

Tired, hungry and covered with dust, we get off the bus in the evening, amongst the teeming crowds of Arusha, a most popular African tourist destination. Many people start their journey to Mount Kilimanjaro or various safaris to the surrounding national parks from here.

First thing next morning, we head straight to the district office, where a very unpleasant surprise awaits us.

"Sorry Madam, you've not come to the right place!"

I cannot believe my own ears, but the clerk shakes his head and gives me a very determined look.

"But why is that?"

His rejection has caught me off guard.

"This is not the competent office. You belong to the Manyana region and must thus apply for your papers in Babati," he tells us.

What a drag, I swear inwardly. I had not seen that one coming. My two travel companions cast questioning looks at me. Is our journey to fail on the very first attempt? The date for the boot camp has already been scheduled, we cannot show up later.

"We've got two options. Either we return to the village or we travel to Babati," I explain the two men.

They exchange a quick look and agree right away.

"Babati! We won't give up that easily!"

Luckily for us, Babati is only a two-hour bus drive away from Arusha. We rush back through the dense crowds to the bus station where I hastily buy tickets for the three of us, after having spotted our bus waiting at some distance. We drop on our seats, panting. It is already noon by now. We should be able to make it before the office closes. Normally.

But then, having lived in Africa for so long, I should know by now that the clock ticks differently here. As it is, the bus will not start.

"Hey, when are we leaving?" I call out of the window to the driver, who is presently enjoying a nice little chat with a few colleagues.

"We're leaving when we're leaving."

The driver's colleagues burst out laughing.

"We'll leave when there are more people on the bus."

All right then, it seems a little patience is required. It is actually two hours before enough travelers have got on the bus. We leave for Babati at about two o'clock and thus do not reach the office before closing time, naturally. No use getting angry, though, we will have to accept our present situation.

Once again, we find ourselves looking for an affordable accommodation, stomachs rumbling. What does a Masai eat on a trip? It is indeed quite a challenge for my travel companions.

"What are you eating, Stephanie? Worms?" the *olaigwenani* asks me, a skeptical look on his face.

I cannot help laughing. Whenever I get the chance to enjoy a more varied menu than my usual diet, I certainly take it! Yet these are not worms I am eating, but a plate of steaming hot spaghetti bolognaise.

"This is really good, try it! This is pasta made of flour and eggs," I reply, pushing my plate toward the two men. Gingerly, they load a small portion of spaghetti on their forks, their first ever pasta dish. They chew up and swallow a mouthful before exchanging a surprised look.

"Mmh, not so bad."

They go on trying other new dishes, such as chicken for instance, but in the end, seem quite happy to discover many stalls selling traditional food such as *ugali*, rice and meat with milk.

On the next morning, we finally get lucky. After a very long wait in the waiting room of the district office, it is our turn at last and we obtain the necessary travel papers without further difficulties. We have finally managed to overcome this major hurdle! It is, however, already noon and we still have to travel back to Arusha. It seems our mission is not meant to go off without a hitch, as after about an hour our bus suddenly starts sputtering. We stop by the side of the road.

"Breakdown! Everybody gets off please!" the driver announces.

Oh no, please no. We leave the bus and stretch our legs while the driver slips his head beneath the hood. The *olaigwenani* walks toward a small clearing in the bush and disappears in the thicket, probably to relieve himself.

"We're going on. Please get back on the bus," the driver calls after a while.

But our leader has not yet reappeared.

"What is he doing? Can somebody please go and check on him?" I ask the others.

Yet there he is already, hurrying towards us, a small stick in his mouth. Now I get it. He did not need to pee after all; he just got himself a "toothbrush". It had not crossed my mind that he might not have packed a "toiletry bag", an item he has no use of in the *boma*.

The Masai usually use small twigs of the Salvadora Persica, the botanical name of a bush otherwise known as the "toothbrush tree". Not only do the chewed up edges of these sticks clean the teeth quite efficiently, but the sap also disinfects the whole mouth.

Once in Arusha, we rejoin the two others and our little party is finally complete. When we have a moment to ourselves, I talk about the *olaigwenani* with Sokoine.

"I think he did not pack any change of clothes. This could be inconvenient for him," I explain to my husband.

"Let us buy two Masai cloaks and present him with them in thanks for his trust," answers my wise husband. "I'll give them to him."

Quite the diplomatic solution, allowing everyone to save face.

And now a quick dash to the bank. We need to procure Kenyan shillings.

We are able to afford the luxury version of the usual bus to Nairobi, namely a smaller, faster shuttle bus that does not stop at every turn of the road. It would be a much more lengthy journey otherwise. Our fellow travelers are a mix of tourists and locals. We set out for the seven-hour drive at eight o'clock in the morning, driving through the Longido district - a region inhabited mainly by Masai people - with Mount Longido looming in the background, after finally managing to leave the hustle and bustle of the city behind. A lot of Masai live here with large herds of cows and goats. The spectacle before our eyes is deeply concerning: brown steppe as far as the eye can reach. Nothing grows on the gigantic dusty surface. When the rain will set in after the dry season, huge craters will appear in the soil, but no lush vegetation will ever grow here again. All along the way, for dozens and dozens of kilometers across two different countries, the signs of drought are plain to see. This is exactly why we are making the journey in the first place.

Just before we reach the border my pulse quickens slightly. Hopefully there won't be any complications here, I think to myself, clutching the fifty-dollar bill I need for our visas. The driver has us leave the bus at the border station and we wait in line in front of the building with everyone else.

"Papers please!" the border official calls, casting a routine glance at our documents. "Please show your backpacks," he adds, as two dogs are brought in to sniff our belongings.

I notice my companions' questioning looks, but the whole thing is over before it even started.

"You got lucky; you don't carry any drugs," the official says, grinning, before stamping our passports and letting us through.

It is an historical moment for the *olaigwenani* and our mayor Mwenye Kiti: for the first time in their lives, they are crossing the border to another country. Unfortunately, there is no time to properly acknowledge the fact. Our next bus is already waiting for us and we resume our journey until we finally catch a glimpse of Nairobi's skyline in the distance.

The *olaigwenani* looks out of the window, his eyes widening.

"Why are the cars driving so fast, Stephanie? Why are they racing so much and where to?"

We all burst out laughing. He is perfectly right, of course, even though we stopped noticing the fact a long time ago. Even though I travel quite a lot, driving along the urban motorway of Nairobi, the Kenyan capital city, home to four and half million people, I confess I too feel overwhelmed by the pace and density of the city.

I have booked rooms in an affordable YMCA for the night, yet one with a private swimming pool, its sparkling waters calling out to me as soon as we have checked in.

"Do you think I can go and take a swim?" I ask Sokoine once we are alone in our room.

"I think you can."

Seeing me in a bathing suit could prove awkward for the Masai, but I do love swimming and don't want to miss such an opportunity. My entire life in the *boma* consists in adjusting and showing consideration. It is quite easy to lose sight of one's own needs. My body longs for the cool water and I manage to go to the pool unnoticed. We are all much too tired to do anything special tonight and early on the next morning, we set out for the last stage of our journey, Narok — yet not before having taken a stroll through the neighborhood.

I suddenly lose sight of the *olaigwenani* and start looking around frantically in search of him. He cannot have gone very far. Indeed I discover him, lying on a small patch of grass, with his eyes closed.

"*Olaigwenani*! Are you all right?" I call anxiously.

Opening his eyes, he gives me a tired look and smiles.

"I just want to lie down here for a little while," he replies, his voice filled with longing.

I understand his predicament. Here he is, a proud, almost two meters tall Masai leader, lying on a small stretch of grass in one of Africa's biggest cities. He needs grounding, in the truest sense of the word. How incredibly exciting and tiring all this must be for a man who usually lives in the bush, surrounded by silence and his animals. A foreigner in a world that is not made for him. What such a journey into the "modern" world might mean for a man of the bush makes me very thoughtful. We did not think to prepare him for what he would see, for this cultural shock; but then perhaps it is never really possible to properly prepare anyone for such overstimulation of the senses. I feel for him. I too have become accustomed to the quiet pace of the *boma*. Even for me, this racing, pulsating city is a bit of a challenge.

I am very moved by this scene. This journey turned out to be revealing and precious for me on so many levels, as I got to know the people from my village even better.

The Mara Training Center

On the next day, we travel for two hours in the direction of the city of Narok, on small, overcrowded intercity buses called Matata, a word meaning "problem" in Swahili. I wonder why that is...

Narok is the gateway to the legendary Masai Mara, the largest contiguous nature reserve of the Masai, bordering on the Serengeti National Park. Lying directly at the border to Masai Mara, our training center is very remote and rural. We all take a deep breath and stretch our legs. This is a place where the men will feel at ease. It is almost like home.

The next morning after breakfast, we meet our two trainers in the seminar room.

"My name is Richard Hatfield, but you can call me Richard. And here is my colleague, Mussa. We shall guide you through the next three days."

Here we are, sitting together in the Mara Training Center, three of us attending classes for the first time in their life. The contents of the boot camp are divided thematically. On day one, we are being taught practical agriculture: crop rotation, resistant varieties of grasses, irrigation, rain, soil condition, lots of biology. In the afternoon, we go to the adjoining fields and meadows to learn how to read the grass and the ground. We learn which plants are strong and resistant enough to thrive and grow even in desiccated soil.

The men listen closely to our trainers, Mussa translating his colleague's words whenever communication problems arise. Kaipai and Sokoine ask lots of question, feeling obviously at ease in this environment and fully trusting the two trainers. The matter of trust is actually quite essential. The *olaigwenani* is too timid and mostly listens. Not wishing to push myself into the foreground, I try to hold back to leave room for the others, as they will need to pass on their knowledge to the other men in our village.

On day one, everybody is still pretty much in his element. On the next day, however, the trainers get really down to business, tackling serious subjects related to the social sphere. My companions had not expected this. Richard talks about the role of women, children and culture, and how they are all connected to the entire community's future. The men wriggle in their chairs uneasily.

"You have many children, but with the increasing number of farms, you also have less and less land for the cows to graze. And then even more land disappears because of the drought. How do you expect to be able to feed your children in the future?"

These are difficult questions for the Masai – difficult, but also necessary. For the first time in their life, they are confronted with questions that challenge their long-standing culture and way of life. It is not easy for them.

I can literally hear their thoughts swirling about in their heads. But Richard does not let go.

"If each one of you has three wives and eight to ten children, and if, at the same time, the land and animal feed dwindles, what do you think will happen?" he asks the men between two meaningful pauses. "You will starve. Less land and less cattle also mean fewer children."

This is definitely hard on proud Masai men. Even though they don't speak openly about birth control and polygamy, they can still figure things out.

Having fewer children is one part of the solution. Merging the numerous smaller herds into a large one is the other part.

"Each small herd of cattle grazes here and there until there is nothing left. There is no structure, no possibility for grass to regenerate."

This makes sense to the men.

"If you think about things on a larger scale and allow the animals to graze together, then other larger meadows and pasture lands may have time to regenerate and grass will be able to grow undisturbed during the wet season. This creates a cycle that we call rotational grazing."

It all sounds logical and coherent; yet it is no easy matter for the Masai men, who would have to gather all the cows from the entire village district, about 130 *bomas*, and create an entirely new system for approximately 10,000 cows. Until now, the cattle herders have only watched over their own herds, which constantly graze the same surrounding meadows. They would henceforth have to lead their animals quite far from their own *boma*. This in turn means setting up new camps and appointing a few shepherds to watch over the entire herd – an utterly unconceivable situation for someone who works daily with his own animals. But then it would indeed allow the pasture land to recover during the period of time it is not being used, until it is once again available for grazing.

The group discusses all these matters extensively, also after class, Sokoine and the men sitting up together late into the night. They understand that everything the two trainers have told them is right and makes sense, yet they also know convincing the others will not be easy.

"If you want to protect your culture, you have to change it."

After three days of seminar, and with Richard's powerful message in mind, we set off for the journey back home.

Persuasive Efforts

Our trip has left a deep impression. The men want to capitalize about what we have just learned and pass on their newly acquired knowledge. Two days after our return, the *olaigwenani* and the mayor invite everyone for a meeting.

"Hey, they have even invited the women!" I realize with surprise.

Typically, the men keep to themselves. This time however, the women are also welcome to join the meeting. I am impressed. Could this be a first positive sign?

"Can I come too? What do you think?" I nonetheless ask Sokoine to be on the safe side.

The fact that I am a driving force of the project does not necessarily imply that I should take part in everything.

From all directions, the Masai head toward the square in the center of the village, gathering beneath a gigantic acacia tree and taking place on tree trunks or on the ground. A few chairs are provided for special guests. Excitement is in the air, snatches of serious conversations mingling with easy chatter. Everybody looks on expectantly, not knowing what this is all about. With great enthusiasm, the *olaigwenani* proceeds to explain what we have learned in Kenya, sticking to general issues for this first meeting. Wishing to gradually bring his audience to the heart of the matter, he has obviously decided to engage in a little "promotion."

At the second meeting, though, he gets to the point. Unsurprisingly, the initially positive atmosphere shifts at once.

"What? A herd with 10,000 cows?"

"Why should I give up my farm?"

"But how are we supposed to get food while the cows are away? The women and the children need milk."

"They're going to steal my cattle!"

"Never!"

"Hey, I only have one cow. I earn my living with my farm and you want to take that away from me?"

The Masai express a lot of fears. Quite understandably, the atmosphere of the meeting becomes quite heated. So many fears, questions, and problems arise. For many shepherds, the idea of merging the herds of the entire village is simply inconceivable. The flaw in the system appears quite plainly: there was always a land management system of sorts in our region, yet no one bothered to observe its rules and used the land at will, a land that, over the years, saw the emergence of many farms. Furthermore, one also needs to remember that for a Masai, a farm does not necessarily imply growing animal feed crops, as this does not correspond to their understanding as shepherds. Masai only grows corn or beans for their own use. Then, a few clever words are spoken:

"A Masai is a Masai, because he possesses cows, not because he is a farmer. If you value your farm more than you value your animals, our culture will disappear sooner or later."

The cows remaining in the *boma* would also need grazing land, which unfortunately is missing. This dilemma has not been brought about solely by the Masai, though. A lot of Swahili people have also settled in the area, setting up farms and claiming land for themselves. Sometimes, Masai have leased their land to the Swahili. How would a restitution of land even be possible?

The more I get involved in the matter, the clearer I recognize why it cannot work. The scale of the problem becomes increasingly overwhelming, a vast area having been divided into tiny plots of land that now need to be merged. Still, we need unity if we want to put the rotational grazing system into practice and thus protect our pasture land.

The problem is simply much too big. Attending one seminar is not enough to change things, let alone raise much enthusiasm. The villagers understand the benefit of the project, but its implementation is just too complex.

The conflicts also show quite plainly that the *olaigwenani* does not possess the necessary assertiveness to hold such meetings. He simply is not able to prevail upon the enraged crowd. Not being a man of opposition, he gradually drops the matter in the face of such vehement protests, his initial euphoria soon fizzling out.

"Couldn't we try to put the system in place on a smaller portion of land and with fewer animals?"

This question keeps going through our minds. Would that be a viable compromise?

In the end, the project comes to nothing. I am badly disappointed, but I still accept the fact. No one dares tell me so, though. The Masai are much too polite to turn me down, or give me a direct rejection. It happens rather incidentally.

"The *olaigwenani* no longer does anything," I complain to Sokoine.

"Leave him be. We have called up another meeting," my husband retorts right away to placate me. "You should stay at home, though; it might get a little trying."

All right then, a small muzzle for Steph, I think to myself. Three months after our trip to Kenya, I address a short note to the mayor and the traditional leader. He cannot read that well, but he did teach himself the basics, and I made sure to write extra large letters. On the note, I list everything that we have already achieved along with all the things that still need to be done. No reaction. Nothing. That makes me very sad.

"Why won't they even react?" I ask Sokoine, upset.

"Stephanie, you can tell people once, and you can tell them twice. But if you have to go and tell them a third time, you might as well drop the whole thing. It won't get better just because you insist."

Still, I keep trying to take small steps forward all the while understanding people's concerns very well. Their cows are their most precious possession; they spend their whole life with them. It feels to them as if someone would ask them to abandon their children in the steppe. They are afraid and change always causes fear. Plus, for a person who owns 5 or perhaps 30 cows, it is difficult to comprehend how a megaherd could actually make more sense.

It is as if I would attempt to pass an elephant through the eye of a needle. The epitome of an impossible enterprise. In the end, I realize that my influence as a white woman does not matter.

Is this the end of the land management project, then? Has it all been in vain? For a long time, this is how it feels to me. I have worked so hard for this, with a specific goal in mind, praying to raise enough money and moving heaven and earth to make things happen. But then, the project has not failed. It has just found another ending. It is all about process work. We are in transition, but things don't happen as fast as I had imagined they would. I confess to being a little frustrated, but I will not be discouraged. I shall simply continue.

Perhaps they need to learn things the hard way, through another drought that is, to give the whole project another thought - whether there will still be enough time for that is another question. Climate change is gaining massive momentum and not enough is done, worldwide, regarding environmental protection, to stop the process. The best land management project won't be of any use when temperatures rise even more and water becomes not only scarce, but disappears altogether. No water, no life.

CHAPTER 12

Memut elukunya nabo eng'eno

One single mind cannot be all-wise.

"Hey Stephanie, you're doing amazing things! I frequently travel to Tanzania to organize trips for women to climb Mount Kilimanjaro. Do you want to meet?" Cate Butcher writes to me.

Cate is Australian and engages in many exciting projects. I like her right away. Scrolling through her Instagram profile, I realize we share the same kind of commitment. Cate herself first came to Tanzania in 2017 to climb Mount Kilimanjaro.

"This trip changed my life," she writes to me in one of our chats. "The magic of the mountain, the connection with the guides, the country, all this deeply moved me."

How well I understand her! Five weeks after her first trip, she returned to the country. Abraham, the guide who took her up Mount Kilimanjaro and who belongs to the Chagga people, took her to his village, where she witnessed great poverty.

Many families sleep on the floor in very primitive huts, having barely enough to live on. Cate would like to help and as it is, she finds different ways to do so, focusing especially on single women, abandoned by their husbands. Together with the Days for Girls international organization that campaigns worldwide for better menstrual hygiene, she decides to start a project of washable sanitary pads in Tanzania, all the while offering trekking tours for women to Mount Kilimanjaro on her Internet page *Wanderlust Women's Adventures*, where she also collects donations.

We started writing to each other on a regular basis and soon became close friends. It was Cate who gave me the idea for my new project.

It is some time before I manage to get over the disappointment I felt at the failure of our land management project. But it just was too big a project for us and my influence on the men in this village is not strong enough. Still, I do hope all the helpful insights we were able to gain won't remain in vain. Someday, all this knowledge will pay off.

I will not be deterred from my plan, though, and I shall continue to try and think of possible ways to help my family in the *boma*.

If men are too complicated and the former project is too big, what about women? Let's reduce the scale of our ambitions a little and focus on the women around me, I think, my head buzzing with thoughts as I research. What would help women? Thanks to my friendship with Cate, I suddenly see what has been under my very nose all along: menstruation and monthly hygiene.

"Stephanie, how do women in your *boma* deal with menstruation?" Cate asks, leaving me pensive.

"I think most of them don't do anything about it. Many don't even possess underwear."

Why have I not tackled that specific issue before? I still cannot quite believe this; perhaps the Masai's reserve and introversion might account in part for the fact. Menstruation is a matter of shame, respect, and boundaries. So many subjects are not addressed among Masai women. Anything intimate and private is off-limits. I, for one, am not especially uptight, but I do respect their culture too much to break any taboo.

"Ask the women if they would be interested in a visit from me. I'll bring sanitary pads, and we can talk about women's health."

I take Cate's offer to heart; it is probably better that she, as an outsider, should be the one broaching these subjects.

Finding the right moment to organize such a meeting is no easy matter, though. One day, however, Mama Klaudia, Yeolei, Ngallande and I all sit together with other women, the atmosphere between us suddenly close and intimate.

"A friend of mine will come visit us soon. She would like to bring something for you," I say, mustering up my courage.

"What kind of thing?" they ask, curious.

"Something for women."

I cannot put things plainly right away and decide to take a more cautious approach. "Something very practical for when you have your period."

A few women start giggling with embarrassment, others lower their eyes.

"That sounds interesting," Mama Klaudia declares after a little while. "Your friend is most welcome. I would like to hear more about it."

Encouraged by Mama Klaudia's reaction, other women venture to display a cautious interest. One big hurdle has just been overcome.

In August 2018, Cate visits us in the *boma*. She starts the reunion by handing out to each woman lovely cloth bags containing a set of sanitary pads mostly made of removable and replaceable components. Cautiously, almost with reverence, the girls and women unfasten the strings of the bags to take out the sets. The general mood is both tense and relaxed, the women obviously delighted by the lovely items. Afterward, as we sit together in a circle, they start talking.

"We're among us. There's no man around listening."

Cate tells them how often the pads need to be washed, how it is done, and how they are supposed to be used in the first place.

"Menstruation connects women all around the world. We all bleed, no matter the color of our skin or whether we possess a lot of money or not."

She finds exactly the right words to conquer the women's hearts, who listen to her, spellbound, nodding in agreement.

"This is not something we should feel ashamed about. Let us talk about it openly."

The spell is broken. Even though not all women dare to ask questions during our gathering, many conversations arise afterward in private, the women confessing to me all manner of awkward situations they found themselves in due to lack of supplies.

"I was about to make tea for my husband when my period started, staining my clothes, the blood trickling down my leg. My husband grew very impatient, and I did not have time to clean myself," one of Sokoine's aunts told me.

Another elderly aunt, who often comes to visit, also recalls extremely embarrassing occurrences quite openly.

"Here you are, riding a motorbike to attend a ceremony and when you get off, you discover your clothes are ruined. Of course, you don't have any change of clothes, and you cannot possibly wash off the stains either. So unpleasant. I'll take a set for my daughters and granddaughters, too."

Sendo, Sokoine's sister, is enthusiastic too.

"Stephanie, these things are just great. It is a huge help. Could I have another set?"

Not only does she get another one, but she also gets a few extra ones for the women in the neighboring *boma*.

The demand is huge. Female visitors keep knocking on my door, asking for pads sets, the enthusiasm about the subject of menstruation steadily rising since Cate and I exchanged our first messages. For me, the women's strong wish to have and use the pads is quite instrumental. They would never have broached the subject on their own, but once Cate introduced them to the topic, they dare express their needs. After some more research, I set up my next two crowdfunding campaigns, making sure to narrow my target this time, so as not to repeat the same mistakes as in my first project.

Who needs sanitary pads the most while being utterly unable to afford them? Young girls have no income and they certainly don't dare mention such issues. This is why I chose the secondary school in Lesoit for my project. About 250 girls attend that school, some of them even living inside the building, their home being too far away. Their parents struggle a lot to afford school fees, and there is no money left for other things. One kit costs 10 dollars. I will need at least 2,500 dollars to provide a set for every girl in the school.

At first, I have to discuss the project with the school administration to make sure they support and agree to it. As a matter of fact, they appear very open-minded and glad that the girls should be offered such an opportunity. I get to work. It takes half the time to set up the campaign than it did on my first attempt, but then I do know how to go about things now. The structures are in place, and my channels have expanded.

"Stephanie, this is great, I'll gladly support this!"

"Great project!"

Once again, I get a lot of positive feedback. Less than four weeks after opening the fundraising page in August, we collected the necessary money and even a little more. I travel to Arusha to meet with the Umoja organization that will sew the pads sets; then I return to the *boma*, heavily loaded.

The twelve-hour ride allows a lot of time for thinking. The more people involved in producing the pads, the more money I need to make. The long bus ride to Arusha is also extremely time and energy-consuming. So many women and girls in our area still have no supplies. And then the sets, no matter how carefully people will use them, certainly won't last forever. How about setting up a sewing workshop here, which incidentally would also create jobs? It would be a source of income for our family and help the women reach economic independence – making them also independent from their husbands. The idea comes to me in a flash. It is the birth of the Masai Women Enterprise, a sanitary pad manufacturer in our *boma*.

First I bring the sets I bought to the students, which unsurprisingly results in quite a lot of giggling and whispering on their part. We are all gathered in a sheltered place, far from the boys' prying ears. I have to go about it even more carefully than before. The sense of shame is far more significant in this age group. But then perhaps this is the perfect opportunity to show them that menstruation is no shameful matter. These girls will grow up differently than their mothers and grandmothers.

We need sewing machines and fabric for my new project. First of all, we need to learn how to use the machines. My knowledge is not strong enough to teach the other women to use the machines.

"Evelyn, could you train us if I come to see you with a few women?"

Evelyn is a cheerful, lively woman I met during the Umoja project, and I feel certain that she is the right person for that job.

"With pleasure, Stephanie. How many women do you plan to come with? You should schedule about four days of training. It'll definitely take as much."

I ponder this for a while and decide to travel to Arusha with two other women. We need food, accommodation, money for the training course, and bus fare. Moreover, the whole thing only makes sense if we can purchase our own sewing machines quite soon and start working right away in a dedicated place.

The surplus from the second crowdfunding not being enough to pay for everything, I decide to launch a third campaign right away. It will have to be the last time I resort to this solution. I don't want to keep asking people for money, which is why I have decided to create this new "company."

Who is best suited for the training among the women in the village? Sendo's name comes to mind at once. Sendo is my sister-in-law, and she is always open to new ideas. She also lives only twenty minutes away from our *boma*.

"Stephanie, this is great. I want to be part of this!" she enthusiastically replies when I tell her about it.

Finding the right people, however, is not such an easy matter. Most women already have very busy days. Lots of them are pregnant or else have just given birth, while others don't trust themselves to be able to take part in the training. After all, many of them have never seen a sewing machine before, let alone used one. I must confess I, too, feel a little uneasy using the foot pedal while holding the fabric in place to create a neat pad. It will definitely take a lot of training, but then I cannot possibly expect to create a company without being able to handle the equipment myself. Perhaps the other women will feel less timid once they see our sewing workshop with their own eyes.

"Stephanie, I would like to learn how to sew and work with you," Rehema, one of Sendo's neighbors, declares.

Even though Rehema was not my first choice, I am still very happy to see her that interested. We don't get along very well yet, but I will give her a chance.

The three of us set out in January 2019. Rehema has already traveled to Arusha before as part of a church mission, but for Sendo, it is a first. She has never left her *boma* and has never been on a bus before. Both women have slept in Yayai's house so we would be able to leave together at five o'clock in the morning, first on motorbikes to Songe, and then from there with the bus. The big difference with the trip to Kenya I took earlier lies in the fact that women show their feelings much more than men. They are not afraid to lose face and watch the passing landscape and animals with open enthusiasm. A women's community is indeed something quite different.

We finally reach Arusha at six o'clock in the evening, completely worn out. Sendo is not quite at ease with the bustling city life and is understandably, very afraid. The noise, the dense crowds, the honking cars make her very jittery. We go to buy some food before checking into our rooms in the hotel, which is not far from the training center. Sendo and Rehema share one room, while I sleep alone in the other one.

"Stephanie, come quickly! Someone is standing in front of our window and keeps peeping into our room."

Around nine o'clock, I was roused from half-sleep by a loud knocking on the door.

"Sendo is seeing ghosts," Rehema says, rolling her eyes, while my sister-in-law casts an anxious look at me.

"No, Stephanie. There was someone."

I, too, believe that the state of her nerves, added to her exhaustion, must have played a trick on her. If this was my first night ever in a big city, I would be very much afraid too and I suddenly recall my terrifying encounter with a leopard during my second stay in Africa. Surely the noises of the city sound just as dangerous and menacing to Sendo as the leopard did to me.

"You know what? We'll close the windows and draw the curtains so no one will be able to take a look inside anymore. Perhaps this will help."

As it is, I was right and the rest of the night goes by without any further incidents.

Sendo likes Evelyn and the atmosphere at Umoja right away. She carefully observes the women's easy and precise gestures, watching them talk together and show their completed models. She absolutely wants to learn how to make these too. At first she leaves all the talking to me, yet after a while she gradually comes out of her shell, asking questions and engaging in conversation with the other women.

"I'd like to try the mandazi biscuits with chai first and then have some meat," Sendo declares, becoming even bolder during the meal we all share after the training.

Sendo herself also draws the other guests' attention. She truly is a beauty and people's eyes are fixed on the proud and tall Masai woman. Most Masai in Arusha belong to the Kisongo tribe. The Parakuyo, the tribe our family belongs to, are far less represented. The Parakuyo women's jewelry is more striking and Sendo, as a married woman, wears several rows of silver headbands wrapped around her head, while long silvery earrings dangle from her ears.

As we sit in the restaurant, I notice one man in particular, who can barely take his eyes off my sister-in-law.

"Look, Sendo, you've caught someone's eye already," I say teasingly, discreetly pointing at the guy.

Sendo giggles, embarrassed. When the guy starts following us out of the restaurant, we no longer laugh, though.

"Steph, we should run!"

I can hear the panic in her voice.

"No, we don't run. We will not show that guy that we are afraid. But we won't return to our hotel. We'll go to another one," I whisper to the two women.

Sendo and Rehema give me an anxious look. We don't know that man's intentions, and I don't want him to know where we are staying. I am starting to get nervous myself. After all, I am responsible for the two of them. What if he attacks us? On an impulse, I turn at a corner, and we step into another hotel.

"May I help you?" the security guard, a Masai himself, asks us kindly.

We explain the situation to him.

"You sit down here for a while. I'll go check things out," the security guard replies, clearly proud to protect us.

Ten minutes later, our pursuer gives up the chase, the fierce expression on our protector's face seemingly having made quite an impression on him. Very much relieved, we quickly walked the remaining 500 meters to our hotel. We never saw that guy again, fortunately.

Four days later, our training completed, Sendo is once again put to the test, as she and Rehema will return to Lesoit without me. I would like to stay a few more days in the city to do some shopping and run some errands. Some time off just by myself will do me good.

"You can do this!" I exclaim encouragingly, waving goodbye to the departing bus.

Now that we halfway know how to sew, all we need are sewing machines. Acquiring these shall be our next step.

"I believe it will be no trouble finding sewing machines in Handeni," Sokoine declares in support of the project.

That he should be the one buying the machines makes sense because, as a white woman, I will probably get charged much more than he would.

"No problem, I'll go with my cousin," he agrees willingly.

Transportation turns out to be a whole different story, though, as two bulky sewing machines, floor stand included, cannot possibly be carried back to the *boma* by bus, being far too expensive and fragile to risk damaging them during the ride. I suggest the men travel to Handeni by bus and then rent a car for the journey back.

And that is how they do it.

After the two men have returned to the *boma* with their precious load, we start to assemble the machines at once and soon notice that two important screws are missing. The machines are inoperable. The huge structures were fastened to the car's roof during the ride. Either the screws fell off during the bumpy drive, or they never were included in the package in the first place. I had anticipated the arrival of these machines with such joy and now justifiably feel devastated. I am so upset that I take it out on Sokoine – regrettably, I have to admit.

"You go all the way to Handeni only to return with two non-functioning machines? Couldn't you have checked them before?" I snap.

Quite predictably, Sokoine does not find my outburst very amusing.

"Go get them yourself next time!" he retorts angrily.

The next morning, however, as the nice man he is, Sokoine sets out once again on the three-hour journey to Handeni, and after that final trip, we can finally assemble the sewing machines and start working.

Our enterprise has one flaw. I don't have the necessary funds to pay the two women, Sendo and Rehema, without making money first. What is more, the three of us do not yet sew well enough to be able to sell our products. Practice, practice, practice - is the motto that will turn crooked, uneven stitches into decent pieces. We also need to work on our pace. Producing one single pad still takes far too much time. It will not pay off this way. But all of this is not a problem for Sendo.

"I thank you for your patience and the opportunity, Stephanie," she declares in answer to my doubts.

During the next few weeks, she walked the distance between our bomas to toil away on the sewing machine almost every second day. Her enthusiasm is plain to see, as is her obvious talent. A humming sound like a litter of purring kittens soon fills our hut, as the fabric slides smoothly under the rattling needles.

Rehema, on the other hand, turns out to be a total disappointment.

"I won't work here if I don't get paid," she says testily.

"Look Rehema, I don't get paid either while I practice here with you."

She does not seem to realize the importance of the workshop I have financed in advance and simply stops showing up, a fact I find extremely upsetting, quite understandably.

"I need to organize orders and also think about advertisement, so we can start to make money. Do you think you can manage on your own, Sendo?"

My sister-in-law beams at me.

"No problem, Stephanie! You do your job and I'll do mine and sew."

I use my social media channels as advertising platforms, posting a few pictures and videos of our production.

"Stephanie, could you do a hundred sets for us? I'd love to hand them out here. Love, Annika!"

I barely dare believe my own eyes after reading Annika's mail. Whenever she comes to visit from Germany, she too lives with a Masai, in Kwediboma, a village about one hour away from our *boma*. Annika's is our first order. We need to show her that the Masai Women Enterprise runs perfectly well.

"Sendo, we're about to earn our first money!"

My sister-in-law's face lights up. We both set to work, dividing up the different work steps between us so we could be as efficient as possible. I cut the fabric, and Sendo, being a much faster seamstress than I am, sews. Once all the different pieces are spread out before us, we start sewing, our machines rattling against the clock. This is not the only order we get, though, and our flourishing small enterprise soon picks up speed.

Our Village Goes Viral

"Could you teach me Swahili?"

I have regularly taught language classes, being constantly on the lookout for occasions to earn money and provide for our family. It will be some time before the sanitary pad manufacturing starts paying off, not to mention that Sendo and I are the only ones currently working. I rely on my social media channels to draw people's attention to the language classes or the manufacturing.

One particular request, however, stands out from the rest of the messages. Dagmara manages Mambo View Point Lodge, located in the Usambara Mountains in East Tanzania.

"I have read your post in Expats in the Arusha Facebook group," she writes.

A friend of mine, whom I met in Ifakara, has created this group. I know now where my services might be needed.

It is 2020, the first year of COVID-19, and Tanzania is one of the few countries still open to tourism.

"I am new here, and because of COVID-19, there are almost no travelers," she continues. "I have plenty of time to learn the language better."

We exchange emails at first, but soon talk over the phone. I will visit for two weeks, staying and eating at my friend's place for free and teaching her two or three hours of Swahili every day.

The best news, however, is yet to come.

"You can come with your husband and your son. It is wonderful out here and we've got lots of toys."

What a lovely offer! Things are just perfect. Shortly before, I have also accepted the invitation of another German woman to take part in a market in Arusha, where we will be able to sell our pads. The Usambara Mountains, about 260 kilometers away from our *boma*, are situated in the Lushoto district. From Arusha, it is about 360 kilometers - almost a small world tour. But it will also be a nice adventure, as we have never been there before. We decide to combine the two trips and look forward to this family excursion with much anticipation and joy.

The market proves very successful. We sell many sets, which we present discreetly, having deliberately chosen a spot visited mainly by women. Unlike the shy Masai, women belonging to other ethnic groups are far less reserved. They are also familiar with washable pads - selling our products proves much easier than in our village.

By then, the COVID-19 pandemic had left its mark in Arusha: there are fewer tourists, a major problem for many locals whose income comes from tourism.

Before setting out for the day-long journey to the Usambara Mountains, we decide to buy some food for the road.

"Mama, Mama, when will we be there?" Yannik keeps asking, very excited.

"We won't be there before tonight, darling, but there will be a lot to see on the way."

We tackle the main part of the journey to Korogwe on a bigger bus, then switch to a smaller vehicle for the last part that steadily climbs up steep paths toward the mountains. Despite the tarred road, the journey still proves rather unpleasant, the small bus often teetering quite close to the edge.

"I am a little afraid," I whisper to Sokoine in a low voice so Yannik won't hear me.

Sokoine squeezes my hand for courage.

Planted by German colonial rulers, huge fir trees line the road as strange and foreign reminders of the colonial past of the region, a small Black Forest within the Tanzanian landscape. The fir trees were probably supposed to lend stability to the roads and cushion the impact of falling rocks. As it is, they also block the view of the deadly precipice, which suits me just fine. With my fingers dug deep into the seat, I try to take deep breaths and not think about what would happen if the driver, with his fast driving style, misjudges the distance to the edge. In the end, we arrive in one piece in the small city of Lushoto, which rests at about 1,400 meters and shares its name with the local district. The path leading to the small village of Mambo is becoming increasingly steep and challenging, so we rent a car for the last part of our journey, which is another two-and-a-half-hour drive.

"I am not riding on a bus on this bad road, no way!" I warned Sokoine.

Yannik is traveling with us, and I don't want to endanger him. Sokoine did not even try to convince me. Adventurous and frightening as the ride might have been, the view and the location of Mambo View Point Lodge is breathtakingly beautiful. Mambo Poa means very good in Swahili, and the exceptional view makes up for the journey's exertions.

"Welcome, it's so nice to have you here!" Dagmara exclaims, greeting us with open arms.

She takes us for a small tour of the compound that stretches over the hilly grounds, where white roundhouses with thatched roofs, nestled in small plateaus, are connected to one another by small paths and narrow climbs. Dagmara then shows us where we will take our meals for the next three weeks. Mountain Cottage, at the highest point of the compound, offers an extraordinary panoramic view of the Usambara Mountains. There won't be any excursion for us today, though. We are all completely worn out. Yannik marvels at our room, which, of course, is nothing like his home in the *boma*. Lots of cushions and thick blankets cover two large double beds and there is even a fireplace in the room, which we will actually need as we are soon about to find out.

"Mama, I am cold!" Yannik says, coming up to me, teeth chattering.

He is right; it is cold, the wind blowing up here in the mountain nothing like the wind we are accustomed to in the *boma*. It is August, the coldest season of the year. We clearly did not bring the right clothes, although I did buy an extra sweater in Arusha, Dagmara having warned me about the cold temperatures. However, one sweater was not halfway enough. We resort to wearing all our clothes, like many onion layers. Dagmara fetches extra blankets for us and a pair of woolen leggings for me. I am very grateful. The three of us look really weird now, but we don't care. Most of the time we sit close to the fire, enjoying our time despite the cold. On clear days one can spot Mount Kilimanjaro in the distance. Yannik soon turns into a small mountain goat, fearlessly climbing every hill and elevation while I struggle to keep his adventurous spirit in check as he speeds along the narrow trails.

There are two other guests in the Lodge apart from us, Kaja and Mateusz.

"Where are you from?" Yannik asks them, breaking the ice at once.

It is quite an extraordinary feeling, the five of us having the normally well-booked location all for ourselves.

"We're from Poland; we are here for work."

This is no chance encounter. Dagmara, the manager of the lodge, also comes from Poland. The three of them have met in the Polish embassy. As filmmakers and bloggers, Kaja and Mateusz travel the world, an enterprise currently very much limited by the pandemic. We like each other from the start and, as it seems we share some kind of community of fate, we decide to take our meals together.

"We like to take a look behind the scenes. We also want to clear up prejudices, which is why we started our channel, Globstory. 'One earth, many worlds', this is our motto," Kaja explains. "We have been full-time travelers for seven years now and have been traveling all around the world."

We enjoy deep and engaging conversations. Dagmara does not have as much time as she had initially hoped and our lessons are not as long as anticipated, which means we are able to take many walks in the area. After one week, Sokoine has had enough of the trip. He is bored.

"I think I'll go back home with Yannik," he announces.

I am okay with this. I would not be able to teach lessons with my bubbly four-year old anyway, if Sokoine decided to go home on his own. We enjoyed some nice family time here and did a lot of things together, but I will have just as nice a time here on my own. After the two of them leave, I will perform translation work for Dagmara to help her and write a lot. I also go climbing and generally enjoy the company of the Polish couple.

"Stephanie, would you like us to visit your village and make a film? I have been thinking about that for a few days now. Your story is very moving and would fit in on our channel."

I am not surprised by Kaja's question and I don't need to give it a lot of thought. I feel honored that such a successful filmmaker should choose us of all people. Yet there is something I need to clarify from the start.

"I am very pleased by your offer, Kaja, but I don't want to be the center of attention. I'd much rather talk about the Masai's problems."

Having spent two very intense weeks with Kaja and having watched many of her videos on her YouTube channel, I do know that she is far from being superficial. Quite the contrary. Her films are extremely documented and insightful. Still it seems important to me to state that I do not wish to be the focus of attention.

"I understand your reservations and we shall weave your story into the film, because a German woman living with the Masai, and committed to them for so long, is also very interesting," she replies. "But the focus will be on the Masai's living conditions, their fight for the preservation of their culture and the consequences of climate change. I am interested in the living conditions of the people you chose to make your home with."

This sounds good to me and I readily agree. I can see we share the same values – which unfortunately is not always the case. I get a lot of messages from journalists and bloggers, but not everyone does a quality job, though. I always try to consider the various proposals with a critical eye, more often than not rejecting a particular project if it seems dubious to me. Part of the problem lies in the fact that many Masai are being marketed as a "tourist attraction." The resulting "business model" fills me with unease as I see fake *bomas*, plastic jewelry, and allegedly authentic Masai rituals that are not true to the reality of the indigenous tribe's everyday life. It is therefore a major concern to me that the videos should not expose them, gloss over their lives or make them appear in any way different than they actually are. I want to show the people with all their facets and emotions, not only neatly staged Masai lightheartedness. I want people to see what it actually means to tackle everyday life under such difficult and changing circumstances.

It is agreed. I need a little time if I am to travel to Lesoit next week. I also need to see to a few sewing orders, but after that, Kaja and Mateusz are most welcome. By the end of September, they come to visit us in the *boma* for three days.

I have prepared my family as best I could ahead of their visit.

"Look here, this is what it will look like," I said, showing them some of their other YouTube videos and telling them how things could be done in our case, Kaja having told us in advance what kind of pictures she would like to take.

"I know this is all very exciting for everyone, but perhaps they'll manage to take things a little easy," she says hopefully.

In that hope, we first share a cup of tea upon their arrival.

The children are literally beside themselves with excitement. After they have set eyes on the huge camera and the drone hurtling above our heads, it grows even more. The scenes of our *boma* seen from above turn out positively amazing, providing a whole new perspective that enchants us all.

Kaja and Mateusz have prepared a rough script for the video but also want to leave room for things to happen organically. They repeatedly attempt to film the children playing, but as soon as they notice the camera aiming at them, all the children come running to the camera.

"Stephanie, what can we do?" Kaja asks, laughing, after yet another take has failed.

"Keep trying!" I answer, laughing too.

Having my own YouTube channel, I am somewhat accustomed to the whole filming process and don't feel overly nervous. I can just keep on working the way I always do. We stroll through the village as I answer her questions and tell her about our life. Kaja and Mateusz are very talented professionals. They work at a very slow pace and leave us a lot of space, their pictures allowing even me to consider our village with new eyes. 25 minutes of our daily routine, our daily work, without any special effects and not too much editing. Unaltered, including the tears I very often cannot hold back when talking about my close relation with Yayai or my love for the Masai. But we also laugh just as often.

On the first evening, Kaja is very enthusiastic about the fading warm light of day as we drive the cattle back.

"I would love to capture that," she explains to me.

This, however, requires some preparation, as the young shepherds must be told beforehand that they will need to drive the cattle back to the *boma* from the "right" angle on the following evening. Indeed the shepherds do everything just like they did on the previous day. We, on the other hand, slightly miscalculated the time - the whistling and the ringing and tinkling of the bells echoing before the camera is even in position.

"They're coming, they're coming!" we cry, rushing madly to the dedicated spot.

"Done, it's a wrap!" Kaja declares, relieved.

When Kaja and Mateusz leave after three days, I am exhausted but also confident that they will piece together the right moments. And now we wait.

They made three films out of the raw footage, one of them a very long interview with Sokoine. This video, posted eight weeks after their visit, is much celebrated in the village. I watch Sokoine react to his interview; he is very moved, his eyes are moist, and the expression on his face clearly shows he feels he has been seen and understood. It is some time before Kaja posts the next video. She has been sick and it is not before two months later, on December 29, that I get a message from her saying: "Stephanie, I have posted it."

Four hours later, she writes again: "I cannot believe this! 50,000 people have watched the video already!"

And then again a few hours later: "Stephanie, the video is going viral!"

The term "viral" used to make me smile. Now, however, I get a first-hand experience of what it actually means - along with what it does to people.

None of us can quite believe it until things really get crazy. Something happens that up to this day I still cannot comprehend.

Kaja makes awe-inspiring videos, yet most of her followers are in Poland, as she films and explains her videos in Polish. Only few of her videos have English subtitles. But because we spoke English together, she used Polish subtitles for our videos, which meant we could reach more people.

The following days and weeks are sheer madness. Everyday, at least 100,000 people from all around the world watch our Masai video. Everyday, I sit in front of my small screen and shake my head in disbelief. After ten days, the million mark is crossed.

My Instagram page has gone wild, as has my Facebook account, my YouTube channel, my mailbox and the news channels. The 5,000 followers I had before the videos were posted soon became 60,000. It is absolutely overwhelming. I cannot answer to the countless messages I receive and feel both enthusiastic and swamped. I was not aware that something like that was even possible and I had certainly not anticipated what it would feel like. Sheer madness, that's what it is. It takes three or four hours daily to try and answer as many messages as I possibly can. People write to me from India, America, South America, the Philippines, Australia, Germany, Africa. There is no end to it. We are flooded by an ocean of praise, interest and sympathy. I won't ever forget that feeling - so many people taking interest in our lives. By 18 million followers I stop checking the numbers. It is simply too much.

The video also draws the attention of other journalists and requests from TV channels from all around the world start coming in every day. I do Zoom interviews with Australian, Polish, and Bulgarian channels. Even the press of my home country contacts me and I do a major interview with the *Süddeutsche Zeitung* newspaper.

I feel relieved once the madness has subsided a little. For all the joy and excitement it brings, going viral is exhausting, both mentally and physically. Because we still need to proceed with our daily chores. The high numbers of viewers demonstrate people's interest, but they do not secure a livelihood. This is not an income model despite what some people seem to imply from time to time.

All in One: A Blessing and a Curse

There is a dark side to that massive visibility, the violence of which I had not in the least expected.

"You're exploiting the Masai."

"You're profiteering."

"Another white **woman showing** off her proud Masai."

Upon reading such comments at first, my heart nearly broke.

Words can be as harmful as swords. I do pay a high price at times for my work on social media. People who do not know me judge me, insult and accuse me. That hurts. It is unfair and untrue. At first, I tried to respond and explain myself, but I soon realized some people are not interested in discussing it with me. They will stick to their opinion without really knowing anything. Fortunately, other followers often step in in my defense, replying to the discriminating and insulting posts. I feel grateful that most of my followers are peaceful and appreciative, but I must confess that the reproach and the blame get to me. But then, I guess it just cannot be avoided.

I have been living in the bush for eleven years now, under rather simple circumstances, and I am co-responsible for a large family of more than 40 people, who rely on me. Sokoine and I have decided on that path as a couple, so he can live like a Masai and not work as a security guard on Mafia, and also to preserve our family. I have invested my entire inheritance in our lives and would do it again without a moment's hesitation. But that money is all spent now. The drought has taken a heavy toll on us and we do not know what to expect in the future. This is why I seize every possible opportunity to secure our living, whether with the sanitary pads project, the Swahili lessons, the lectures – or this book. It all flows into the family and this makes me really proud. It truly is my life's work.

The verbal attacks no longer hurt me as much as they did in the past. It only gets harder when they involve my son.

"You're robbing your son of his chances at a better future."

I have heard this and so much more.

"Why doesn't Yannik learn German?"

People often blame me for that. Apart from Maa and Swahili, Yannik currently learns English at school. It would not be wise at this point to impose on him a fourth language. A language he does not even use in his daily life. Apart from the fact that this specific issue is nobody's business, there are many questions I have not yet found an answer to myself. My son has grown up a very happy child who is very close to nature. He is loved and free, and has so many invaluable experiences. If there is one thing I have come to understand in the past few years, it is the fact that we can learn more from the Masai than during many pointless classes. Sokoine and I will always, as parents, consider Yannik's future and decide together what is right for him.

Fame does not put food on our table, nor does it change the climate, but I can use the media to draw attention to the Masai's fate. And that is not all. The awareness of the people following me is changing. I can move people's hearts all around the world simply by telling them about my daily life and the consequences of climate change on my village's fate. This, indeed gives me a lot of hope. If I can achieve something when I'm nothing but a tiny speck in a small village in Tanzania, imagine what we could all accomplish if we put our insights and visions into practice. Just as the Masai need to change to preserve their way of life, people in Europe and in the rest of the world need to do so too.

I am not a Masai

I am not a Masai! I have to make that clear time and again. I am married to a Masai, I live in a Masai village and I am part of a Masai family. My son grows up in his father's culture. But I am not a Masai. I need to state this clearly. One is born a Masai. Marriage alone cannot turn me into a Masai. The respect I have for the culture of my husband's and my son's people is far too great. This is also why I only wear traditional clothes and jewelry on very special occasions, when the others expressly wish me to. It would not feel right otherwise.

Looking back, I recognize that most of the decisive turning points in my life have occurred by chance, and because of my trust in life. I rarely knew where one particular decision would lead me, whether it was going abroad, meeting my English friends, studying in Great Britain, or coming across a flier and volunteering to go to Africa. If I had not traveled to the lodge for a language class, I would never have met Kaja. And without her video about our *boma*, all these people all around the world would never have heard about us in the first place. Nor would this book have been written. I did not plan all this. It was brought forth by my own curiosity and thirst for adventure, as well as the chance fact that led me to a remote village in Tanzania. I have quite a journey behind me - a journey people can only relate to with great difficulty, which has often made me feel isolated and abandoned. It was too much for some friends, and they could not accept the path I had chosen. These friends I have lost. But in the end, one can only ever make decisions for oneself.

"Stephanie, do you want to live with the Masai forever?" my followers ask me.

"I don't know," I reply truthfully. "I don't know what life has in store for me."

One thing is sure, though: the Masai people will forever be in my heart.

EPILOGUE

For a long time, I wondered whether or not I should write this book.

It took extraordinary people, whose job is to tell extraordinary life stories, to convince me that I had something to say.

In the end, I made up my mind to write the book, because I wanted to tell people about the Masai as I see and experience them. I want to convey the value of their culture, the same value shared by all indigenous people, who genuinely are the protectors of the earth.

Feelings are very important to me. Much of what I know today, I know only with my heart. Just like a child knows his mother loves him, I know the Masai have chosen the right way of living for themselves and the only right way for our planet.

Many people tell me I cannot expect everybody to live like the Masai. That is not my point at all. To me, the question is about what we humans want.

Do we want a healthy planet and a future for our children? If such is the case, we might take guidance from the Masai and the indigenous way of life. Living a simple life does not only have a beneficial effect on nature, it also has a positive impact on our very souls. By sitting quietly. By letting go of the urge to do something constantly and learning to be alone with one's thoughts. If we do not allow ourselves time to breathe and exist, we will never figure out what we want for ourselves and all of us.

The ability to change our lives positively starts with listening to our thoughts. Our thoughts are our soul, and our soul tells us what we need.

It has cost me a great deal to understand this. It was years before I could let go of my Western way of life and adjust to the Masai's. Writing as much is easy, but it was in fact a journey to my innermost self, a struggle with so many demons that finally enabled me to reach this new level of understanding of myself and of the world surrounding me.

This is what I wanted to share with you. Perhaps what I have come to learn in my twelve years with the Masai could prove helpful to you, too.

People like the Masai people, who live amid nature, have more knowledge, understanding, and respect for our environment and our earth than we can ever hope to learn again. They live off the land without abundance, using very little water and no electricity, thus keeping their ecological footprint very small.

Indigenous people know better than we do how to manage the land sustainably. A land they were born and bred in, they know its natural cycles, its plants and animals, and the latter's behavior. They understand how all beings live together in harmony. And when this no longer is the case, as the great drought has made all too apparent, then only because they were stripped of their habitat. Farms have gradually occupied their formerly huge pasture lands, so they no longer have enough land to sustain their animals. This also prevents the pasture lands from properly regenerating. We have learned as much in our land management class.

The Masai do not aim to profit from their land. Their goal is to live a peaceful life in harmony with nature. They want the right to live according to their culture and have enough to live on.

It is incredibly wrong when Western environmental organizations drive indigenous people out of their land in the name of animal protection and/or profit. The Masai have been driven out of Serengeti despite the Serengeti being a wildlife paradise thanks to them. The Masai have been protecting the animals there for centuries.

I studied environmental protection but was trapped in Western ways of thinking. I know now how wrong this was. And I can only consider myself lucky that fate should have brought me to the Masai so I could learn everything anew.

The Western world teaches us to evaluate and assess to understand when, in truth, the only way we can ever hope to gain understanding is to ask questions and sometimes agree to leave some of these questions open. We do not need an answer to all questions. Usually, it is exactly when we don't have answers that we really learn something.

Our culture often considers other cultures negatively because of traditions we view negatively. Specific ceremonies have us grit our teeth. We want to bring people from different cultures to our own culture and change them because we believe they would be happier. What do we hope to achieve? Do we expect all cultures to assimilate? Do we wish to erase all cultural specificities? What kind of world would that be? In a world still marked by racism, I would rather commit myself to the preservation of cultural diversity.

The most important lesson I have learned from the Masai is that there is no such thing as an ultimate truth. Our truths are subjective and very much subjected to the different cultural socialization models we grew up in. What I feel is true might be the opposite in another person's view. What I consider right might be regarded as wrong by somebody else.

I wish the story of my life with the Masai might help us view one another with more tolerance of the different truths conveyed by other people and cultures.

We are all humans. We all have our own truths. We can all learn from one another.

GLOSSARY

Masai: One can only guess the exact number of Masai. Between 500,000 and one million people belonging to the indigenous group live primarily in Tanzania and large parts of Kenya. They speak Maa, and the younger generation also speaks Swahili.

The Masai are regarded as the protectors of wildlife in the Serengeti National Park, as they live alongside the wild animals but do not hunt them. The once nomadic people have been driven out of many territories, such as national parks, nature reserves, or large-scale farms, which were established on "their" land. The loss of their land also robbed them of their food supply, the confiscated areas formerly serving as vital pasture land. But the nomadic people returned to these places, particularly in periods of drought. The consequences of global climate change that brought forth more frequent and more dire droughts and water shortages have severely aggravated the Masai's situation, who - to make matters worse - have no lobby.

Masai men go through several specific life stages in their lifetime, which in turn are associated with certain rights, duties and tasks. Young boys before the age of circumcision belong to a group called *olaiyoni* (plural, *laiyok*), they are in charge of looking after the cattle. Celebrated by the entire village, the *emuratare*, or circumcision ceremony, occurs within the circle of men and marks the transition to the next life stage. It is of particular importance for the adolescents, who from now on are called *morani* and belong to the group of adults. As *ilmoran*, warriors, they look after the cows and goats, provide for their families, protect the village and participate in meetings. Men who have reached the age of 35 no longer need to fight, thus entering a new life stage: they become *olpaiyan* (plural, *lepaiyan*), masters for the new generation of warriors, but remain responsible for their family, assuming more responsibility in meetings and conflict resolution.

Auolo: The place in the *boma* where the animals rest in the morning, after having been led out of their enclosure, and go to in the evening, upon their return from grazing. The men also spend a lot of time together in the *auolo*, eating and talking.

Boma: Family settlement; also, enclosure for the protection of the animals.

Emuratare: Circumcision.

Emutu: Maa for *Ugali*.

Engaang: At home - the translation into Maa of the Swahili word *boma*.

Engangalani: Earrings.

Enkaji: House.

Enkalash: Glass bead necklace.

Enkitok: Woman.

Enkoti: A receptacle to keep milk made from a hollowed-out pumpkin. (Maa)

Eromboi: Metal plates used to decorate jewelry.

Esankoi: Metal strips worn around the legs.

Esime: Warrior's knife.

Esosi: Round neckwear made by Masai women.

Esufiria: Cooking pot (Maa).

Ilmoran: Warriors.

Kabila: Tribe (Swahili).

Maa: Language of the Masai.

Mperre: Spear.

Mstai lelekonyak: Headdress.

Mstai lekenju: Ankle bracelet.

Mzungu (pl. Wazungu): White person.

Olaiyoni: Boy.

Olale: Enclosure for goats, both outside and inside the houses.

Olkati: Neck jewelry adorned with silver-colored metal plates.

Olkipere: Wooden cooking vessel, carved by hand, used to prepare *ugali* (Maa).

Olkuma: Warriors' club (used as a throwing weapon).

Olmeg: Dismissive Masai term designating all non-Masai people and meaning something like corrupted/lost.

Olmorani: Warrior.

Olpaiyan: Any man who no longer is a warrior.

Olpul: A place at some distance from the *boma*, where animals are slaughtered and where the men take their meals. Women are not allowed inside the *olpul*.

The term also refers to a ritual. To accomplish said ritual, men spend one or two months in the bush, far away from the *boma*, living exclusively on goat and beef meat and herbal decoctions. It is intended to detoxify and strengthen the men while creating a strong bond between them. You are not a Masai man if you have never been to the *olpul*.

Ugali: The basic Tanzanian food is made of corn flour (Swahili).

ACKNOWLEDGMENTS

I want to thank my husband, who brought me to the Masai.

Thank you, Yayai, for your affection, protection, and respect.

Thank you, Yeyolai, for your bright laughter and wonderful soul.

Thanks to my German friends, who have always been by my side and supported me through my darkest days: Sandra and your whole family, Nadja, Heike and Lisa.

Thank you, Eleni, for always being there for me without ever judging me.

Thank you, Mark, for bringing me from Australia to England and thus to Tanzania.

Thank you, Mark and Maureen, from the San Francisco Fudge Factory; I have called Bath my home thanks to you.

Thank you, Marieke and Renate, for your true friendship.

Thank you, Cate, for inspiring me to create our *Masai Women Enterprise* and for supporting me in countless other ways. Thank you for being my friend. More than just a friend, actually - a soulmate.

Thank you to my parents, who have brought me into this world.

Thank you, Mel, for saving me without even knowing it. You allowed me to find myself again after Yannik was born.

Thank you, Christoph, for your kind soul and readiness to help.

Thank you, Kaja and Mateusz from *Globstory*. Without you, I would not be here.

Thank you to all my Tanzanian friends for all the stories that led me to contemplate the world anew.

Thank you to all the people who have shown kindness and love to me, even for only one second. The memory of you all is very much alive inside me.

Thank you, Tanzania, a country of love, strength and warm-heartedness.

All my thanks go to the Masai in Lesoit, who have welcomed me in their midst.

Last but not least, thank you to the wonderful women who have made this book come true. Christine Proske from Ariadne Buch: Thank you for believing in me and my story.

Alexandra Brosowski: Thank you for your extraordinary talent as a storyteller and for your ability to see others. Thank you for your warmth and understanding. Thank you, Tracy C. Ertl, Publisher, Dominique Rotermund, English Translator, and everyone else at TitleTown Publishing, LLC., for all your hard work on this book. I am so grateful to you for making this happen.